STREETWISE FRENCH

DICTIONARY/THESAURUS

STREETWISE FRENCH

DICTIONARY/THESAURUS

The User-Friendly Guide to French Slang and Idioms

Ian Pickup, BA, PhD
Rod Hares, MA (Cantab.)

McGraw-Hill

Chicago New York San Francisco Lisbon London Madrid Mexico City Milan New Delhi San Juan Seoul Singapore Sydney Toronto

Library of Congress Cataloging-in-Publication Data

Pickup, Ian.
Streetwise French dictionary/thesaurus : the user-friendly guide to French slang and idioms / Ian Pickup and Rod Hares.
p. cm.
ISBN 0-658-00417-4
1. French language—Slang—Dictionaries—English. 2. French language—Idioms—Dictionaries—English. I. Hares, Rod. II. Title.

PC3741 .P5 2002
443′.21—dc21 2001054655

McGraw-Hill

A Division of The ***McGraw-Hill*** *Companies*

6 7 8 9 0 DOC/DOC 1 0 9 8 7

ISBN 0-658-00417-4

Other titles in the Streetwise Series:
Streetwise French, Isabelle Rodrigues and Ted Neather
Streetwise Spanish, Mary McVey Gill and Brenda Wegmann
Streetwise Spanish audio package, Mary McVey Gill and Brenda Wegmann
Streetwise Spanish Dictionary/Thesaurus, Mary McVey Gill and Brenda Wegmann
Streetwise German, Paul G. Graves

This book was set in Minion and Myriad by Village Typographers, Inc.
Printed and bound by R. R. Donnelley—Crawfordsville

Cover design by Nick Panos
Cover photograph copyright © Stone
Interior design by Village Typographers, Inc.
Illustrations by Luc Nisset-Raidon

This book is printed on acid-free paper.

Contents

Introduction

The language used by those we can label *streetwise*—the jargon used by the young, by students, hookers, musicians, and so on—differs greatly from *standard* language. It can be impenetrable, even to native speakers who do not belong to a particular subculture or group or who do not share the same cultural assumptions.

When we use the word *slang*, we describe language that deviates from standard language: it is informal, specific to a particular group or subculture, or used exclusively by people of a certain age. We may sometimes find it difficult to draw a clear distinction between a *familiar* and a slang expression. Another related difficulty is the fact that certain expressions are acceptable to some groups but may cause offense to others. What is mildly vulgar or amusing in the eyes of one person may be considered highly offensive by another.

If we sometimes hesitate, when speaking in our native tongue, about whether to use a phrase or set expression in a given context, for fear of offending or of creating the wrong impression, how much more difficult is it for the foreign language learner who wishes to show that, linguistically, he or she is streetwise? Once we feel fairly proficient in standard French, for example, we soon want to explore words and phrases that will enable us to speak the same jargon as someone our own age or someone who belongs to the same subculture or group as ourselves. And this is where learning a foreign language becomes really difficult. *Register* and *context* are potential minefields for the student of a foreign language.

The authors of this *Streetwise French Dictionary/Thesaurus* were mindful of these concerns when they set about their task. They quickly decided that, for ease of use and reference, the reader would be presented with an alphabetically arranged list of topics. This is intended to give a rapid shortcut to the reader who is looking for streetwise expressions in French relating to a specific category. The authors have, therefore, selected broad subject categories, which are then divided into subcategories. An example is the topic headed *Business* which is then split into the subcategories *Banking and Money Matters; Building Trades; Business Titles/Job Descriptions; Buying and Selling/Wheeling and Dealing; Employment (Normal/Occasional/Illegal); Factories and Factory Work.* The reader can therefore concentrate on a specific area of human activity and explore the streetwise words and phrases available in French and listed under the appropriate heading with English translations. Examples of usage are also given, in complete sentences or in mini-dialogues. The reader can then test his or her knowledge at the end of each topic by working through the related exercises. An answer key is provided at the back of the book.

The alphabetical dictionary/index is a second source of reference for the reader who may have come across a particular expression not contained or explained in a standard bilingual dictionary. Page reference(s) send the reader to the page(s) in this book where the expression is used and translated into English.

Streetwise French will be used and reacted to differently, depending on the age or the particular group or subculture to which the person or persons addressed belong. A series of symbols are therefore provided to indicate register and to warn about usage. They are complemented by notes giving more detailed advice on where and when the words and phrases in question should or should not be used. The symbols, which progress from noting standard language to indicating highly offensive expressions, are as follows:

- (ok) placed after a word or phrase to indicate that it is part of the standard language and can be used in any formal or informal context without causing offense
- (?) placed after a word or phrase to indicate that it is considered to be very familiar or slightly vulgar
- (!) placed at the beginning of a list or sentence or after a word or phrase to indicate that everything contained in the list or sentence, or that the specific word or phrase, is highly vulgar, crude, or offensive. The reader should use everything labeled (!) at his or her own risk!

These symbols are included for guidance. They should—if heeded—prevent learners from using language that, in the wrong context, could get them into hot water.

Language is constantly changing and evolving, none more rapidly than the categories that are labeled *slang*. Some of the words and phrases included in this dictionary/thesaurus are set expressions that have stood—and will continue to stand—the test of time. Others may already be a little dated, while, at the other extreme, others may not yet be commonly used outside restricted circles. It is hoped that the *Streetwise French Dictionary/Thesaurus* will open new horizons for students of French who wish to go beyond conventional textbooks and bilingual dictionaries. Further reading is suggested in the short bibliography, which lists other works that beat a path, in their different ways, toward a better understanding of streetwise French. «Amusez-vous bien!»

Thesaurus

Gestures: Speaking Without Words

BOREDOM

J'en ai ras le bol!
I've had it up to here!/I'm totally pissed off(?)!

Quelle barbe!
What a drag!/[Br.] What a bloody bore!

COST

C'est pas donné!
It'll cost you!/It's expensive!

DISBELIEF

Mon œil!
My eye!/My foot!

Tu me racontes des histoires!
You're telling fibs!/You're lying!

DRINK AND DRUNKENNESS

À boire!
Give me a drink!

Juste un chouïa.
Just a drop.

Il/Elle est complètement bourré(e).
He's/She's loaded./
[Br.] He/She is completely pissed⑦.

FEAR

Les boules!
Scary!/It scared me to death!

T'as la pétoche ou quoi?
Are you scared or what?

HOPE

Pourvu que ça marche!
Fingers crossed!

INSULTS

Va te faire foutre!(!)
Fuck you!(!)/[Br.] Get stuffed!(!)
NOTE: This gesture is known ironically as the *bras d'honneur.*

Ça va pas la tête?
Are you crazy?/off your rocker?/[Br.] off your trolly?

Complètement dingue!
Absolute nutcase!/[Br.] Barking mad!

LEAVING QUICKLY

Barrons-nous!/Je me barre/tire!
Let's get out of here!/I'm off!

PERPLEXITY

Alors là...
I don't really know . . . /I'm not sure about that . . .

QUOTATIONS

Entre guillemets.
In quotes./[Br.] In inverted commas.

SILENCE

Chut!
Quiet!

TELEPHONING

On s'téléphone.
I'll give you a call/ring/[Br.] bell.

THREATS

La ferme!
Shut your mouth/face!

Tu vas voir ta gueule!
I'm gonna smash your face!

Acronyms and Initials

NOTE: When we speak colloquial English, we use large numbers of acronyms (such as AWOL, KO, OK, OTT, US), often unconsciously. Exactly the same thing happens in French and in order to be confidently streetwise, we need to be aware of the most common acronyms French speakers use in place of whole phrases. The following list shows the most common and will give you a working knowledge.

BCBG [bon chic bon genre] preppy, [Br.] Sloane(-ranger)

NOTE: Also, **bourge [bourgeois]** (classy/[Br.] Sloane-rangerish).

BD [bande dessinée] cartoon, comic strip

le CRS [Compagnie Républicaine de Sécurité] riot-policeman

NOTE: The CRS are not greatly loved because of the public perception of their tendency to overreact at times of public disorder. Some people consequently treat them with a slightly fearful humor, referring to the CRS as **centres de rattrapage scolaire**, that is, a place where young people can catch up on their schooling (that is, detention centers)!

GDB [gueule de bois] hangover

H [haschisch] hash, [Br.] blow

HP [hôpital psychiatrique] psychiatric hospital

HS [hors service] bust, kaput, out of order, [Br.] knackered

JT [journal télévisé] television news

LSD⁈ **[elle suce debout**⁈**]** shorty, squirt, [Br.] titch; [Br.] lofty (reverse humor)

NOTE: In polite circles, this would be very offensive, since it refers to a woman who is short enough to perform oral sex while standing up.

NAP [Neuilly-Auteuil-Passy] preppy, [Br.] Sloane(-ranger)

PD(!) **[pédé(raste)**(!)**]** fag, queer

pédégé [PDG, président-directeur général; humorous spelling of **PDG]** CEO, [Br.] MD

PQ/papier Q [papier-cul] TP, [Br.] bog roll

RU [restaurant universitaire] university cafeteria, canteen, [Br.] refec[tory]

la SF [science fiction] science fiction

WW marking on temporary license plates

la X [ecstasy] X

EXERCISES

C'est à vous maintenant!

A *Match each situation with an appropriate acronym from the box.*

CRS	SF	WW	HP	BD	PDG	RU	JT

1. You are on the way to visit a friend who is mentally ill and are looking for the right sign: ________
2. Your friend has just started at the university and you have arranged to meet there. You follow this series of signs: ________
3. You are in a large bookstore and are looking for a book on the *Star Wars* series. The section you need has the sign: ________
4. You are studying the TV program listings and wish to find a television news channel, to which you are guided by this acronym: ________
5. You have to meet a friend with a brand-new car and temporary plates. You can't remember the number, but these initials tell you the right car: ________
6. You have a job interview in a large office building and are told to go to the CEO's/MD's (managing director's) office. You can't remember her name, but are saved by recognizing this acronym on the door: ________
7. You witness a mugging and are looking for the police. You cannot see the usual type of police car but spot a car from which you will get help, with the following acronym: ________
8. Once again, you are in a bookstore. This time you are looking for comic books, to which you are led by this sign: ________

B *To what are the following people referring?*

1. Pour lui, c'est la GDB chaque matin! ____________________
2. Ma voiture? Mais, elle est HS! ____________________
3. Maman, il n'y a plus de PQ ici! ____________________
4. Mon petit, ne dis pas PD! Ce n'est pas gentil! ____________________
5. Elle est LSD tandis que lui, c'est un géant! ____________________
6. Il s'appelle Xavier Hugolette, mais le week-end, les initiales X et H, ont une signification tout à fait différente pour lui! ____________________

Animals

For expressions involving animals, see also "The Human Body," "Sex."

BARNYARD ANIMALS

Familiar words used by children

le cochon piggy

la cocotte hen

le dada horsey, [Br.] gee-gee

la meu-meu moo-cow

Idiomatic expressions involving barnyard animals

«Ce qu'il a fait, c'est un travail de cochon.» "He's made a mess of it./[Br.] He's made a pig's ear of it."

«Elle est écervelée. Elle saute du coq à l'âne.» "She's harebrained/featherbrained. She jumps from one subject to another."

«Alors, regarde-moi ça! C'est un mouton à cinq pattes.» "Just look at that! It's really unusual/a genuine rarity."

Elle saute du coq à l'âne.

«Il me pardonnera quand les poules auront des dents.» "He'll never forgive me in a month of Sundays."

«J'ai failli être écrasé par une vache à roulettes(?).» "I was almost knocked down by a motorbike/motorcycle cop."

«Elle a une peau de vache(?).» "She's a real bitch(?)/[Br.] rotten cow."

«Il a été très vache avec toi.» "He's been really nasty to you."

«Il pleut comme vache qui pisse(?).» "It's raining cats and dogs./[Br.] It's pissing(?) down."

«Elle est pleine comme une vache.» She's as drunk as a skunk/[Br.] pissed(?) as a newt."

«Lui, il parle français comme une vache espagnole.» "He speaks pidgin/lousy French."

«Mort aux vaches!» "Down with the cops!/Kill the pigs!"

«La famille est dans la mouise/la panade. Elle mange de la vache enragée.» "The family's living in poverty/[Br.] in queer street. It's going through hard times."

«Ça (ne) vaut pas un pet(?) de lapin. "It's totally worthless./[Br.] It's not worth a monkey's fart(?)."

NOTE: In familiar and slang French, **ne** in the negative **ne... guère/jamais/pas/plus/rien** is often omitted.

«Elle lui a posé un lapin.» "She's stood him up."

«Ils baisent(?) comme des lapins et après, lui, il souffle comme un bœuf.» "They fuck(!)/[Br.] shag(!) like rabbits, and afterwards he has to fight for every breath."

«Il est monté comme un âne(?)/comme un cheval(?).» "He's hung like a horse(?). He's got a really big prick(?)/dick(?)."

CATS

le greffier, le minet, la minette, le minou puss, pussy, pussycat ▪ **«Viens voir la gamelle, mon minet.»** "Come for your food, pussy."

NOTE: **Gamelle** is a feeding dish for cats or dogs. See also "The Human Body."

Idiomatic expressions involving cats

«C'est imbuvable! C'est du pipi de chat(?).» (*lit.*, cat's piss) "It's undrinkable./[Br.] It's gnat's piss(?)."

NOTE: The expression **du pipi d'âne**(?) (*lit.*, donkey piss(?)) has the same meaning as **du pipi de chat**(?).

«Elle a toujours appelé un chat un chat.» (*lit.*, "She has always called a cat a cat.") "She's always called a spade a spade."

«Excuse-moi, j'ai un chat dans la gorge.» (*lit.*, "I've got a cat in my throat.") "Sorry, I've got a frog in my throat."

«Il a d'autres chats à fouetter.» (*lit.*, "He has other cats to whip.") "He has other fish to fry/better things to do."

«Il n'y a pas de quoi fouetter un chat.» (*lit.*, "There's no [not enough] reason to whip a cat.") "It's not worth making a fuss about it."

«Il n'y a pas un chat.» (*lit.*, "There's not a cat about.") "There's not a soul about."

«Ils vivent comme chien et chat.» "They go at it like cat and dog."

DOGS

le toutou, le cabot, le cador, le clébard, le clebs mutt, pooch, doggy, doggie ▪ **«Viens, mon toutou, on va sortir et je vais te promener.»** "Come on, doggy, I'm going to take you out for a walk."

NOTE: Both **cabot** and **cador** also take on the meaning "boss," [Br.] "gaffer" in slang French. (Compare with "top dog" in English.)

Idiomatic expressions involving dogs

«Depuis qu'il m'a foutu(!) dans la merde(?), je lui garde un chien de ma chienne.» "Since he dropped me in the shit(?), I've been wanting to get even with him./I've had it in for him."

«Elle a du chien.» "She's a real good looker./She's really dishy."

«Je me suis donné un mal de chien pour te rembourser.» "I've done everything I could./I've tried my very best to pay back the money I owe you."

«Quelle chienne de vie!» "Life's a bitch!"

«Quel métier/Quel temps/Quelle vie de chien!» "What a crummy job!/ What lousy weather!/What a rotten life!"

«Quel radin! Il a toujours été chien avec toi.» "What a tight-assed(?)/[Br.] arsed(?) bastard!(?) He's always been stingy with you."

NOTE: **Être chien avec quelqu'un** also means "to be nasty to someone."

WILD ANIMALS AND INSECTS

Idiomatic expressions involving wild animals and insects

«Elle a une araignée au plafond. Elle est à l'asile depuis trois ans.» "She has bats in the belfry./She has a screw loose. She's been in the nuthouse for three years."

«C'est une punaise de sacristie./C'est une grenouille de bénitier.» "She's a narrow-minded old bigot."

«Il a bandé(!) comme un cerf quand elle s'est mise à poil(?).» "He got a real hard-on(?)/an enormous erection when she stripped (off)."

«Je la déteste. C'est un vrai chameau.» "I can't stand her. She's a nasty piece of work."

«On n'apprend pas à un singe comment faire la grimace.» "You can't teach an old dog new tricks."

«Quelle mouche te pique? Tu montes sur tes grands chevaux chaque fois que tu en parles.» "What the hell's got into you? You get on your high horse every time you talk about it."

TERMS OF ENDEARMENT INVOLVING ANIMALS IN ENGLISH AND FRENCH

mon chéri, mon canard duck
mon petit chou sweetie, [Br.] duckie
ma poule, ma cocotte chicken, honey
mon petit canard, chaton darling
mon gros/petit loup (my) pet
mon biquet, ma biquette my love

EXERCISES

C'est à vous maintenant!

A *Fill in the blanks in the sentences in French with the name of an appropriate animal or insect.*

1. Your friend has just offered you some pretty undrinkable wine.
   Le vin qu'il m'a offert, c'est du pipi de ______________.

2. Your brother has been in a bad mood all morning and you want to know why.
   Alors, toi, quelle ______________ te pique?

3. Your neighbor believes that she's far superior to you. She's convinced that she's always right about everything.
   Ma voisine, dès que je lui parle de n'importe quoi, elle monte sur ses grands ______________.

4. The old woman you just met strikes you as having a closed mind because of her religious views.
   Cette vieille dame est une ______________ de bénitier.

5. Your male friend is extremely vulgar and boasts to you about his sexual prowess. The very thought of sex is a real turn-on for him.
   «Moi, je bande comme un ______________, rien qu'à y penser.»

B *Fill in each blank in the sentences below with one of the French words listed. Then, translate the sentence into English.*

chameau	chat	chien	chienne
lapin	mouton	singe	vache

1. J'ai un ____________ dans la gorge.

   ____

2. Ma mère et moi, nous vivons comme ____________ et ____________.

   ____

3. Elle mène une vie de ____________.

   ____

4. Le fauteuil qu'il a acheté est un ____________ à cinq pattes.

   ____

5. Depuis qu'elle l'a quitté, il lui garde un ____________ de sa ____________.

   ____

6. Ses bijoux ne valent pas un pet de ____________.

   ____

7. Je déteste cette femme: elle a une peau de ____________.

   ____

8. Toute la famille parle anglais comme une ____________ espagnole.

   ____

9. Cette femme est insupportable. C'est un vrai ____________.

   ____

Art

See also "The Human Body," "The Movies," "Music."

ART AND ARTISTIC PEOPLE

Arte culture vulture ■ **«Tu sais, Madeleine est très Arte!»** "You know, Madeleine is quite a culture vulture!"

NOTE: **Arte** is a Franco-German cultural television channel, launched in France in 1992. Compare the British English of the 1970s, "He's very BBC2!"

le beau linge (*lit.*, fine linen) beautiful people, celebs, top people ■ **«T'as vu tout ce beau linge à l'opéra?»** "Did you see all those celebs/top people at the opera?"

la co-vedette féminine/masculine (*lit.*, female/male co-star) leading woman/man

le dirlo [directeur] director

le/la fana de théâtre [fanatique (fanatic)**]** theater buff

le genre artiste (*lit.*, artistic type) artsy-fartsy, [Br.] arty-farty ■ **«Il se donne un genre artiste!»** "He makes out he's/comes off as real artsy-fartsy!"

le gigolo des bars (*lit.*, bar gigolo) bar lizard, lounge lizard

le premier rôle leading role, lead part, [Br.] leading light (male or female)

le vrai Beaubourg! real bit of contemporary design

NOTE: Beaubourg is the name given to the **Musée des arts contemporains** in the Beaubourg quarter of Paris. Because of its mix of metal towers and scaffolding it is seen by many to resemble a gasworks and has consequently been given the affectionate nickname of **l'usine à gaz**.

DESCRIBING ARTISTIC PEOPLE AND TEMPERAMENTS

branché (*lit.*, branched, plugged in), **câblé** (*lit.*, cabled), **chébran** [*verlan* for **branché**] with it, trendy, [Br.] switched on

brancher to interest, to turn on ■ **«Cette pièce ne m'a pas vraiment branché.»** "That play didn't really turn me on."

se vouloir artistique to think of oneself as artsy-fartsy/[Br.] arty-farty ▪ **«Il se veut artistique, sans avoir le talent.»** "He makes out he's/comes off as artsy-fartsy without the talent to go with it!"

beaufⓉ **[beau-frère], mimile**Ⓣ (*diminutive of* **mimi** [cute]), **ringard(e)** square (old-fashioned)

faire du cinéma to put on an act, a performance ▪ **«Pas de cinéma, vieux—t'as pas de public ici!»** "Don't put on an act, buddy/[Br.] mate—there's no one watching!"

NOTE: Used even in the theater, almost certainly because it confirms theater people's prejudice that film is, for them, the inferior art form.

en décor naturel on location

Note the expression **aller dans les décors** (to go crashing off the road).

guindé(e) uptight, stiff, starchy, anal retentive

intello [intellectuel] intellectual, egghead

la locomotive trendsetter, leader ▪ **«*La Haine* est la locomotive pour le nouveau genre hyper-réaliste.»** "*La Haine* sets a new trend in hyper-realism."

NOTE: *La Haine* is a trendsetting film of the super-realist genre, similar to the British *Trainspotting*, dealing with drugs and the myriad problems of those living in the rundown suburbs.

la Marie-Chantal (a common name in pretentious families) highbrow snob

monter sur les planches (*lit.*, to climb up onto the planks) to go on the stage

SUCCESS AND FAILURE

le bide (*lit.*, belly/gut), **le four** (*lit.*, oven) failure, flop ▪ **«Pour moi, la mise en scène a été un vrai four!»** "For me, the production was a real flop!"

le grand manitou (*lit.*, Algonquin Indian chief, possessed of supernatural powers), **le ponte** (*lit.*, punter [in a game of chance]) the big boss, big shot, big white chief ▪ **«Ne me demande pas ça! Adresse-toi au grand manitou dans la loge!»** "Don't ask me that! Take it to the big boss up in the box!"

oublier son texte to forget one's lines

se ramasser (*lit.*, to pick oneself up), **se planter** (*lit.*, to plant oneself [down]) to fail, flop ▪ **«Il s'est ramassé avec son exposition.»** "His exhibition was a flop."

le roman de gare [le romancier de gare] (*lit.*, train station novel) pulp/trashy novel

tâter de to try (to), to take up, [Br.] to have a go at ■ **«Tu sais ce qu'elle fait maintenant? Elle tâte de la sculpture!»** "You know what she's doing now? She's taking up sculpture!"

Lui, c'est une grosse légume.

le ténor, le gros bonnet (*lit.*, big bonnet), **la grosse légume** (*lit.*, big vegetable) big noise, star performer, [Br.] leading light, VIP ■ **«Elle est d'un naturel rigide. Elle ne sera jamais une grosse légume!»** "She has a rigidity about her. She'll never be a star performer!"

le trac (*lit.*, nervousness, fright) stage fright ■ **«Il a tellement le trac, qu'il vomit toujours juste avant le début!»** "He gets stage fright so badly that he always gets sick/throws up just before the start!"

le virus bug, passion ■ **«Son virus à lui, c'est le théâtre!»** "His real passion is the theater!"

EXERCISES

C'est à vous maintenant!

A *Match the expressions on the left with the definitions on the right.*

____	1. **un vrai Beaubourg**	a. a lounge lizard
____	2. **un gigolo des bars**	b. a director
____	3. **faire du cinéma**	c. Beaubourg
____	4. **Arte**	d. the beautiful people
____	5. **le beau linge**	e. put on an act
____	6. **un genre artiste**	f. a real piece of contemporary design
____	7. **l'usine à gaz**	g. an artsy-fartsy
____	8. **un dirlo**	h. culture vulture

B *Fill in the blanks in the French sentences with a word from the box.*

branchée	Marie-Chantal	Marie-Antoinette	artistique
décor	planches	locomotive	

1. Your friend is enthusiastic about a filmmaker's location shots.
   Tu sais, il fait des merveilles en ______________ naturel!
2. Your landlady is irritated by a woman's snobbish behavior.
   Elle s'appelle Marie-Hélène, mais elle est plutôt une ______________!
3. Your neighbor is totally against her daughter going on the stage.
   Je ne veux absolument pas qu'elle monte sur les ______________!
4. A party guest is explaining who is the real driving force behind a new theater.
   La ______________ dans ce théâtre est assurément Guy Bernard.
5. Your landlady's daughter is saying just how different her parents are.
   Maman est très ______________, mais papa est vraiment beauf!
6. A fellow guest at an art exhibition points out someone full of airs and attitudes.
   Elle se veut ______________, mais elle n'a aucune idée de la peinture!

C **Saying what you think.** *At an "arty" party, you hear the following comments from French-speaking friends and acquaintances. You then reply in French.*

1. **Est-ce que tu as lu le nouveau roman de Gilbert Herschel?**
   Say you think it's a pulp novel.

   ____

2. **Le nouveau film de Billy Bingles, c'est un succès?**
   Say no, Billy has had a flop.

   ____

3. **L'actrice Sarah-Louise Gardiner, elle est bien vue aux USA?**
   Say she's a star performer.

   ____

4. **Pourquoi Adam Paradise n'obtient-il pas les meilleurs rôles?**
   Say he forgets his lines.

   ____

5. **Jeannette est normalement si impolie. Pourquoi est-ce qu'elle est si polie envers ce monsieur-là?**
   Say he's the big boss at the studio.

   ____

6. **Ton amie, Pauline, qu'est-ce qu'elle fait en ce moment?**
   Say she's taken up sculpture.

   ____

Beauty

See also "Clothing."

COSMETIC SURGERY

Having an operation: the breasts; the face

se faire refaire les nichons(?) to have a boob job(?)

NOTE: **Nichons**(?) is of a similar register to "tits"(?) or "boobs"(?) in English and should not be used in polite company or formal situations.

se faire faire un ravalement/se faire ravaler la façade (*lit.*, a cleaning/ to reface a façade) to have a face job/a face-lift

«Elle est allée voir un chirurgien parce qu'elle a décidé de se faire refaire les nichons.(?) **L'année dernière elle s'est fait faire un ravalement/elle s'est fait ravaler la façade et ça lui a coûté les yeux de la tête.»** "She went to see a surgeon because she's decided to have a boob(?) job. Last year she had a face-lift and it cost her an absolute fortune/[Br.] packet."

NOTE: The standard French expression for having a breast implant is **se faire refaire les seins** while breast enlargement is **une augmentation mammaire**. The standard French expression for having a face-lift is **se faire faire un lifting** while cosmetic surgery is **une opération de chirurgie esthétique.** "To have a nose job" is **se faire refaire le nez.**

Defects that may lead to cosmetic surgery

avoir une culotte de cheval (*lit.*, "riding breeches") to have saddlebags

avoir la fesse triste/tombante to have drooping buttocks

avoir des poches/des valises sous les yeux to have bags under the eyes

«Regarde-moi cette connasse(!)**! Elle a des valises sous les yeux et la fesse tombante.»** "Just look at that bitch(!)! She's got bags under her eyes and drooping buttocks."

See also "The Human Body."

DIETING

être maigre comme un clou (*lit.*, to be as thin as a nail) to be as thin as a rake

affûter la forme to get into top shape

le gros lard (*lit.*, fat streaky bacon), **un gros-plein-de-soupe**⑦ (*lit.*, lots of/full of soup) (man) fatty, fatso⑦, big fat slob⑦

la grosse dondon⑦ (woman) fatty, fatso⑦, fat cow⑦

«Ma copine est une grosse dondon⑦ mais moi, je suis maigre comme un clou car ça fait six mois que je suis un régime amaigrissant qui m'a permis d'affûter la forme. Mon mec, par contre, est un gros-plein-de-soupe⑦. Il devrait essayer de manger moins gras.» "My friend's a fat cow⑦ but I'm as thin as a rake because I've been on a diet/[Br.] a slimming course for six months that let me get into shape. My boyfriend/[Br.] bloke, on the other hand, is a big fat slob. He should try to cut down on fatty food."

NOTE: The expressions used here describing overweight people should be used with discretion; they are far from complimentary!

NOTE: Anorexia/[Br.] slimmer's disease in French is **anorexie mentale**; a dieters'/[Br.] slimmers' magazine is **un magazine de diététique**; a reducing/slimming aid is **un produit amincissant.**

EXERCISING

Being in good shape

une armoire à glace, une armoire normande (*lit.*, a wardrobe with a mirror/a Norman-style wardrobe) well-built man, hunk, [Br.] hulk ■ **«Il passe des heures sur son vélo d'appartement et dans sa salle de musculation. Le résultat? C'est une véritable armoire à glace/armoire normande.»** "He spends hours on his exercise bike and in his weight room. As a result he's a real hunk/hulk of a man."

NOTE: **La musculation** (bodybuilding) is **la muscu** in familiar French.

C'est une véritable armoire normande.

canon⑦/une nana canon⑦ stunning/a stunner/a stunning chick ■ **«Elle fait de l'aérobic tous les jours. Elle est hyper canon./C'est une nana canon.»** "She does aerobics every day. She's a real stunner."

NOTE: **Canon** is used both as an adjective and as a noun (stunning; a stunner, stunning chick).

HAIR

le coiffe-tifs hairdresser ▪ **«Elle est allée chez le coiffe-tifs mais lui est resté à la maison parce qu'il se déboise.»** "She went to get her hair done, but he stayed at home because he's losing his hair/[Br.] barnet."

NOTE: An alternative to **coiffe-tifs** is **coupe-tifs**. The standard French word for hairdresser is **coiffeur/coiffeuse** (m/f); a hairstyle or hairdo is **une coiffure.**

MAKEUP—MANICURE—PEDICURE

ravaler sa façade (*lit.*, to renovate one's façade) to put on one's war paint/ makeup ▪ **«Elle a ravalé sa façade après s'être reloquée. Tout le monde l'a reluquée.»** "She put on her war paint after getting dressed. Everybody ogled her/ [Br.] eyed her up."

se sucrer la gaufre (*lit.*, to sugar one's waffle/honeycomb) to do one's face ▪ **«Elle n'a pas eu le temps de se sucrer la gaufre. Elle est vraiment moche!»** "She didn't have time to do her face. She looks really scuzzy/grungy/ugly!"

NOTES: Other slang expressions for putting on makeup are **se griffer la tronche** (*lit.*, to scratch one's face/mug) and **se griffer la devanture** (*lit.*, to scratch one's shop window/frontage). The standard French for "to put makeup on" is **se maquiller.** A more standard (but familiar) French alternative for the English noun "face" is **frimousse**, used in the slang phrase **ravaler sa frimousse** (to put on one's makeup).

While **se reloquer** means simply "to get dressed" (**s'habiller** in standard French), two slang expressions for getting "dolled up" are **se nipper** and **se saper.**

Care should be taken to differentiate between **(se) reloquer** and **reluquer** "to ogle (someone)/[Br.] to eye (someone) up."

se faire les ongles to manicure one's nails

se faire soigner les pieds to have a pedicure

«Elle se fait les ongles tous les jours mais il est impossible de lui faire rentrer dans la tête qu'il faut aussi se faire soigner les pieds. Quelle drôle de gonzesse!» "She manicures her nails every day, but it's impossible to make her realize that she should have a pedicure too. What a weird chick/[Br.] strange bird!"

NOTE: Manicure in French is **manucure** (f); **se faire manucurer** is "to have a manicure"; pedicure is **pédicurie** (f); the French word also means "podiatry."

SPAS

le club/l'établissement (m) **de remise en forme, l'établissement pour cures d'amaigrissement et de rajeunissement** spa, health club/[Br.] farm ■ **«Elles se paient une cure dans un club de remise en forme mais elles sont toujours aussi moches. Elles ont toutes les deux une drôle de forme.»** "They treat themselves to sessions in a health club, but they're still just as ugly. They're both an odd shape."

NOTE: **Moche** refers to someone who is physically ugly, but also to someone who is morally reprehensible. The vulgar expression **être moche à chier**Ⓥ means "to be as ugly as sin." A "reducing program" ([Br.] slimming course) in a spa is **une cure d'amaigrissement.**

NOTE: **Moche** is a familiar rather than vulgar term but should generally be avoided in such phrases as the last one cited above.

EXERCISES

C'est à vous maintenant!

A *What is the standard French for the following slang expressions?*

1. Elle va **se faire refaire les nichons.** ______________________
2. Sa fille **s'est fait faire un ravalement.** ______________________
3. Elle est allée **chez le coiffe-tifs.** ______________________
4. Sa fille **s'est griffé la tronche.** ______________________

   NOTE: The past participle **griffé** does not have a feminine agreement because the direct object (**la tronche**) follows. Compare **Elle s'est cassé la jambe**, where the direct object is **la jambe** and the reflexive pronoun (**s'**) is the indirect object.

B *Complete the following slang expressions in French and give an English translation.*

1. **Sa petite sœur a la** ______________ **tombante.**

   ____

2. **Elle va se sucrer la** ______________ **avant de sortir.**

   ____

3. Son père a des ________________ sous les yeux.

____

4. Il est maigre comme un ________________.

____

5. Son fils est une véritable ________________ à glace.

____

Business

BANKING AND MONEY MATTERS

la Grande Boulange (*lit.*, the big baker's), **La Boulange aux faffes** La Banque de France, the Bank of France ■ **«Si la Grande Boulange fait faillite, on est tous dans une merde noire.»** "If the Bank of France goes bankrupt, we're all up shit creek without a paddle."

le pognon; le blé (*lit.*, wheat) money

les économoques (fpl) savings

le chèque en bois (*lit.*, wooden check/cheque) bad check/[Br.] cheque, a check/[Br.] cheque that bounces ■ **«Quel connard! Il lui a filé un chèque en bois.»** "What a stupid bastard! He gave him a bad check/cheque."

> NOTE: **Un chèque en bois** is used in relaxed, informal situations. **Un chèque sans provision** is the standard French expression for "a bad check/[Br.] cheque."

le chèqueton check/[Br.] cheque

«Je vais faire des économoques et je mettrai mon pognon/mon blé en banque.» "I'm going to save up and I'll put my dough/bucks in the bank."

> NOTE: French has a lot of slang expressions for units of money (some of which change their meaning from time to time).
>
> 5 francs: **une thune**; 10 francs: **un keuss/un keusse**; 20 francs: **un linvé**; 100 franc note: **un petit format**; 500 franc note: **un grand format**; 1000 francs: **un kilo** (compare with "a grand" in English); 10,000 francs: **un pavé**, **une brique**.

«Voilà un pavé de foutu en l'air.» That's 10,000 francs down the tubes.

> NOTE: **Francs** were replaced by **euros** in January 2002 and were no longer legal tender by the middle of the following month. The words and phrases listed will still be found in films and books, however.

> NOTE: There are many slang words for money, including **une balle [un franc], le beurre, le fric, le grisbi, l'oseille** (f), some of which are used in set expressions:

faire son beurre (*lit.*, to make one's butter) to make lots of dough

mettre du beurre dans les épinards (*lit.*, to put butter in the spinach) to improve one's living standard(s), to grease the wheels

être bourré(e)/plein(e) de fric (*lit.*, to be bulging with/full of money) to be filthy rich

faire son oseille (*lit.*, to make one's sorrel), **coûter la peau des fesses** (*lit.*, to cost the skin on one's buttocks) to make money/a buck

coûter les yeux de la tête (*lit.*, to cost the eyes in one's head) to cost an arm and a leg

la faire à l'oseille à quelqu'un (*lit.*, to do it to someone's sorrel) to con someone, [Br.] to take the Mickey out of someone

le faffe greenback, banknote

les faffes (m) ID, identity papers

montrer ses faffes to show one's ID

NOTE: The above expressions should not be used in formal business situations but reserved for more relaxed, informal contexts.

«Ils voulaient mettre du beurre dans les épinards mais le pavillon qu'ils voulaient acheter leur aurait coûté les yeux de la tête.» "They wanted to improve their living standard(s), but the house they wanted to buy would have cost an arm and a leg."

BUILDING TRADES

l'arpette (m), **l'arpète** (m) bricklayer's apprentice/laborer

le barbouilleur painter

le contrecoup foreman

NOTE: An alternative slang word for "foreman" (**contre-maître** in standard French) is **contrefiche** (f).

l'électro (m) electrician, [Br.] sparkie, sparks

le maçon bricklayer, [Br.] brickie

le manœuvre laborer, unskilled worker

la menuise carpenter, [Br.] chippie, chips

NOTE: **Maçon** is standard French. The familiar noun **menuise** is derived from the standard term **menuisier** while **électro** is derived from the standard term **électricien.**

l'ouvrier (m) **du bâtiment** construction worker

le plombard plumber

NOTE: The familiar noun **barbouilleur** has pejorative connotations; the familiar noun **plombard** is derived from the standard term **plombier.**

le sous-entrepreneur/sous-traitant subcontractor, [Br.] subbie

le chantier building site

l'industrie (f) **du bâtiment** the building industry/trades

la baraque cowboy firm, crap⑦ company

NOTE: **Baraque** is also used to mean the place where one lives ("pad").

le fumiste cowboy, [Br.] skiver

la bicoque jerry-built house

NOTE: The standard French expression for a "jerry-built house" is **maison** (f)/ **pavillon** (m) **(construit[e]) en carton-pâte.**

la masure (f) dump, hovel

«Il est dans le bâtiment mais sa baraque a un chantier où l'on n'embauche que des fumistes. Même son contrecoup habite une bicoque.» "He works in the construction business but his lousy firm has a site that only employs cowboys/[Br.] skivers. Even his foreman lives in a jerry-built house."

«Le barbouilleur et le plombard ont accusé le maçon d'avoir construit des bicoques.» "The painter and the plumber accused the bricklayer of being a jerry-builder."

BUSINESS TITLES/JOB DESCRIPTIONS

NOTE: French has a large number of familiar and slang words and expressions for business titles and job descriptions. The majority describe those at the top or in the higher echelons of the business community, but some (often humorous) words and phrases designate those at the bottom end of the hierarchy.

PDG [Président-Directeur Général] CEO, [Br.] Chairman and Managing Director ■ **«La Jaguar, ça fait très PDG.»** "A Jaguar is a real boss's/director's car."

le staff personnel (with the emphasis on "staff," the executives)

le boss boss, director

le cador boss, top dog

le négrier boss employing illegal immigrants, slave driver

le singe boss man, [Br.] guv'nor

le taulier, le tôlier owner, boss (of bar, restaurant, pub, lodging house)

le bistrot bar owner; bar

le troquet bar owner; bar

les grosses légumes top brass, men in (gray, [Br.] grey) suits

le roi de l'épicerie

les supérieurs, les gros bonnets top brass

l'huile (f) important person, VIP, big cheese, big shot

les huiles top guys, big guns

le nabab mogul

le roi tycoon

le roi du béton (*lit.*, the king of concrete) concrete tycoon

le roi de l'épicerie (*lit.*, the king of the grocery trade) supermarket tycoon

le roi du pétrole (*lit.*, the oil king) oil tycoon

le roi de l'édition (*lit.*, the king of publishing) publishing tycoon

le roi de l'immobilier (*lit.*, the king of the property/real estate business) property tycoon

NOTE: The noun **roi** in the sense of "tycoon" is used ironically in the phrase **le roi des cons**⚠ which means "a prize idiot," "a real dickhead⚠," "a complete prick⚠." A civil servant who is particularly despised—a tax inspector—is known as **un père presseur** (a deformation of the standard term **percepteur**).

«Ce roi du pétrole se fout⚠ pas mal du négrier qui, lui, ne connaît aucun des gros bonnets. Mais ces deux types détestent également le père presseur.» "This oil tycoon couldn't give a shit⚠ about the guy who employs illegal immigrants and who doesn't know any of the top brass. But both of them can't stand the tax inspector."

NOTE: In French, there are a number of slang and familiar words and phrases to designate those at the opposite—the bottom—end of the job market:

un cul de plomb (*lit.*, a lead ass⚠/[Br.] arse⚠) office worker (often used to describe civil servants, **fonctionnaires**)

le sous-fifre, le sous-verge, le porte-coton humble employee, underling, junior

le burlain, le burlin, le burelain office worker ■ **«Les cols blancs sont des burlains.»** White-collar workers are employed in offices.

un nègre (*lit.*, a slave) the one who does the donkey work/shit⚠ work ■ **«C'est moi le nègre dans cette boîte.»** I'm the chief cook and bottle-washer/[Br.] the dogsbody in this place.

NOTE: **Boîte** means "workplace, firm, business, school" and also "nightclub" (**boîte de nuit**).

NOTE: All the expressions in this subcategory referring to individuals, with the exception of the "standard" abbreviation **PDG**, should not normally be used when addressing the person to whom they refer.

BUYING AND SELLING/ WHEELING AND DEALING

le combinard, le traficoteur, le magouilleur wheeler-dealer

l'affairisme (m) wheeling and dealing

NOTE: A standard but pejorative term for a "wheeler-dealer" is **un affairiste**.

magouiller to do some wheeling and dealing

la combine, l'arnaque (f) scam, racket, caper

arnaquer to scam, to rip off

carotter to swindle, to con

la camelote worthless goods, junk, [Br.] trash gear

fourguer to palm off, to unload, [Br.] to flog

le fourguem, le fourgat receiver (of stolen goods), fence

fusiller (*lit.*, to shoot) to overcharge, to rip off

NOTE: In slang French, **fusiller** (*lit.*, to shoot) also means "to wreck," "to smash up," [Br.] "to knacker."

laver (*lit.*, "to wash") to launder (money), to sell off (stolen goods), to fence

toc (adj.) counterfeit, fake; (nm) junk, [Br.] phony gear

«Ce magouilleur a trouvé une sacré combine: il a trouvé facile d'arnaquer les touristes en leur fourguant de la camelote/du toc. Il connaît un fourgat qui fusille ses propres parents et qui lave des sommes énormes chez un rital⚠.» "This wheeler-dealer has discovered a real scam: he finds it easy to rip off tourists by unloading fakes on them/[Br.] flogging them trash gear. He knows a fence who overcharges his own relatives and who launders huge amounts of money through a wop(!)/eyetie(!)."

EMPLOYMENT (NORMAL/OCCASIONAL/ILLEGAL)

embaucher, engrainer to employ, to hire ▪ **«On l'a engrainé la semaine dernière mais il s'est fait lourder hier.»** "He was hired last week but they fired him/[Br.] sacked him yesterday."

licencier, virer, lourder to fire, to dismiss, [Br.] to sack

le petit boulot (illegal) odd job, occasional employment ▪ **«Il a un petit boulot et ça va sans dire qu'il est payé sous la table.»** "He has a moonlighting/[Br.] casual job and it goes without saying that he doesn't declare it/he's paid cash (in hand)."

NOTE: **Être payé(e) sous la table** (compare "under the table payments" in English) is an illegal form of payment which allows the recipient to avoid taxes, etc.

le travail de proximité job in the neighborhood (denotes fairly menial work)

le travail/le boulot précaire casual/occasional job with no security

le travail au noir (*lit.*, work in the dark) illegal employment ▪ **«Même sur les chantiers de construction des grosses entreprises, énormément d'ouvriers travaillent au noir.»** "Even on the building sites of large companies, a lot of workers are illegal/a lot of workers are paid cash (in hand)."

être au chômage/au chômedu; être/faire chômedu; pointer à l'ANPE/au chôm'du to be unemployed/[Br.] on the dole/out of work

NOTE: **Pointer à l'ANPE [Agence Nationale pour l'Emploi]** means literally "to sign up/[Br.] clock on at the job center/employment office."

«Je suis (au) chôm'du depuis trois mois et tout ce que j'ai pu trouver c'est du boulot précaire.» "I've been unemployed/[Br.] on the dole for three months and all I've been able to find is casual/occasional work/jobs with no security."

se faire licencier/virer/lourder avec prime à la clé to get the golden handshake ▪ **«Elle s'est fait virer avec prime à la clé, alors elle ne rouspète pas trop.»** "She got the golden handshake so she's not complaining/moaning/bitching(!) too much."

SMIC [Salaire Minimum Interprofessionnel de Croissance] minimum gross hourly wage for French workers eighteen and over ▪ **«Les patrons sont persuadés que le SMIC est trop élevé.»** "The bosses/employers are convinced that the (official) minimum wage is too high."

le treizième mois annual bonus (equal to a month's salary) ▪ **«Elles, elles ont de la veine: elles reçoivent un treizième mois.»** "These women are (bloody) lucky; they get an annual bonus of a month's salary."

FACTORIES AND FACTORY WORK

pointer (sa fiche horaire) to clock in/on, to clock out

NOTE: **Se pointer** means "to turn up, [Br.] to roll up, to put in an appearance."

le boulot, le job, le turbin work, job

la boîte firm

boulonner to work really hard, [Br.] to graft

la planque, la planquouse easy job, [Br.] cushy number

le/la planqué(e) person with an easy job, [Br.] cushy number

le métallo steelworker ▪ **«Ces métallos ont des postes de dix heures.»** "These metal workers do ten-hour shifts."

le pue-la-sueurⓉ (*lit.*, a stink-of-sweat) workman ▪ **«Ce pue-la-sueur**Ⓣ **est obligé de boulonner. Alors, après le turbin, il s'en jette un derrière la cravate.»** "This worker really has to work hard/[Br.] graft. So after work he goes for a drink."

NOTE: **Un pue-la-sueur**Ⓣ is derogatory and should not be used as a form of address.

avoir des postes de dix heures to work ten-hour shifts

faire un travail posté to work (on) shifts

c'est de la crème/c'est une bonne gâche it's a piece of cake/[Br.] a doddle/an easy number (job) ▪ **«Quand il a pointé (sa fiche horaire), il se dit tous les soirs ‹Ce boulot, c'est de la crème/c'est une bonne gâche›.»** "When he clocks out, he says to himself every evening, 'This job's a piece of cake/[Br.] doddle.'"

EXERCISES

C'est à vous maintenant!

A *Explain the following terms and give a translation.*

1. PDG

___

2. SMIC

___

3. ANPE

____

4. **La Grande Boulange**

____

B *Give the slang equivalent of the following standard French terms for tradesmen/workers.*

1. **menuisier** _______________
2. **électricien** _______________
3. **plombier** _______________
4. **peintre** _______________

C *Translate into English the slang words and phrases that are in bold in the following sentences.*

1. Lui (a) **a fait son beurre** et son fils (b) **est bourré de fric.**

   a. _______________ b. _______________

2. (a) **Les grosses légumes** ne parlent pas souvent aux (b) **cols blancs.**

   a. _______________ b. _______________

3. Je connais (a) **des combinards** qui seraient prêts à (b) **carotter** leurs meilleurs amis.

   a. _______________ b. _______________

4. Lui (a) **est au chômedu** et sa femme (b) **s'est fait lourder** hier.

   a. _______________ b. _______________

5. Ce (a) **pue-la-sueur** (b) **est payé sous la table.**

   a. _______________ b. _______________

Cars

See also "City."

ACCIDENTS

Accidents: damaging a car

amocher un phare to smash a headlight/[Br.] headlamp ■ **«Il a fait un sacré dérapage et sa bagnole s'est écrasée contre un arbre. Il a amoché un phare.»** "He went into a hell of a skid and his car/[Br.] motor crashed into a tree. He smashed a headlight."

bousiller sa bagnole to wreck/smash up/[Br.] write off one's car ■ **«Il a bousillé sa bagnole dans un accident; elle était bonne à envoyer à la casse.»** "He smashed up his car in an accident; it was a complete wreck."

Accidents: road rage

perdre la boule (*lit.*, to lose one's head/[Br.] nut) to go nuts/bonkers/crazy ■ **«Dès qu'il a sa vieille bagnole entre les pognes, il perd la boule.»** "As soon as he gets behind the wheel of his old jalopy/[Br.] banger, he goes nuts/crazy."

NOTE: **Les pognes** are "paws, mitts (hands)"; the standard French expression for "to get behind the wheel of a car" is **prendre le volant** or **se mettre au volant**.

NOTE: Suitable for any situation in which a person "sees red."

Accidents: sustaining injuries

voir trente-six chandelles (*lit.*, to see thirty-six candles) to see stars ■ **«Sa bagnole a fait un tonneau et il a vu trente-six chandelles.»** "His car turned over and he saw stars."

NOTE: Suitable for any physical knock or bump which causes the victim to see stars.

Sa bagnole a fait un tonneau et il a vu trente-six chandelles.

le coup du lapin (*lit.*, rabbit punch) whiplash injury ▪ **«Ça ne va pas? Qu'est-ce que tu as?» «Ça m'a fait le coup du lapin.»** "Are you hurt? What's the matter?" "I've got a whiplash injury."

NOTE: In addition to the above usage, the phrase **le coup du lapin** is used in boxing to designate a "rabbit punch." **Faire le coup du lapin à quelqu'un** means "to give somebody a rabbit punch."

MY CAR

l'amazone (f) (*lit.*, amazon, a mythical, fearsomely strong woman fighter) prostitute who works from a car

amocher la bagnole (*lit.*, to bash about the jalopy), **amocher la tire**⚠ to smash up one's car/jalopy/wheels ▪ **«C'est la troisième bagnole qu'il a amochée!»** "It's the third set of wheels he's smashed up!"

le bolide (*lit.*, meteor) rocket, fast car, hot rod ▪ **«Son bolide? C'est plutôt une fusée qu'une voiture!»** "His fast car/hot rod? It's more like a rocket than a car!"

la borne (*lit.*, milestone) kilometer

la brêle scooter, moped

NOTE: Secondary meaning: fathead, jerk, [Br.] tosspot.

«À chaque brêle, sa brêle!» "Every jerk has his scooter!"

la caisse⚠**, le char** (*Québécois*)**, la chignole, le clou, la guimbarde, le tacot, le tape-cul**⚠**, la tire** old car, [Br.] banger, [Br.] boneshaker, [Br.] crock ▪ **«Avec cette guimbarde-là, tu peux t'inscrire pour la course des vieux tacots!"** "With that old [Br.] banger, you can sign up for the old crocks' race!" ▪ **«Lui, et son vieux tape-cul**⚠**!»** "Him and his old jalopy/[Br.] boneshaker!"

NOTES: **La course des vieux tacots** means "the old heaps'/[Br.] crocks' race"; **la chiotte** (normally, "the shithouse⚠") can also be used to mean "an old [Br.] banger/rust bucket," but is current slang among young people for a motor scooter: **une mobylette.**

déglingué(e) bust, busted, falling apart, [Br.] knackered

la deuche Citroën 2CV [deux chevaux] Citroën 2CV (2 horsepower) ▪ **«Cette vieille deuche pue l'huile!»** "That old *deux chevaux* stinks of oil!"

la gumbarde heap, rust bucket, [Br.] banger

le lance-fusées rocket launcher ▪ **«Ça accélère comme un lance-fusées!»** "It accelerates like a rocket launcher!"

le mastodonte large, heavy truck; [Br.] juggernaut

être motorisé(e) to have transportation/wheels, to be mobile

peugeotiste Peugeot owner and loyalist ■ **«Tu peux bien t'acheter ta nouvelle Mercédès! Moi, je suis peugeotiste pour de bon!»** "You can go and buy your new Mercedes! I'll always be a Peugeot man!"

NOTE: Peugeot is the only French car for whom the French public have coined a name for the owner, due to a long-standing mutual affection.

le/la pilote driver ■ **«Elle se voit plutôt comme pilote de course!»** "She's more inclined to think she's a race car driver!"

le propergol rocket fuel ■ **«Sa voiture roule au propergol!»** "Her car runs on rocket fuel!"

NOTE: **Propergol** is more frequently heard referring to strong drink, e.g., **Ce calva est plutôt du propergol!** (That Calvados is more like dynamite!)

le siège à morts death seat (front passenger's seat)

le VTT [véhicule tout terrain] 4×4, off-roader

NOTE: **VTT** is more commonly used for **un vélo tout terrain** (a mountain bike).

DRIVING

à tout berzingue at top speed, like sixty, [Br.] like the clappers

blinder, bomber to bomb/[Br.] belt along

brûler un feu (rouge) (*lit.*, to burn a [red] fire/light) to go through a red light, [Br.] to jump the lights

le chauffard road hog

(se) crasher to crash

dépoter to go like a bomb/the wind

le diable au volant devil at the wheel

esquinter to bust (up), to wreck, [Br.] to knacker

faire du lèche-cul(!) to drive bumper-to-bumper, [Br.] to drive nose-to-tail

NOTE: Compare current English: "to drive up someone's ass(!)/[Br.] arse(!)." The French expression normally refers to [Br.] arse-licking(!) in its general sense.

brûler un feu (rouge)

faire du stop (*lit.*, to do some stopping), **faire du pouce** (*lit.*, to do some thumb), **lever le pouce** (*lit.*, to lift the thumb) to hitchhike, to thumb a ride, [Br.] to thumb it

faire un tour (*lit.*, to go for a tour/trip) to go for a spin

freiner à mort (*lit.*, to brake to death) to slam on the brakes

pédibus (*lit.*, with the foot [Latin]) on foot ■ **«Il a eu une panne d'essence et y est allé pédibus!»** "He ran out of gas (fuel) and had to go there on foot!"

la pétrolette moped ■ **«Les temps sont durs. Tu vois, comme il a échangé sa Mercédès contre une pétrolette!»** "Times are hard. See how he's traded his [Br.] Merc for a moped!"

piloter to drive (race cars) ■ **«T'as vu la façon dont il pilote sa bagnole?»** "Have you seen the way he drives his car?"

> NOTE: **Piloter** is often used to imply that a driver should be on the racetrack, not the public roads!

rater l'écrit to fail the written test

rater le pratique to fail the practical/the road test

le rodéo joyride (in a stolen vehicle)

rouler au pas (*lit.*, to roll at a step) to crawl along

mettre le turbo (*lit.*, to switch on the turbo) to get a move on

EXERCISES

C'est à vous maintenant!

A *Supply the French equivalents below.*

1. Give two slang French verbs which mean "to smash," [Br.] "to write off" (a car or part of a car).

   ______________________ ______________________

2. Give two standard French expressions for "to get behind the wheel of a car."

   ______________________ ______________________

3. The English expression "to see stars" does not translate literally into French. What is the equivalent of "stars" in the corresponding French expression?

   ____

B *Find the intruder in each string of expressions.*

1. la caisse	le tacot	la guimbarde	le rodéo
2. le propergol	le lance-fusées	la deuche	la pétrolette
3. le bolide	le lance-fusées	le propergol	le chauffard
4. piloter	rouler au pas	faire du stop	mettre le turbo
5. chauffeur	peugeotiste	amazone	pilote
6. faire du stop	faire du lèche-cul	faire du pouce	lever le pouce
7. bomber	blinder	esquinter	dépoter

C *You are having a conversation with a friend who contradicts every statement you make. Fill in the blanks with the correct word from the box.*

pédibus	pétrolette	VTT	déglingué(e)
pratique	pas	diable	

1. Vous — Sa BMW n'est pas neuve!
   Ami(e) — Ah, si, elle est ______________!
2. Vous — Il blinde toujours!
   Ami(e) — Non, il roule au ______________!
3. Vous — C'est un conducteur calme.
   Ami(e) — Pouah! C'est plutôt un ______________ au volant!
4. Vous — Il prend toujours sa voiture.
   Ami(e) — Ce n'est pas vrai! Il va ______________!
5. Vous — Il a déjà réussi à l'écrit et demain, il va avoir son permis de conduire.
   Ami(e) — Non! À mon avis, il va rater le ______________!
6. Vous — Elle est très riche et elle se donne des airs!
   Ami(e) — Non! Tu n'as pas vu comme elle a une ______________ pour se déplacer!

D *Using your sense of logic, rewrite each group of expressions in rising order.*

1. a. **à tout berzingue** ____, ____, ____
   b. **pédibus**
   c. **à brêle**
2. a. **un VTT** ____, ____, ____, ____
   b. **une pétrolette**
   c. **un lance-fusées**
   d. **un tape-cul**
3. a. **mettre le turbo** ____, ____, ____, ____
   b. **blinder**
   c. **rouler au pas**
   d. **faire un tour**
4. a. **dépoter** ____, ____, ____, ____, ____
   b. **brûler un feu**
   c. **esquinter**
   d. **faire du lèche-cul**
   e. **cracher**

City

See also "Entertainment," "Food and Eating."

EATING

la bouffe, la boustiffe, la boustifaille, la mangeaille chow, food, grub

la BGV fast food ■ **«La BGV va remplacer le sandwich chez les jeunes en France.»** "Fast food is going to replace the sandwich for young people in France."

NOTE: **La BGV [la Bouffe à Grande Vitesse]** is based on **le TGV [le Train à Grande Vitesse]**, France's celebrated high-speed train. The standard French expressions for "fast food" are **la restauration rapide** (the industry) and **le prêt-à-manger** (the actual food). French has also adopted the phrase **le fast-food** (plural: **les fast-foods**) which also designates a fast-food restaurant.

becter, becqueter, bouffer, croûter, grailler, grainer to chow down, to nosh, to grab a bite (to eat)

la beuverie binge, [Br.] piss-up⑦

le gueuleton blowout, [Br.] nosh-up

le croque [un croque-monsieur] toasted ham and cheese sandwich

la gaufre waffle

le casse-croûte (*lit.*, break-crust) snack, sandwich

le croque-madame (*lit.*, bite/crunch-madame) toasted ham and cheese sandwich with an egg on top

le macdo [McDonald's] hamburger, burger

la formule à 120 francs menu at 120 francs (appetizer/[Br.] starter and main course or main course and dessert)

se faire un macdo to go for a burger

le restau, le resto, le restif restaurant

le restau(-)U, le resto(-)U [Restaurant Universitaire] student restaurant/ canteen

le marchand de soupe (*lit.*, soup seller) owner of a cheap restaurant ▪ **«Le marchand de soupe m'a dit qu'il est fermé.»** "The boss of this dive/cheap restaurant told me that he's closed."

NOTE: There are other slang French words meaning "food": **la bectance, la briffe** (food or meal), **la croûte, le fricot, la graille** (food or meal), **la grinque, la jaffe** (food or meal), **le rata** (food or meal; the noun also refers specifically to a bean and potato stew), **la tortore** (food or meal).

Other slang French words meaning "meal" include **la becqtance, le frichti, la ventrée** (copious meal).

«J'ai tellement envie de grailler que je propose qu'on aille se foutre une ventrée tout de suite.» "I'm so (damn/[Br.] bloody) hungry I suggest we go and stuff our faces/[Br.] go and have a blowout right away."

«Lui, il préfère se faire un macdo mais elle aime mieux aller au resto et se payer une formule à 80 francs.» "He prefers to go for a burger but she'd rather go to a restaurant and have an eighty-franc meal."

«Après leur beuverie, ces étudiants ont bouffé au resto-U.» "After their drinking binge/[Br.] piss-up⑦, the students had a meal in the university/student restaurant."

«On va becqueter un casse-croûte? Moi, je vais prendre un croque.» "Shall we go and have a snack? I'm gonna/going to have a toasted ham and cheese sandwich."

See also "Entertainment," "Food and Eating."

SHOPPING

le magaze shop

le grand magasin department store

la grande surface supermarket, [Br.] hypermarket

le marché aux puces flea market, [Br.] rag market

faire du lèche-vitrines to go window-shopping

faire/courir les magasins/magazes to go shopping, [Br.] to go around the shops

se payer quelque chose to treat oneself to something

les fringues (fpl) clothes, [Br.] gear

le blot discount, special price

faire de la chine, chiner to hunt for antiques/secondhand goods ■ **«Il adore chiner/faire de la chine mais la plupart du temps il trouve que dalle.»** "He loves hunting for antiques/secondhand goods, but most of the time he finds nothing at all/[Br.] damn all."

la brocante, la chine secondhand trade

la brocasse secondhand goods

le broc, le broco secondhand goods dealer

le pinardier wine merchant, [Br.] plonk seller

le commerçant (market) trader, shopkeeper

«Je me suis payé du gros rouge dans la grande surface située près de l'autoroute car il coûte moins cher que chez le pinardier de mon quartier.» "I bought some red [Br.] plonk from the supermarket/hypermarket near the expressway/[Br.] motorway because it's cheaper than at my local liquor store/wine merchant's/[Br.] offie/[Br.] off-license."

«Ma gonzesse aime faire du lèche-vitrines mais plutôt que de courir les grands magasins, elle est obligée de passer son temps au marché aux puces car on est presque fauchés. La semaine dernière elle a trouvé des fringues sensass.» "My babe/chick/[Br.] bird likes to go window-shopping but instead of going to department stores, she has to spend her time at the flea market because we're almost broke/[Br.] skint. Last week she found some great threads/[Br.] gear."

«J'ai demandé au broc de me faire un blot mais... nib de nib.» "I asked the secondhand dealer for a discount but got nothing/[Br.] sweet FA⑦/[Br.] sod-all."

TAXIS

le bahut, le sapin, le taco(t) taxi, cab

le noirot, le nuitard late-night taxi

la loche cabbie, cabdriver

le galérien driver of a taxi that has a roof rack

NOTE: In standard French, a "roof rack" on a vehicle is **une galerie.**

être/rester en strasse (of taxi) to be/to wait at a taxi stand/[Br.]taxi rank

le Jacquot, le mouchard, la pendule (taxi) meter

le copeau short journey, trip

la maraude soliciting fares/[Br.] touting for clients away from taxi stands/[Br.] ranks

le maraudeur taxi driver soliciting fares/[Br.] touting for clients away from taxi stands/[Br.] ranks

marauder to solicit/[Br.] tout for hire, to solicit/[Br.] tout for customers on the streets

défoncer la plaque to work beyond permitted hours

NOTE: **Défoncer** in slang French means "to work hard"; **la plaque** is a license/registration plate.

faire du tout-debout not to switch on the meter

«La loche qui m'a conduit à mon hôtel était un nuitard qui maraudait quand il m'a chargé. Mais le sacré connardⓉ **a fait du tout-debout et je suis certain qu'il avait défoncé la plaque.»** "The driver who took me to my hotel was a late-night cabbie/cabdriver who was soliciting fares/[Br.] touting for hire when he picked me up. But the goddamnedⓉ bastardⓉ didn't switch on the meter and I'm sure he was working beyond his permitted hours."

SUBWAY/UNDERGROUND

le dur, le métral, le tromé subway, [Br.] metro, [Br.] tube, [Br.] underground

NOTE: **Le tromé** is yet another example of *verlan* and is derived from the standard word for subway/underground, **le métro**; **le métral** is a deformation of the same word.

brûler le dur to travel on the subway/[Br.] tube/train without a ticket

la bouche de métral/métro subway/[Br.] underground entrance ▪ **«Comme la station était fermée, on a passé la nuit sur une bouche de métral.»** "As the station was closed, we spent the night in the subway entrance."

le ticson, le biffeton, le bifton ticket (for transportation, theater)

NOTE: In slang French, **le biffeton, le bifton** also mean a "banknote" and a "doctor's prescription/[Br.] certificate."

la carte orange (*lit.*, the orange card) long-term ticket for public transportation in the Paris region

le carnet (de tickets) book of ten tickets (which gives a discount)

la RATP [Régie Autonome des Transports Parisiens] the Paris transport authority

le RER [Réseau Express Régional] rapid-transit train service in the Paris region (which goes well beyond the **métro** lines to the suburbs)

«Il a perdu son bifton mais le contrôleur était persuadé qu'il brûlait le dur.» "He lost his ticket but the conductor/[Br.] ticket inspector was convinced that he hadn't bought one."

WALKING

le chauffard road hog, dangerous driver

se payer un piéton (*lit.*, to treat oneself to a pedestrian) to hit a pedestrian

brûler un feu rouge (*lit.*, to burn a red light) to go through a red light

la viande à pneu (*lit.*, lump of meat/carcass with tires) imprudent pedestrian

(se) bagot(t)er to walk, to go on foot

se baguenauder to wander, to saunter around

faire un footing to go for a jog

faire le bitume/le macadam to walk the streets, to be a hooker, [Br.] to be on the game

NOTE: The standard French expression for **faire le bitume/le macadam** is **faire le trottoir.**

«Ce chauffard a brûlé le feu rouge et s'est payé un piéton.» "This road hog/[Br.] speed merchant/dangerous driver went through a red light and hit a pedestrian."

«Moi, je voulais tout simplement me baguenauder mais ma copine est partie faire un footing.» "I just wanted to saunter/wander around but my girlfriend went for a jog."

«J'avais envie de bagoter mais je ne m'attendais pas à voir tant de putes qui faisaient le bitume.» "I wanted to go on foot/go for a walk, but I didn't expect to see so many hookers/[Br.] pros walking the streets/[Br.] on the game."

PARIS

Paname, Pantruche Paris

le parigot, la parigote Parisian

NOTE: There are many slang words and phrases for the streets, monuments, and civic buildings of Paris. Here is a list of the most obvious or famous ones, classified according to the **arrondissement** (the numbered administrative district) in which they are situated:

1er arrondissement (Right Bank)

la Cigogne (*lit.*, the stork) law courts, the police headquarters

NOTE: In standard French, law courts are **Le Palais de Justice**; police headquarters are **la Préfecture de Police**.

la Grande Boulange the Bank of France

la Tour pointue (*lit.*, the pointed tower) police headquarters

2ème arrondissement (Right Bank)

l'Embrouille (la Bourse) the Stock Exchange

3ème arrondissement (Right Bank)

la Quincampe la rue Quincampoix

4ème arrondissement (Right Bank)

le Pompidolium, la Raffinerie (*lit.*, the refinery), **l'Usine à gaz** (*lit.*, the gasworks) the Pompidou Center

le Sébasto, le Topol le boulevard Sébastopol

5ème arrondissement (Left Bank)

le Latin, le Boul' Mich Latin Quarter, Boulevard St-Michel

le Baz Grand lycée Louis-le-Grand

Sainte-Ginette Sainte-Geneviève library

la Mouffe Mouffetard quarter

la Mutu Palais de la Mutualité

6ème arrondissement (Left Bank)

le Lucal, le Luco the Luxembourg Gardens

Saint Ger Saint-Germain-des-Prés

7ème arrondissement (Left Bank)

le Poireau (*lit.*, the leek), **la Tour Cifelle** the Eiffel Tower

la Terre sainte (*lit.*, the Holy Land) area between the **esplanade des Invalides** and the Champs-Élysées

les Invalos, les Invaloches Invalides

8ème arrondissement (Right Bank)

les Champs the Champs-Élysées

11ème arrondissement (Right Bank)

la Bastaga, la Bastoche the Bastille

13ème arrondissement (Left Bank)

Tonguinam Chinese quarter at the Porte d'Ivry

14ème arrondissement (Left Bank)

Montparno Montparnasse

la Santaga, la Santoche Santé prison

16ème arrondissement (Right Bank)

le Troca Trocadéro

20ème arrondissement (Right Bank)

Ménilmuche Ménilmontant

EXERCISES

C'est à vous maintenant!

A *Match the slang French words below with their English translation, remembering that some words have a dual meaning.*

beuverie	casse-croûte	frichti	gueuleton	tortore

1. blowout/[Br.] nosh-up ______________
2. meal ______________
3. binge/[Br.] piss-up ______________
4. snack, sandwich ______________
5. food, meal ______________

B *Match the English words and phrases below with their slang French equivalent.*

clothes/[Br.] gear	discount/special price	store/shop
secondhand dealer	secondhand trade	

1. magaze ______________
2. blot ______________

3. **fringues** ________________________
4. **brocante** ________________________
5. **broc** ________________________

C *Give the slang French for the following English words and phrases.*

1. a taxi driver soliciting fares/[Br.] touting for hire away from taxi stands/[Br.] taxi ranks ________________________
2. taxi, cab ________________________
3. a short journey or trip (in a taxi) ________________________
4. a subway/[Br.] underground entrance ________________________
5. a book of tickets (on the Paris subway/[Br.] underground) ________________________

D *Match the following slang French expressions with their English equivalent.*

brûler un feu rouge	**faire le bitume/le macadam**
faire un footing	**se payer un piéton**

1. to go for a jog ________________________
2. to hit a pedestrian (when driving a car) ________________________
3. to go through a red light ________________________
4. to walk the streets/to be a hooker/[Br.] to be on the game ________________________

E *Give slang French alternatives for the following slang expressions referring to Paris and to monuments or areas of Paris.*

1. **la Santoche** ________________________
2. **le Boul' Mich** ________________________
3. **Pantruche** ________________________
4. **le Pompidolium** ________________________
5. **la Tour Cifelle** ________________________

Clothing

See also "Immigrants and Immigration."

DRESSES

des fringues (fpl) clothes, [Br.] gear

se fringuer (chic) to get dolled up/[Br.] tarted up

être tiré(e) à quatre épingles (*lit.*, to be pulled [down]/drawn by four pins) to be dressed (up) to the nines

la serpillière (*lit.*, the mop/[Br.] floorcloth) dress, rag

la roupane dress

la robe de quatre sous cheap dress

collant(e) skintight, tight fitting, clinging

«Elle aime bien se fringuer pour sortir mais hier soir elle portait une robe de quatre sous.» "She loves to get dressed up to go out but yesterday evening she was wearing a cheap dress."

«Maman a mis du sent-bon et une roupane de satin blanc très collante. Elle est sensass!» "Mommy's/[Br.] Mummy's put on some perfume and a skintight, white satin dress. She looks sensational/brilliant!"

NOTE: **Sent-bon** (m) is an expression used by children.

«Lui, il était tiré à quatre épingles mais elle avait mis une serpillière qu'elle s'était payée au marché des puces.» "He was dressed (up) to the nines, but she put on a dress she bought at the flea/[Br.] rag market."

FASHION/FASHION ACCESSORIES

l'esclave (m/f) **de la mode** fashion victim, slave to fashion

les grands couturiers great fashion designers

du beau linge (*lit.*, fine linen) high society, jet set

le dernier cri (*lit.*, the last cry/shout) latest fashion

s'habiller mode to wear the latest fashion

NOTE: In the expression **une robe très mode**, the noun **mode** is used adjectivally; it is used adverbially in the expression **s'habiller mode**.

être mal fagoté(e) to be badly dressed, [Br.] to be dressed like a dog's dinner

être ficelé(e) (*lit.*, to be tied up) to be dolled/[Br.] tarted up, to be very chic

se nipper to get dressed up, [Br.] to tog oneself up

la robe très mode really trendy dress

le bénard, le culbutant, le falzar pants, trousers, [Br.] bags, [Br.] strides

NOTE: There are several alternative slang words for pants/trousers: **le froc, le fendard, le fendant, le fendu** (men's pants/trousers), **le fourreau, le futal, le fute, le grimpant, le rofou, le valseur.**

la limace, la limouse, la liquette shirt

l'imper (m) raincoat

NOTE: **Imper** is an abbreviation of the standard term **imperméable.**

le cuir leather jacket

le zomblou bomber jacket

NOTE: **Un zomblou** is an example of *verlan* and is based on the noun **blouson.**

des lisses (fpl) stockings, nylons

le bitos hat, [Br.] tifter

le galure, le galurin hat

le larfou scarf

NOTE: **Un larfou** is an example of *verlan* and is based on the noun **foulard.**

des tirants (mpl) stockings (worn with suspenders/garters)

le tire-jus⑦**, le tire-moelle**⑦ snot rag, [Br.] nose wipe

«Il y a toujours du beau linge chez les grands couturiers.» "There are always members of the jet set/high society in the houses of the great fashion designers."

«Elle prétend s'habiller mode mais chaque fois que je la vois, elle est mal fagotée.» "She claims to wear the latest fashions, but every time I see her, she's dressed like something the cat dragged in/[Br.] a dog's dinner."

«Elle est toujours bien ficelée: elle se nippe chez Givenchy et cette semaine elle cherche un galurin et un imper.» "She's always well dressed/dressed to the nines; she buys her clothes/[Br.] gear at Givenchy's, and this week she's looking for a hat and a raincoat."

«Il a acheté un fendard et un zomblou mais les limouses et les larfous ne lui plaisaient pas.» "He bought some pants/trousers/[Br.] bags and a bomber jacket, but didn't like the shirts and scarves."

FASHION MODELS

NOTE: The terms marked (ok) are standard French expressions.

le mannequin(ok) fashion model

le défilé de mannequins(ok) fashion parade

le podium(ok) catwalk

la présentation de modèles/de collection(ok) fashion show

faire les collections parisiennes/londoniennes(ok) to go to the Paris/London fashion shows

le modèle(ok) model, design

le top model, le modèle top model

avoir un look d'enfer to look great/cool/[Br.] wicked

«J'ai rencontré ce top model quand je faisais les collections parisiennes. Quand je l'ai vu(e) dans un défilé de mannequins, je me suis dit, ‹Pige-moi ça! Elle a un look d'enfer›.» "I met this top model when I was doing the Paris fashion shows. When I saw her in a fashion parade, I said to myself, 'Just get a load of that! She looks really cool/[Br.] wicked.' "

Elle a un look d'enfer.

SHOES

NOTE: Slang French has many words and phrases for shoes, including **des asperges** (f) (high heels; also, penis, "beanpole"), **des basks** (f) (basketball shoes, [Br.] trainers), **des croquenots** (m) (large shoes), **des écrase-merde**⚠ (m/f) (large shoes, *lit.*, "shit-stompers⚠"), **des godasses** (f) (very commonly used in slang French), **des grolles** (f), **des lattes** (f) (*lit.*, boards/slats), **des patins** (m) (the standard meaning is "skates" as in **patins à glace** [ice skates] and **patins à roulettes** [roller skates]), **des péniches** (f) (*lit.*, barges), **des peupons** (f) (*verlan* slang, based on **pompes**), **des pompes** (f), **des ribouis** (m), **des sorlots** (m), **des targettes** (f) (clodhoppers; also means "feet" in slang French), **des tartines** (f) (*lit.*, slices of bread), **des tatanes** (f), **des tiges** (f) (feet, penis), **des trottinets** (f) (feet).

«Lui avait mis des baskets et son frangin des écrase-merde; la frangine n'avait rien aux arpions.» "He'd put on some basketball shoes/[Br.] trainers and his brother some clodhoppers/shit-stompers⚠; their sister had nothing on her feet."

SPORTSWEAR

des basks (fpl) basketball shoes, [Br.] trainers

des chaussures de jogging running shoes, [Br.] trainers

le jogging sweat suit, sweats, tracksuit

faire son jogging quotidien to go for one's daily jog/run

le survêt' sweat suit, sweats, tracksuit

NOTE: **Le survêt/survêt'** is an abbreviation of the standard term **le survêtement**; **la veste de survêt(ement)** (sweat jacket, tracksuit top); **le pantalon de survêt(ement)** (sweat pants, tracksuit bottom/pants).

«Elle met des basks et son survêt pour faire son jogging quotidien.» "She puts on running shoes and her sweats to go on her daily jog."

SUITS

le costard suit

s'habiller en pingouin (*lit.*, to dress as a penguin) to wear a dinner/dress suit; to wear tails

«Lui ne met jamais son costard mais son copain adore s'habiller en pingouin.» "He never puts on a suit/[Br.] whistle and flute, but his buddy/[Br.] mate loves to wear a tux/[Br.] dinner suit."

UNDERWEAR

des fringues (fpl) **de coulisse** underwear, lingerie

la minouse panties, [Br.] knickers, pants

le barsli, le bénouze, le calcif briefs, underpants

NOTE: **Le bénouze** can be used for a man's or a woman's briefs/panties. Other words for men's underpants are **le calbar, le calebar, le calfouette, le caneçon** (all of which mean "boxer shorts"), and **le slibar** (briefs).

le cache-frifri, le string G-string, skimpy panties

le sostène, le soutif bra, [Br.] boulder-holder

«Elle a des tiroirs pleins de fringues de coulisse—minouses, soutifs et même des cache-frifri. Son mari manque de caneçons.» "She has drawers full of underwear/lingerie: panties/[Br.] knickers, bras/boulder-holders and even G-strings. Her husband is short of boxer shorts/boxers."

VACATION CLOTHES

NOTE: The terms marked (ok) are standard French expressions.

la casquette de baseball(ok) baseball cap

le chapeau de soleil(ok) sun hat

le pare-brise (*lit.,* windshield/[Br.] windscreen) glasses, [Br.] specs, goggles

des lunettes noires/de soleil(ok) shades, sunglasses

des bernicles (fpl), **des carreaux** (mpl) glasses, [Br.] specs

NOTE: A humorous alternative to **bernicles** is **besicles** (fpl).

des espagas (fpl), **des espadoches** (fpl) espadrilles, fabric sandals

le short(ok) shorts

le string, le cache-frifri G-string, thong

NOTE: A standard alternative to **un string** is **un cache-sexe.**

le maillot de bain(ok) swimsuit, [Br.] swimming costume

le slip de bain(ok) swim(ming) trunks

le monokini(ok) topless swimsuit

le bikini(ok) bikini

Le topless est interdit. Topless bathing is forbidden.

«Il a enlevé ses lunettes noires et a mis ses bernicles car il avait vu deux gonzesses; la première d'entre elles portait seulement un string et l'autre un monokini minuscule—et ça sur une plage où le topless était interdit!» "He took off his shades and put on his glasses/[Br.] specs/goggles because he'd seen two chicks/babes: the first was only wearing a G-string and the other just a skimpy bikini bottom—and on a beach where topless bathing was forbidden/banned!"

EXERCISES

C'est à vous maintenant!

A *Give the slang or idiomatic French equivalent of the following English expressions.*

1. to be dressed like something the cat dragged in/[Br.] a dog's dinner ____________________
2. to look great/cool/[Br.] wicked ____________________
3. to wear a tux/dinner suit/dress suit ____________________
4. to be dolled up/[Br.] tarted up ____________________
5. to be dressed (up) to the nines ____________________

B *Translate the following sentences into English.*

1. **Maman porte une robe de quatre sous.**

   ____

2. **C'est un esclave de la mode.**

   ____

3. **Elle a fait les collections parisiennes.**

   ____

4. **Le topless est interdit ici.**

   ____

5. **Je mets mon survêt' pour faire mon jogging quotidien.**

   ____

C *Give the slang French equivalent of the following words and phrases.*

1. panties/[Br.] knickers ______________________
2. large shoes, "shit-stompers"⑦ ______________________
3. a bomber jacket ______________________
4. a dress ______________________
5. a G-string/thong ______________________

D *Translate the following slang French words into English.*

1. **des godasses** ______________________
2. **des basks** ______________________
3. **un calcif** ______________________
4. **une limouse** ______________________
5. **des lisses** ______________________

Conversations and Invitations

See also "Emotions," "Sports," "Weather."

COMPLAINING

faire de la musique (*lit.*, to make music), **renauder** to complain, to bitch(?)

aller au chagrin (*lit.*, to go to the grief/sorrow), **porter le pet**(?) (*lit.*, to carry/take the fart) to lodge/register/put in a complaint

> NOTE: The standard French verb for "to complain" is **se plaindre**; "to register a complaint" is **porter plainte.**

piailler to whine

> NOTE: The verb **piailler** tends to be used of children.

le piailleur, une piailleuse whiner

rouspéter to moan, to grouse

le rouspéteur, la rouspéteuse moaner, complainer

«Tu n'a fait que rouspéter toute la matinée. Qu'est-ce que t'as?» «Y'en a marre! Je vais voir mon patron pour porter le pet.» "You've done nothing but moan all morning. What the heck's wrong with you?" "I'm really pissed(?) off!/ I've really had enough! I'm going to see my boss to put in a complaint."

«C'est un véritable rouspéteur qui passe sa vie entière à renauder.» "He's a real moaner who spends his whole life bitching(?)/complaining."

DISCUSSING YOUR HEALTH

comment va la santé? how are you?/[Br.] how are you keeping?

être en pleine santé, avoir bon pied bon œil (*lit.*, to have sound feet and eyes) to be hale and hearty

> NOTE: **Avoir bon pied bon œil** is used of older people to indicate that they continue to be in good health.
>
> NOTE: The above expressions can be used in relaxed and semi-formal situations.

couci-couça so-so, fair to middling

se lever du pied gauche (*lit.*, to get up on the left foot) to get up on the wrong side of the bed, [Br.] to get out of bed on the wrong side

NOTE: The above expressions should be reserved for fairly relaxed situations.

avoir le cafard to feel blue

elle n'est pas dans son assiette (*lit.*, she is not in her plate) she isn't feeling too well

la crève cold, flu

NOTE: **La crève** can refer to various (more or less serious) illnesses but usually refers to a cold or flu.

attraper/choper la crève to catch a stinking/nasty cold

raide plastered; drugged

lever le coude (*lit.*, to lift the elbow) to be a heavy drinker

le laziloffe, le nase(?), **le naze**(?) venereal disease, the clap

cloquer le nase/le naze(?) to get/to pass on a dose of the clap

être à deux doigts de la mort (*lit.*, to be two fingers' distance from death) to be at death's door

passer l'arme à gauche (*lit.*, to pass one's weapon to the left), **avaler son bulletin de naissance** (*lit.*, to swallow one's birth certificate) to kick the bucket, to croak, [Br.] to snuff it

manger les pissenlits par la racine (*lit.*, to eat dandelions by their roots) to be pushing up (the) daisies

«Comment va la santé, mon pote?» «Oh, couci-couça: je ne peux pas me plaindre.» "How are you, pal?/[Br.] How are you keeping, mate?" "Oh, fair to middling; I can't complain."

«Le pépère qui habite à côté a bon pied bon œil mais sa bobonne mange les pissenlits par la racine.» «Ah bon? Je n'savais pas que la vieille avait passé l'arme à gauche.» "The old guy who lives next door is hale and hearty but his old lady/old dear is pushing up the daisies." "Really? I didn't know that the old lady had croaked/[Br.] snuffed it."

avaler son bulletin de naissance

«J'ai vraiment le cafard ce matin car je suis persuadé que je vais choper la crève.» «T'as de la chance, toi! Moi, j'ai cloqué le naze⑦ à vingt-deux balais et je suis sûr que je vais avaler mon bulletin de naissance d'ici peu.» "I've really got the blues this morning; I'm convinced I'm going to get a stinking/nasty cold." "You're lucky! I caught the clap when I was twenty-two and I'm sure I'm going to kick the bucket/[Br.] snuff it any time now."

«Ce mec n'est pas dans son assiette aujourd'hui. Qu'est-ce qu'il a?» «Il a passé la nuit à lever le coude, alors, qu'est-ce que tu veux?» "This guy isn't himself today. What's the matter with him?" "He spent all night drinking, so what do you expect?"

DISCUSSING THE WEATHER

aujourd'hui c'est la canicule it's a real scorcher today

le temps est au beau fixe the weather's fine/it's going to be beautiful/[Br.] the weather is set fair

il fait un temps de chien (*lit.*, it's a dog's weather) the weather is lousy

il pleut/tombe des hallebardes (*lit.*, it's raining halberds) it's raining cats and dogs/[Br.] it's bucketing down

il pleut des cordes (*lit.*, it's raining ropes) it's pouring/[Br.] it's bucketing down

le pébroque, le pépin umbrella/[Br.] brolly

NOTE: **Pépin** also means a "hitch" or "snag" in slang French; **J'ai un pépin** (Something's come up); **avaler le pépin** (to get pregnant).

le zef the wind

NOTE: The above locutions are fairly standard but the nouns cited are to be restricted to informal contexts.

«Quel temps fait-il chez toi? C'est la canicule comme ici?» «Non, t'es vraiment à côté de la plaque. Il fait un temps de chien: il pleut des cordes depuis ce matin!» "What's the weather like there? Are you having a heat wave like us?" "No, you're way off the mark. The weather's lousy; it's been pouring/[Br.] bucketing down since this morning!"

«Qu'est-ce qu'elle fait avec son pébroque? Le zef est trop fort pour l'ouvrir.» "What's she doing with her umbrella/[Br.] brolly? The wind is too strong to put it up."

GREETING A FRIEND/STRANGER

Salut, les gars! Hi, you guys! Hello, guys!

Salutas! Howdy!

Enchanté(e)./Très heureux(-euse). Pleased to meet you.

Heureux(-euse) de vous revoir. Nice to see you again.

faire la bise à quelqu'un to kiss someone (on both cheeks) ■ **«Quand j'ai rencontré ma copine, je lui ai fait la bise.»** "When I met my girlfriend, I kissed her on both cheeks."

NOTE: Meeting a stranger for the first time in France tends to be quite a formal affair, and slang or even relaxed expressions should not be used in order to avoid causing offense. It is advisable to use **Monsieur/Madame/Mademoiselle** when greeting a stranger for the first time; the **tu** form should be avoided! An integral part of greeting one's friends in France is kissing them twice (four times for close friends) on the cheeks.

«Salut, les gars! Ça boume?» "Hi, you guys! How's tricks?/How're things?"

«Salut, mon pote! Oui, ça gaze.» "Hi, pal/[Br.] mate! It's going good./Yeah, life's a gas."

«Bonjour, Madame. Je suis très heureuse(-eux) de faire votre connaissance.» "Hello, ma'am. I'm very pleased to meet you."

«Bonsoir, Monsieur. Très heureux(-euse) de vous revoir.» "Good evening, sir. Nice to see you again."

INTERRUPTING

Ta gueule!(?)**/Ferme ta gueule!**(?) Shut your face!(?)/trap!(?)

Vos gueules!(?) Shut up, all/[Br.] the lot of you!

NOTE: The standard French expression for "to interrupt somebody" is **interrompre/couper quelqu'un**; "to cut someone short" is **couper la parole à quelqu'un**.

«Ta gueule!(?) **Si tu dis ça encore une fois devant ma gonzesse, je te casse la figure.»** "Shut your mouth/face! If you say that once more in front of my chick/girl, I'll smash your face in."

INTRODUCING YOURSELF/A FRIEND

Voici mon frangin. This is my brother./Meet my brother.

Voici mes parents. These are my parents./Meet my parents.

C'est moi... (Jean-Claude, etc.) I'm . . . (Jean-Claude, etc.)

Ce sont mes meilleurs amis. They are my best friends.

Voici mes meilleurs amis. These are my best friends.

NOTE: In formal situations, it is much safer to use formal expressions such as **«Je vous présente mes parents»** or **«Je m'appelle Marc»** rather than the more familiar expressions used above.

«Salut, Michel! Voici mon frangin, Jean-Jacques.» "Hi, Michel. This is my brother, Jean-Jacques."

«Salutas! C'est moi Marc, le frangin de Marie-Claire.» "Hi, I'm Marc, Marie-Claire's brother."

INVITING A FRIEND/A STRANGER

becter, becqueter (*lit.*, to peck) to chow (down), [Br.] to nosh

boire un coup to have a drink

la gambille dancing, [Br.] bopping

gambiller, guincher to dance, to boogie

le ciné, le cinoche flicks, movies

pieuter to crash, [Br.] to kip

la piaule pad, place, joint

NOTE: The above expressions should be used in relaxed situations with friends or acquaintances of the same age. If inviting a stranger, it is far safer to stick to more formal invitations such as **«Voulez-vous dîner/danser/aller au cinéma avec moi?»**

«Si on allait becter ensemble? Et après, on pourrait guincher toute la nuit.» "How about a meal/[Br.] nosh together? Afterwards, we could dance the night away."

«Tu peux pieuter chez moi si tu veux. Ma piaule est à cinq minutes d'ici.» "You can crash/[Br.] kip at my place if you like. My pad is only five minutes away from here."

«Veux-tu aller au cinoche avec moi? Ou si tu préfères, on ira boire un coup dans ce bar.» "Would you like to go to the flicks/movies with me? Or if you prefer, we'll go and have a drink in this bar."

MEETING A FRIEND/A STRANGER

le rembour, le rencard, le rancard appointment, meet(ing), date ■ **«On n'a qu'à se filer rencard quelque part.»** "Let's just plan/[Br.] fix a meet(ing) somewhere."

NOTE: The standard French expression for "to arrange to meet someone (at six in the evening)" is **donner rendez-vous à quelqu'un (pour dix-huit heures)**. It is advisable to use such standard expressions when arranging to meet a stranger.

rancarder/rencarder quelqu'un to arrange to meet someone, to make a date with someone ■ **«Elle m'a rencardé pour dix-huit heures mais elle n'est pas venue.»** "She made a date/[Br.] fixed a meet(ing) for six in the evening but she didn't turn up."

être à la bourre to be short of time

«J'avais oublié mon rembour. Et maintenant je suis à la bourre!» "I forgot my appointment and now I'm short of time!"

SAYING GOOD-BYE

Salut!, Ciao! Ta-ta!, [Br.] Ta-ra!, See you!, Bye(-bye)!

un de ces quat' one of these days

«Salut! On se reverra un de ces quat.» "Bye! We'll meet again one of these days."

NOTE: **Un de ces quat'** is a familiar form of **un de ces quatre (matins).**

à la prochaine! be seeing you! ■ **«À la prochaine, mon pote!» «Oui, fais bien attention (à toi).»** "Be seeing you, pal/mate." "Yes, take care."

NOTE: In semi-formal and formal situations, it is better to use **au revoir** and **à la prochaine fois** when saying good-bye to someone.

EXERCISES

C'est à vous maintenant!

A *Give the equivalent slang French expression of the standard words and phrases below.*

1. porter plainte ______________________
2. mourir ______________________
3. boire beaucoup/à l'excès ______________________
4. se plaindre ______________________
5. il fait mauvais ______________________
6. un parapluie ______________________
7. taisez-vous! ______________________
8. danser ______________________
9. aller au cinéma ______________________
10. donner rendez-vous à quelqu'un ______________________

B *Match the corresponding pairs of words and phrases below, placing the more formal or standard expression first.*

EXAMPLE: au revoir, mon ami—à la prochaine, mon pote

salut, les gars	ciao	le zef
becter	manger	ça va
je vous présente mes parents	le vent	salutas
le rhume/la grippe	la crève	voici mes vieux
ça boume	bonjour	au revoir
	bonjour, mes amis	

____________________ — ____________________

____________________ — ____________________

____________________ — ____________________

____________________ — ____________________

____________________ — ____________________

____________________ — ____________________

____________________ — ____________________

____________________ — ____________________

Disputes

NOTE: To help readers to find their way around this section, we have itemized behavior by increasing levels of trouble and seriousness. So, if you are looking for guidance with something relatively minor, start toward the beginning of the section. If you need information on serious aggravation, look toward the end.

BEING ANNOYING

casse-pieds (adj., inv.) annoying, pain-in-the-neck

casse-couilles① (adj., inv.) annoying, pain-in-the-neck

NOTE: Compare with the English: He's a pain in the ass!②/[Br.] nuts!②

faire suer quelqu'un (*lit.*, to make someone sweat) to be a pain to someone

mettre quelqu'un en boîte (*lit.*, to put someone in a box) to annoy someone, [Br.] to wind someone up

remuer le potage (*lit.*, to stir the soup) to stir things up

semer la merde (*lit.*, to sow the shit②) to stir up, [Br.] to wind up ■ **«Il n'est pas mon genre. Il sème la merde n'importe quand!»** "He's not my sort. He's forever making trouble!/[Br.] stirring it up!"

Pas de vagues! (*lit.*, No waves!) Don't make trouble!/[Br.] stir it (up)! ■ **«Dans cette situation, pas de vagues! Mieux vaut un peu de calme.»** "The way things are, don't make waves!/[Br.] stir it (up)! We can do with a bit of calm."

NOTE: Compare English: to make waves.

casser les couilles à quelqu'un① (*lit.*, to break someone's nuts②), **casser les pieds à quelqu'un** (*lit.*, to break someone's feet) to get on someone's nerves, [Br.] to get on someone's wick ■ **«Elle m'a toujours cassé les pieds!»** "She's always got(ten) on my nerves!" ■ **«Tu me les casses!**②**»** "You're getting on my nerves!"

faire tourner quelqu'un en bourrique (*lit.*, to turn someone into an ass) to push someone over the edge, [Br.] to drive someone round the bend/twist

CAUSING TROUBLE

tirer la gueule to pout, [Br.] to pull a (long) face ■ **«Il tire toujours la gueule quand il la voit danser avec un autre!»** "He always pouts/[Br.] pulls a face when he sees her dancing with someone else!"

y mettre son grain de sable (*lit.*, to put in one's grain of sand) to put one's two cents in, to interfere, [Br.] to stick one's oar in ■ **«Elle y met toujours son grain de sable.»** "She's forever putting her two cents in/[Br.] sticking her oar in."

ramener sa fraise (*lit.*, to bring back one's strawberry) to butt in, [Br.] to get stroppy

dire des personnalités (*lit.*, to say/speak personalities) to talk about someone (usually behind his or her back), to bad-mouth

envoyer des vannes à quelqu'un (*lit.*, to send digs/jibes to someone) to get at someone

la ramener (*lit.*, to bring it back) to kick up/make a fuss

forcer la dose (*lit.*, to force the dose) to push it (too far) ■ **«Doucement! Tu forces la dose avec elle!»** "Easy does it! You're pushing it with her!"

faire un fromage(?) (*lit.*, to make a cheese), **faire une montagne** (*lit.*, to make a mountain), **faire un tabac**(?) (*lit.*, to make a tobacco shop), **faire une tartine**(?) (*lit.*, to make a slice of bread and butter) to kick up/make a fuss ■ **«Elle fait un tabac pour un rien!»** "She makes a fuss out of nothing!"

faire chier(?) **quelqu'un** (*lit.*, to make someone shit(?)) to make someone sick

faire une scène to make a scene

se monter la tête (*lit.*, to fit out one's head) to blow one's top ■ **«Ne te monte pas la tête pour une fois!»** "Don't blow your top, just for once!"

faire du tam-tam to make a big song and dance (about something), [Br.] to get the jungle drums rolling ■ **«Écoute-moi ça—il y a encore Bernard qui fait du tam-tam!»** "Just listen to that—there's Bernard getting worked up/[Br.] on the jungle drums again!"

faire un foin terrible (*lit.*, to make a terrible hay) to kick up/make one hell of a fuss ■ **«Je ne comprends jamais pourquoi les gens font un foin terrible pour quelque chose de minime comme ça!»** "I never understand why people kick up/make such a hell of a fuss over something trivial like that!"

mettre quelqu'un en boule (*lit.*, to make someone curl up) to raise someone's hackles, to infuriate someone

Ça barde. (*lit.*, That's bristling/[Br.] barding up.) Things are heating up.

le grabuge trouble ■ **«Il y aura du grabuge!»** "There's going to be trouble!"

la casse (bodily) violence, broken bones ■ **«Avant trop longtemps, il y aura de la casse!»** "Before too long, there are going to be some broken bones!"

Ça va barder. There's going to be trouble.

Ça va chauffer. (*lit.*, It's going to heat up.) There's going to be trouble.

le roussi [fig.] a rise in temperature, things heating up, [Br.] hotting up ■ **«Ça sent le roussi!»** "Things are heating/[Br.] hotting up!"

faire bondir quelqu'un (*lit.*, to make someone jump) to make someone hopping mad

aller faire un malheur (*lit.*, to be about to do something unfortunate) to be about to blow up ([Br.] it)/to do something nasty ■ **«S'il ne s'excuse pas, je sais que je vais faire un malheur!»** "If he doesn't say sorry, I know I'm going to blow up!"

faire râler quelqu'un (*lit.*, to make someone rattle) to make/[Br.] send someone livid

attraper (*lit.*, catch), **engueuler**(!) (*lit.*, roast), **enguirlander**(?) (*lit.*, decorate), **passer un savon à** (*lit.*, soap), **secouer les puces à** (*lit.*, shake fleas at), **sonner les cloches** (*lit.*, ring the bells) to tell someone off

NOTE: The use of any of the above preceded by **se faire** will give the idea of "to get," e.g., **«Je me suis fait attraper par lui!»** "I got told off by him!"

T'occupe!(?) Mind your own (darned) business!

NOTE: This is a shortened and very abrupt form of **Occupe-toi de tes propres affaires!**

secouer les puces à quelqu'un

se chamailler to squabble

faire passer un mauvais quart d'heure à (*lit.*, to give someone a bad quarter of an hour) to give someone a bad time ■ **«Elle m'a fait passer un mauvais quart d'heure pour l'avoir oubliée!»** "She gave me a bad time for having forgotten her!"

se foutreⒾ **en rogne/boule** (*lit.*, to get oneself into a temper/[Br.] ball) to get cross, annoyed

faire du roucan/raffut/barouf to cause a commotion, [Br.] to kick up a stink

être furax/furibard(e)/furibond(e) to be livid

se bouffer le nezⓉ to be at each other's throats ■ **«Elles se bouffent le nez pour cet-homme-là—incroyable!»** "They're at each other's throats for that guy over there—unbelievable!"

NOTE: This is a graphic and not particularly pleasant image. Two people are finger-jabbing at such close quarters that they are liable to ram each other up the nose.

faire une croix dessus (*lit.*, to draw a cross above) to settle, close (it), [Br.] to draw a line under ■ **«On a eu un différend—maintenant, faisons une croix dessus!»** "We've had a difference of opinion—now, let's settle/[Br.] draw a line under it!"

passer l'éponge là-dessus (*lit.*, to wipe the sponge over it) to forget/wipe the slate clean of something ■ **«On est toujours amis? Cette bagarre, passons l'éponge là-dessus!»** "Are we still friends? Let's just forget about this little quarrel!"

VERBAL ABUSE

Pauv' tache! (*lit.*, poor [Br.] stain/blob/blot!) You poor jerk!, [Br.] Sad git!, [Br.] Sad berk!

CAUSING AND SUFFERING VIOLENCE

la baffe, la gifle slap (on/in the face)

allonger/ficher/flanquer/foutre une baffe/gifle à quelqu'un to give someone a slap ■ **«Je lui flanquerai une giroflée à cinq feuilles!»** "I'm going to give him a real slap in the face!"

NOTE: This expression is a poetic and, under the circumstances, almost pretty image. **Giroflée** (stock, wallflower) is a play on **gifle** and the **cinq feuilles** are the five fingers of the hand! So the listener has the mental picture of a scented wallflower with five leaves being applied to the face of the offending person. Because the expression is humorous, it can actually defuse the situation.

donner une fessée à quelqu'un (*lit.*, to give someone a swat/[Br.] bottoming) to give someone a spanking ■ **«Si tu continues comme ça, je te donnerai une bonne fessée!»** "If you carry on like that, I'll give you a good spanking!"

botter les fesses à quelqu'un(?) (*lit.*, to boot the backside) to kick someone up the ass(?)/[Br.] arse(?)

flanquer une beigne/une châtaigne/un gnon/un marron/une pêche/une taloche à quelqu'un (*lit.*, to give someone a slap/a chestnut/a thump/a peach/a cuff) to slug someone, [Br.] to clout/thump someone

la bagarre brawl

chercher la bagarre to look for a fight

c'est la bagarre (*lit.*, it's the battle) to have it in for ■ **«Entre eux, c'est la bagarre, pure et simple!»** "They've got it in for each other, simple as that!"

se bagarrer to brawl

envoyer les cinq/le poing (*lit.*, [Br.] to send one's five/fist) to punch ■ **«T'as vu comment elle lui a envoyé le poing à la figure?»** "Did you see how she punched him in the face?"

se bagarrer, se tabasser, se taper dessus to fight, to go at it, [Br.] to have a punch-up

flanquer (*lit.*, to give)**/ficher**(?)**/foutre**(!) **une trempe** (*lit.*, a soaking) **à quelqu'un** to beat someone up

flanquer (*lit.*, to give)**/ficher**(?)**/foutre**(!) **une raclée** (*lit.*, a scraping) **à quelqu'un** to beat someone up ■ **«Si tu fais de l'œil à sa gonzesse, il te fichera une raclée!»** "If you give his chick/[Br.] bird the eye, he'll beat you up!"

amocher quelqu'un (*lit.*, to make someone ugly), **casser la figure/la gueule à quelqu'un, casser la tronche à quelqu'un** (*lit.*, to smash someone's [Br.] nut/bonce), **casser le portrait à quelqu'un** (*lit.*, to smash someone's portrait) to bash/smash someone's face in ■ **«Je te casserai la gueule, je te le promets!»** "I'll smash your face in, I promise you!"

faire une grosse tête à quelqu'un (*lit.*, to give someone a big head) to bash someone's face/head in ■ **«T'as vu la grosse tête qu'elle lui a faite?»** "Have you seen what a mess she made of his face?"

NOTE: **Une grosse tête** is more commonly an egghead.

«Elle a fait une grosse tête de son mec.» "She made an egghead out of her guy."

abîmer le portrait de/à quelqu'un (*lit.*, to damage someone's portrait) to bash someone's face in ■ **«Il t'abîmera le portrait pour un rien!»** "He'll smash your face in for the hell of it!"

arranger le portrait de/à quelqu'un to rearrange someone's face ■ **«Il t'arrangera le portrait à un prix avantageux!»** "He'll rearrange your face at a bargain price!"

piquer, planter, poignarder quelqu'un (*lit.*, [Br.] to sting/plant/dagger someone) to stab, [Br.] to stick one in on someone ■ **«Si tu dis rien, je te plante!»** "If you say anything, I'll stab you/[Br.] stick one in on you!"

descendre quelqu'un (*lit.*, to drop someone) to do in, to kill, to bump off, to knock off someone ■ **«Il l'a descendue au grand jour!»** "He bumped her off in broad/full daylight!»

faire la peau à quelqu'un (*lit.*, to skin someone) to do in, to kill, to bump off, to knock someone off ■ **«Elle jure de lui faire la peau!»** "She swears she's going to knock him off!"

zigouiller to do in, to kill, to bump, to knock off

le feu, le flingue, le flingo gun, [Br.] shooter, shooting iron

flinguer quelqu'un (*lit.*, to gun someone) to shoot someone

ficher/foutre une balle dans la peau (*lit.*, to put a bullet in the skin) to shoot ■ **«Il a foutu une balle dans la peau de sa nana, salaud!»** "He shot his girlfriend, the swine!"

POLICE AND OTHER INTERVENTIONS

le barbouze plainclothes cop, [Br.] police plant

le flic, le poulet cop, policeman

la flicaille the cops, the fuzz

les vaches the pigs

la vache à roulettes (*lit.*, cow on casters/skates) motor-cop, [Br.] speed-cop

le panier à salade (*lit.*, salad basket) police van, [arch. Br.] a Black Maria

le gorille bodyguard, bouncer ■ **«Gare au gorille!»** "Watch out for the bouncer!"

> NOTE: This expression became immortalized in Georges Brassens's classic song *Le Gorille*, in which it refers literally to a gorilla.

la maison royco police station, [Br.] station house, [Br.] the cop shop

la taule, la tôle prison

EXERCISES

C'est à vous maintenant!

A *Selecting one item from each column, put together the pairs of expressions that mean approximately the same thing.*

____	1. mettre en boîte	a. faire une tartine
____	2. casser les pieds	b. flanquer une baffe
____	3. faire un fromage	c. botter les fesses
____	4. barder	d. semer la merde
____	5. allonger une gifle	e. se tabasser
____	6. donner une fessée	f. chauffer
____	7. se bagarrer	g. faire chier

B *From the list of expressions below, make groups of those that mean the same thing.*

1. roucan	5. une beigne	9. furax	13. un flingo
2. furibond	6. passer un savon	10. une taloche	14. attraper
3. engueuler	7. une châtaigne	11. barouf	15. une pêche
4. un flingue	8. raffut	12. un feu	16. furibard

____—____—____

____—____—____

____—____—____

____—____—____—____

____—____—____

C *There has been a dispute outside a French café. Alex has been hurt. Interpret for him the colorful language used by his assailant to the police.*

1. Ce ricain y a mis son grain de sel!

   ____

2. Il forçait la dose!

   ____

3. Il me faisait bondir!

   ____

4. Il cherchait la bagarre!

   ____

5. Je lui ai dit «T'occupe!»

   ____

6. Puis, ça bardait,...

   ____

7. Et je lui ai fiché une baffe. C'est tout!

   ____

Drinks

GENERAL DRINKING

NOTE: Wine is the natural drink in France, almost to the point of being a national emblem. Consequently, the great majority of the vocabulary and expressions relating to the consumption of alcohol comes from two thousand years of wine drinking!

aimer son pinard to like one's wine (general, very ordinary quality) ■ **«Il a toujours aimé son pinard, celui-là!»** "That fellow's always liked his wine!"

NOTE: Everyday colloquial register for matter-of-fact statements.

le gros rouge ordinary red wine ■ **«On le trouve toujours au zinc avec son gros rouge comme compagnon.»** "You'll always find him at the bar (counter) with his red wine to keep him company."

NOTE: Colloquial/slang register; inoffensive and often used humorously.

NOTE: **Gros(se)** (fat/cuddly).

le rouquin (*lit.*, the red-haired one) red wine with a bit more body ■ **«Lui, il va rester célibataire. Il est déjà marié au rouquin!»** "He'll stay a bachelor. He's already married to his (strong) red wine!"

NOTE: Colloquial/slang register; often used humorously, as above.

la piquette cheap wine, rotgut, [Br.] plonk ■ **«Pour lui, la piquette c'est les grands crus!»** "For him, any rotgut/[Br.] plonk is a great wine!"

NOTE: Originally colloquial/slang register, now acceptable colloquial French, especially as it can convey humor or condescension, as above.

la bébine weak/poor quality wine ■ **«Chez eux, on ne boit que de la bébine.»** "At their place, they only drink the weak/poor stuff."

NOTE: Colloquial/slang register, unlikely to cause offense.

le tord-boyaux rotgut, [Br.] gut-rot ■ **«Tu ne t'attends pas à ce que je boive ce tord-boyaux?»** "You're not expecting me to drink that rotgut/[Br.] gut-rot?"

NOTE: Colloquial, fairly coarse register; in very polite company, it would only be used to add a bit of theater or deliberate color to the conversation.

NOTE: The **tord-boyaux** was a medieval instrument of torture, used on the intestines.

un coup de rouge (*lit.*, a shot of red) glass/drop of red ■ **«Je prendrai un coup de rouge.»** "I'll have a drop of the red."

NOTE: Colloquial, affectionate, slightly colorful, and most unlikely to offend.

NOTE: **Le coup** (strike, blow).

le petit canon (*lit.*, little cannon) small glass of wine (derived from the shape of the glass) ■ **«Tu as suffisamment de place pour un petit canon.»** "You've got enough room for a small glass."

NOTE: A colloquial but universal expression that will raise a smile, even in the most proper company.

NOTE: **Le canon** (tube, barrel); compare current Australian/British English "I'll have a tube" (of lager).

les cadavres (mpl) empties ■ **«Toi, tu peux ranger tes propres cadavres!»** "You can clear away your own empties!"

NOTE: Again, colloquial but universal; likely to raise a smile, whatever the company.

NOTE: **Le cadavre** (corpse); the term arises from the witty idea that an empty bottle, like a dead corpse, is an empty vessel from which the spirit has flown.

DRINKING AND DRUNKENNESS

NOTE: Until relatively recent times, the wine in France was cleaner and, therefore, safer to drink than the water. This state of affairs, together with the abundance of winegrowing areas in France, meant that a certain level of alcoholism was endemic in the rural population. Consequently, of all the major languages, French has the richest fund of expressions to describe drink and the various levels of drunkenness. This thesaurus provides you with a selection of the most common terms that you may encounter.

prendre un pot to have a drink/[Br.] jar ■ **«Tu vas prendre un pot avec nous?»** "Are you going to have a drink/[Br.] jar with us?"

NOTE: Colloquial register for a pleasant drink, usually in company.

NOTE: **Le pot** (pot, jar).

boire un coup (*lit.*, to drink a shot) to have a drink ■ **«Je suis complètement stressé; je vais boire un coup!»** "I'm stressed-out; I'm going to have a drink."

NOTE: Colloquial register for an eagerly anticipated drink.

NOTE: **Le coup** (stroke, blow, [lifting] action).

s'en jeter un dernier (*lit.*, to throw oneself a last one) to have one for the road ■ **«Si on s'en jetait un dernier?»** "How about having one for the road?"

avoir une sacrée descente (*lit.*, to have a hell of a downslope) to be able to put it away/knock it back ▪ **«C'est ton dixième whisky! Tu as une sacrée descente!»** "It's your tenth whisky! You sure know how to knock it back!"

arroser un événement to celebrate an event ▪ **«Viens avec nous! On va arroser l'arrivée du bébé.»** "Come with us! We're going to drink to the baby's health/[Br.] wet the baby's head."

NOTE: Colloquial and universal, with pleasant undertones.

NOTE: **Arroser** (to water, to wash down); **Ça s'arrose!** (This calls for a celebration!)

baptiser son vin to dilute one's wine ▪ **«Pour les gosses au repas, on peut toujours baptiser le vin.»** "For the kids, we can always dilute the wine with the meal."

NOTE: Colloquial and universal; a pleasant image, causing no offense.

NOTE: **Baptiser** (to baptize, i.e., to anoint with water).

picoler to booze ▪ **«S'il picole? Il a toujours eu du vin dans les veines!»** "Does he booze? It's always been wine that's flowed through his veins!"

NOTE: Colloquial/slang; mildly unpleasant and offensive.

le buveur, la buveuse drinker

NOTE: Standard French.

NOTE: The following is a list of the most common colloquial/slang expressions for a "drunkard" and a "boozer," all of which are mildly unpleasant and offensive: **le/la poivrot(e), le/la soûlard(e), le/la soûlot(te), le/la boit-sans-soif, le picoleur/la picoleuse, le/la soiffard(e).**

l'éponge (f) (*lit.*, sponge) sponge, [Br.] soak ▪ **«Elle n'en boit jamais moins de deux bouteilles—c'est une véritable éponge!»** "She never drinks less than two bottles. She's a real sponge/[Br.] right soak!"

NOTE: Colloquial/slang; mildly offensive.

être ivre/soûl(e)/saoul(e) to be drunk

NOTE: Standard French.

s'enivrer, se soûler, se saouler to get oneself drunk

NOTE: Standard French.

NOTE: **Se saouler la gueule**(!) (*lit.*, to get one's mouth drunk) is slang and will often cause considerable offense.

être beurré(e) (*lit.*, to be buttered) to be drunk/plastered ▪ **«'Faut l'éviter, il est complètement beurré ce soir!»** "Keep out of his way, he's plastered tonight!"

NOTE: Colloquial/slang register; it would cause mild offense to some people.

NOTE: The following is a short list of the most common alternatives for "plastered." All belong to the colloquial/slang register and, with the exception of **rond**, they are all mildly offensive: **blindé(e), bourré(e), paf, rond(e) (comme une bille)** (*lit.*, round [as a marble]), **schlass.**

NOTE: The following is a similar list of ways of saying "to get loaded/[Br.] get pissed(?)." All belong to the colloquial/slang register and are mildly offensive: **se cuiter, se payer une bonne cuite, prendre une cuite.**

NOTE: **Une cuite** (a good cooking); compare English "a skinful."

être pompette to be tipsy ■ **«Ta fiancée est un peu pompette ce soir.»** "Your girlfriend's a bit drunk tonight."

NOTE: Colloquial register; mild and slightly picturesque. It tends to be used pleasantly of people who are not habitual drinkers.

avoir un coup dans l'aile (*lit.*, to have something stuck in the propeller blade) to be tipsy, to have been drinking/[Br.] at the bottle ■ **«Je te dis qu'il a un coup dans l'aile—écoute la façon dont il divague!»** "I'm telling you, he's been drinking/[Br.] at the bottle—listen to how he's rambling on!"

NOTE: Colloquial/slang register; picturesque and mildly humorous.

avoir un verre dans le nez (*lit.*, to have a glass up one's nose) to have had one too many ■ **«Elle a un verre dans le nez et pas pour la première fois, je t'assure!»** "She's had one too many and not for the first time, I'm telling you!"

NOTE: Colloquial; picturesque and likely to raise a smile.

Elle a un verre dans le nez et pas pour la première fois.

cuver son vin (*lit.*, to ferment one's wine) to sleep it off ■ **«Elle a une constitution solide. Elle cuve toujours son vin!»** "She's got a strong constitution. She can always sleep it off!"

NOTE: Colloquial/picturesque; will usually raise a mild smile.

avoir la gueule de bois (*lit.*, to have a mouth made of wood) to have a hangover ■ **«Passe moi l'aspirine, j'ai la gueule de bois!»** "Let me have the aspirin; I've got a hangover!"

NOTE: Colloquial/slang; mildly offensive.

INDIVIDUAL WINES AND BEERS

NOTE: Because the French are so attached to the alcohol that goes into their stomachs, a large number of colloquial and slang names for individual drinks and even their containers has developed over the years.

le beaujolpif Beaujolais

la blonde light beer

la boutanche bottle

le calva [calvados] calvados (apple brandy)

le carburant drink that keeps you going

le champ [champagne] champagne, bubbly, [Br.] champers

le cinquante-et-un pastis (after the 51 brand loved in the south of France)

la conso[mmation] drink (in a bar, café, or club)

le gorgeon drink

[boire] la goutte (to have) a drop of brandy

le jaune pastis

la kro [Kronenbourg] Kronenbourg beer

le litron bottle of red wine

la mousse (frothy) beer

le pichtegorne, le picrate, le pinard wine, vino, [Br.] plonk

NOTE: Because the French see themselves, with some justification, as knowing a thing or two about wine, these terms are all a little condescending, but also, as the sound suggests, quite humorous and even affectionate.

le poison officiel (*lit.*, the official poison) pastis

NOTE: **Les pastis**, the aniseed-based range of *apéritifs*, were, like absinthe, traditionally cured in large barrels outside the back door of the farmhouse, hence the term **vin cuit** (see below), a reference to the heat generated when the sun got to work on the barrels. Absinthe, however, was cured in wormwood and the enzymes produced in the process literally rotted the human brain, leading to absinthe's removal from sale at the turn of the twentieth century.

le pousse-au-crime firewater, rotgut, [Br.] gut-rot

le sérieux liter of beer

le tango beer with grenadine syrup

la tomate pastis with grenadine

la valse beer with mint syrup

le vin cuit vermouth

NOTE: Because of the strong sunlight in southern France and in Italy during the summer, the mixture of wine and herbs stored in the farmhouse barrels was often subject to an intense buildup of temperature, which led to very strong mixtures being produced, mixtures which often led to stomach disorders or worse! The term **vin cuit** (*lit.*, cooked wine) is highly pejorative; you would not ask your host or hostess for one, as it implies inferior quality.

(un whisky) bien tassé (*lit.*, [a whisky] well crammed/squeezed in) a good measure (of whisky)

EXERCISES

C'est à vous maintenant!

A *An interested student with little knowledge of French drinking expressions has interpreted a French person's conversation in a very literal way for a fellow English speaker. Look at his rendering, see where he went wrong, and try to produce a more accurate interpretation of the French!*

Le capitaine a trouvé un petit canon pour son numéro deux.
The captain found a little cannon for his number two.

____

Il y avait aussi du tord-boyaux blanc!
There was also a white gut-twisting torture machine.

____

C'était trop terrible!
It was too terrible!

Le capitaine a pris un coup de rouge, aussi!
The captain bled badly as well!

Après, les serviteurs ont rangé les cadavres.
Afterwards the servants cleaned up the corpses.

B *Use the words in the box to complete the following statements and questions.*

aile	ailier	quinze	cinquante-et-un
verre	ver	baptise	baptême
cuve	cure	arsouille	arrosons
peau	pot	carburant	carburer

1. **Il est un peu snob, il ne voulait pas prendre un ____________ avec moi.**
2. **Elle est trop économe. On dit qu'elle ____________ son vin!**
3. **Vous avez gagné le match—félicitations! ____________ le résultat!**
4. **Regarde-la! Elle a un ____________ dans le nez!**
5. **Sophie est en retard? Bien sûr! Elle ____________ son vin.**
6. **Ce n'est pas un ange—il a très souvent un coup dans l'____________!**
7. **Pour elle, le ____________ n'est pas seulement l'essence qu'on met dans le réservoir de sa voiture!**
8. **Il est quel numéro dans l'équipe? Normalement, le sept, mais, les jours de fête, il est plutôt le ____________!**

C *The following statements all include colloquial drinking terms, which can lead to hilarious misunderstandings. Imagine you are interpreting for a friend. Give all the colloquial meanings in English,* ***not*** *the literal ones!*

1. Tu voudrais une tomate?

 ___

2. Après un tango, j'ai toujours une indigestion!

 ___

3. J'ai pris une blonde.

 ___

4. Regarde ce comique avec son sérieux!

 ___

5. Je suis médecin, mais je t'offre le poison officiel!

 ___

6. Nous prenons tous deux une valse.

 ___

7. Il y a une mouche dans le champ!

 ___

Education

EXAMINATIONS

le bac, le bachot the baccalaureate

NOTE: **Le bachot** (**le baccalauréat** in standard French) corresponds roughly to the high-school diploma/[Br.] A levels. Passing the **bac** gives automatic right of entry to most—but not all—courses in French universities.

la boîte à bachot cram[ming] school, [Br.] crammer('s)

le bachotage cramming

bachoter, faire du bachotage to cram/[Br.] to swot for an exam

le bachoteur, la bachoteuse student cramming for an exam

le bachelier, la bachelière student who has passed the bac

la prépa [classe(s) préparatoire(s) (aux Grandes Écoles)]

NOTE: **La prépa** refers to the two-year, post-baccalaureate course (**les classes préparatoires**) that prepares students for the competitive entry examinations (**le concours**) for the **Grandes Écoles** (higher education establishments of the highest repute that train France's top civil servants, business administrators, engineers, and so on). The course is taken in what are reputed to be the top **lycées** by those who get the best results in the **bac**.

le bahut (*lit.*, chest/sideboard) senior high school, [Br.] grammar school, [Br.] sixth-form college, [Br.] secondary school

NOTE: **Bahut** can designate a **lycée**, which caters to 15- to 18-year-olds in three successive years: **la (classe de) seconde, la (classe de) première,** and **la classe terminale** (tenth to twelfth grade/[Br.] fifth form to upper-sixth form).

le lycéen, la lycéenne high-school student, [Br.] sixth-former, [Br.] secondary-school student

l'hypokhâgne, la khâgne first-/second-year preparatory course for the arts section of the **Grandes Écoles**

l'hypotaupe, la taupe first-/second-year preparatory course for the math/science section of the **Grandes Écoles**

l'énarque (m/f) student or graduate of the **ENA**

NOTE: **ENA [École Nationale d'Administration]** is the prestigious **Grande École** for Public Management, which trains France's top civil servants and produces a lot of top-ranking politicians. The (often-criticized) power and influence of the **ENA** has spawned the noun **énarchie**.

le capésien, la capésienne holder of the **CAPES**

NOTE: **CAPES [Certificat d'Aptitude Professionnelle à l'Enseignement Secondaire]** is the secondary-school teaching qualification awarded on a competitive basis (through a **concours**) and determined by the number of posts available.

«Il déteste sa boîte à bachot et sait fort bien qu'il n'aura pas son bac. Sa sœur a bûché et a été reçue; elle est actuellement khâgneuse.» "He can't stand his cram[ming] school/[Br.] crammer and knows full well that he won't pass his high-school diploma/A levels. His sister hit the books/[Br.] swotted and passed; she's now a student in the **khâgne**/she's now in her second year of the arts entry course for a **Grande École**."

NOTE: **Khâgneux** (m)/**khâgneuse** (f) and **taupin** (m) are slang terms for students taking the relevant **classes préparatoires** (see page 78).

«L'énarchie se manifeste dans le gouvernement actuel. Moi, je ne connais aucun énarque mais je fréquente pas mal de capésiens.» "The power/influence of **énarques** is apparent in the present government. I personally don't know a single **énarque**/graduate of the **ENA** but I see/mix with quite a few qualified secondary-school teachers."

SCHOOL

le bahut, la boîte school

la récré recess, break, [Br.] break time, [Br.] time-out

NOTE: **La récré** is an abbreviation of **la récréation. La cour de récréation** is the playground/schoolyard (see "Playground" on page 82).

la cour des grands
(See page 80.)

la cour des grands the older children's playground

jouer dans la cour des grands to play with the big boys/older children; to play in the major league

le pion (*lit.*, pawn [in chess]), **la pionne** supervisor, monitor

le surgé [surveillant général] chief, head, supervisor (in charge of discipline), dean of students

brutaliser quelqu'un to bully someone

brimer quelqu'un to haze/bully/[Br.] rag someone

NOTE: **Un pion** is an older student who is paid to supervise schoolchildren and is answerable to the **surveillant général (le surgé).**

«Dans cette boîte, j'ose pas aller dans la cour des grands car j'ai peur d'être brimé. Et même si un petit dur me cassait la figure, les pions ne feraient rien.» "In this damned school I'm scared of going into the older children's playground for fear of being bullied. Even if a school bully beat me up, the **pions**/supervisors/monitors would do nothing about it."

«‹Tu vas voir ta gueule⑦/tar' ta gueule⑦ à la récré!› me cria un des plus grands.» "One of the biggest pupils shouted to me, 'You're really in for it at recess/[Br.] break time.'"

NOTE: The expression **tar'** (sometimes **t'are**) **ta gueule à la récré** was made famous in a song by the French singer Alain Souchon entitled *J'ai dix ans* (1975).

HAZING IN THE *GRANDES ÉCOLES*

le bizut, le bizuth freshman, first-year student, [Br.] fresher

le bizutage hazing, [Br.] ragging

bizuter to haze/[Br.] rag a freshman/[Br.] fresher

NOTE: **Le bizutage** has been criticized in some quarters because of the humiliation and abuse to which freshmen/[Br.] freshers have been subjected. The practice has been banned in some institutions.

SCHOOLWORK

le devoir sur table class or written test

le cahier de cours workbook, exercise book

le conseil de classe staff meeting (to discuss individual students' progress)

le cahier d'appel attendance register/sheet

le prof teacher, teach

l'instit (m/f) primary-school teacher

NOTE: **Prof** and **instit** are abbreviations of **professeur** and **instituteur,** respectively.

NOTE: Both of these abbreviations are of a familiar and largely inoffensive register.

un problème de maths vachement balaise really hard math(s) problem

manquer to be absent (a lot) from school, [Br.] to bunk off

manquer à l'appel to be absent (at attendance/roll call/registration)

sauter to skip class, to play hooky, [Br.] to bunk off (a class)

filer à l'anglaise (*lit.*, to take English leave) to take unauthorized time off/ [Br.] French leave

«Comme il a beaucoup manqué cette année, le prof est allé voir ses vieux.» "As he's been absent/[Br.] bunked off a lot this year, teach went to see his folks."

«On a eu droit à un problème de maths vachement balaise.» "We got a really difficult math(s) problem."

«Hier elle a sauté la géo et ce matin elle a manqué à l'appel. Alors ça va chauffer au conseil de classe!» "Yesterday she skipped geography/[Br.] geog, and this morning she wasn't at roll call/[Br.] registration. They'll really have it in for her at the staff meeting!"

HIGH SCHOOL

la boum, le guinche hop, dance

l'économe (m/f), **l'intendant** (m) bursar

charrier un prof to hassle/[Br.] to rag a teacher, [Br.] to take the Mickey/ piss(?) out of a teacher

renvoyer un élève to expel a student/pupil

le directeur, le proviseur, le principal headmaster, principal

la directrice, la principale headmistress, principal

NOTE: **Un proviseur** is the head of a **lycée** while the term **directeur** is used for the head of a **collège** (college/middle school).

«Elle a beaucoup charrié ce prof parce qu'il voulait pas aller à la boum.» "She really hassled/[Br.] ragged/[Br.] took the piss(?) out of this teacher because he wouldn't go to the dance/hop."

«Le sacré proviseur a renvoyé Jean-Pierre parce qu'il a cassé la gueule(?) à l'intendant.» "The (damn) principal/[Br.] (bloody) head has expelled Jean-Pierre because he beat up/beat the living daylights out of the bursar."

See also Examinations, School, *pages 78, 79.*

HOMEWORK

les devoirs (mpl) homework

le devoir homework exercise, paper

le cahier de devoirs notebook, homework book

le cahier de textes homework notebook/diary, journal

NOTE: "To do one's homework" in a metaphorical sense ("to get information in advance," [Br.] "to gen up") can be expressed in the following familiar or slang expressions: **se tuyauter, se rencarder.**

«Ils n'ont pas fait leurs devoirs et ils ont paumé leur cahier de textes. C'est le bouquet!» "They haven't done their homework, and they've lost their notebooks. It really is the last straw!"

NOTE: The verb **paumer (quelque chose)** can be used in relaxed situations meaning "to lose" almost anything.

PLAYGROUND

se shooter to inject (drug), to shoot, to mainline

NOTE: A *verlan* alternative to **se shooter** is **se teushou,** and the corresponding noun **teushou** (m) means "a fix."

le shit hashish, shit⑦, dope

la marie-jeanne grass, weed, Mary Jane

la bagarre fight, [Br.] scrap

se bagarrer, se bastonner, se castagner to fight, [Br.] to scrap, to brawl

la baston free-for-all, [Br.] punch-up

jouer à la marelle to play hopscotch

sauter à la corde to skip, jump rope

la corde à sauter jump rope, skipping rope

jouer au foot to play soccer/[Br.] football

jouer au basket to play basketball

la cage à poules (*lit.*, hen coop) jungle gym, [Br.] climbing frame (in playground)

«Je n'en croyais pas mes yeux: dans la cour de récréation, près de la cage à poules, une fille de quinze ans se shootait et deux mecs vendaient du shit et de la marie-jeanne.» "I couldn't believe my eyes; in the playground, near the jungle gym/[Br.] climbing frame, a fifteen-year-old girl was mainlining/ shooting up and two guys/[Br.] blokes were selling shit/hash and grass/ Mary Jane."

«Une bande de salopards s'est pointée dans la cour des grands et en un clin d'œil tout le monde se bagarrait/se bastonnait.» "A gang/bunch of dickheads/scumbags turned up in the older children's playground and in a flash everyone was brawling/[Br.] scrapping."

«Y a de la baston dans l'air! Les filles voulaient jouer à la marelle mais les garcs les ont bousculées parce qu'ils veulent jouer au foot.» "There's trouble brewing!/[Br.] There's gonna be some aggro/violence! The girls wanted to play hopscotch but the guys jostled them because they wanna/want to play soccer/ [Br.] football."

TEACHERS

le prof d'histoire-géo [histoire-géographie] history and geography teacher

le prof de sciences-po [sciences politiques] political science teacher

le prof de maths [mathématiques] math(s) teacher

le prof de gym [gymnastique] gym teacher

le prof de sciences-nat' [sciences naturelles] natural science teacher

«Elle trouve le prof de gym super mais le prof de maths lui file les jetons.» "She thinks the gym teacher is groovy, but the math(s) teacher gives her the willies."

UNIVERSITY

For expressions relating to student restaurants, see "City" (Eating).

Qualifications, services, and courses

la fac university

NOTE: **La fac** is an abbreviation of **la faculté** and is commonly used by students even though the old **facultés** have been replaced by **UFR (Unités de Formation et de Recherche)**.

le DEUG [Diplôme d'Études Universitaires Générales] university diploma

la licence degree (university)

NOTE: **DEUG** is the first national qualification (**diplôme d'état**) taken after two years of university study in a whole range of disciplines. To indicate the level of a qualification, the French say, for example, that the **DEUG** is **Bac+2** (it is awarded after two years of post-Bac study), while the **licence** is **Bac+3**.

le doctorat doctorate

F.L.E. [Français Langue Étrangère] French as a foreign language

le CROUS [Centre Régional des Œuvres Universitaires et Scolaires] Student Welfare and Accommodation (Residence) Service

NOTE: **Le CROUS** is administered through the national center, **le CNOUS**, and is based on the regional **Académie** (for educational purposes, France is divided into **Académies**). The **CROUS** runs student accommodation (residences that are heavily subsidized) and the (heavily subsidized) meal service (including meals for schools). It also offers social and cultural services and organizes trips, etc.

le SUIO [Service Universitaire d'Information et d'Orientation] Student Information Service (offers information and counseling)

le PV, le p.-v. [procès-verbal] student transcript/profile

NOTE: **Le p.-v.** is a transcript of achievement in higher education. In normal French slang **un p.-v./PV** is a police fine/a ticket. **Coller un PV à quelqu'un** means "to book someone."

Lectures and classes

les t.d. [travaux dirigés] (m) seminar(s)

NOTE: These can number as many as seventy or so students and are practical seminar groups where students undertake coursework assignments, etc.

le c.m. [cours magistral] (formal) lecture (that may be given to several hundred students)

l'u.v. (f) **[unité de valeur], l'u.c.** (f) **[unité de compte]** course, module

NOTE: Students must pass a certain number of these course modules (courses) to obtain a given qualification.

la Scolarité (le Bureau de la Scolarité) Registrar, Academic Office, [Br.] Registry Office

«Il est à la fac depuis cinq ans mais il est incapable de suivre des cours Bac+3.» "He's been at the university/[Br.] uni for five years but just isn't up to degree-level courses."

«Elle est allée au Bureau de la Scolarité mais on lui a dit de s'adresser au CROUS.» "She went to the Registrar/[Br.] Registry Office but was told to go to the Student Welfare and Accommodation Services."

«Dans le c.m. le prof leur a dit de poser leurs questions dans les t.d.» "In the lecture, the prof told them to ask their questions in their seminar groups."

Studying and student residences

la RU, la r.u. [résidence universitaire] residence hall

le studio apartment, flat

le directeur, la directrice director, supervisor (of a hall, etc.)

bûcher to cram, [Br.] to swot

la cage à lapins (apartments, etc.) rabbit hutch

la B.N. (old) French National Library [**Bibliothèque Nationale**]

la Grande Bibliothèque (new) National Library [**la Bibliothèque Nationale de France**]

bosser to work/[Br.] slog

le bouquin book

l'amphi [amphithéâtre] (m) lecture hall

«Il est sorti de sa résidence—véritable cage à lapins—à huit heures pile et il bûchait à la B.N. dès neuf heures.» "He left his residence hall—which is a real rabbit hutch—at exactly eight o'clock and was working/[Br.] swotting at the National Library by nine."

«Dans cet amphi, l'on entend que dalle» fit la jeune fille à côté de moi. "In this lecture hall, you can't hear a thing/[Br.] can hear damn all/[Br.] sweet FA⑦," said the girl next to me.

«Elle bosse dans un bar jusqu'à dix heures du soir et puis elle lit ses bouquins jusqu'à trois heures du matin.» "She works in a bar until ten in the evening and then reads her books until three in the morning."

See also Teachers, *page 83; "City"* (Eating) *for student restaurants.*

EXERCISE

C'est à vous maintenant!

Match the slang French words and phrases on the left with their English translation on the right.

____ 1. **un amphi**

____ 2. **se bagarrer**

____ 3. **un bouquin**

____ 4. **le cahier d'appel**

____ 5. **un cahier de cours**

____ 6. **charrier un prof**

____ 7. **un c.m.**

____ 8. **la cour des grands**

____ 9. **un(e) énarque**

____ 10. **faire du bachotage**

____ 11. **filer à l'anglaise**

____ 12. **la récré**

____ 13. **sauter à la corde**

____ 14. **se shooter**

____ 15. **le SUIO**

a. attendance register/sheet

b. book

c. recess/[Br.] time-out/[Br.] break time

d. to cram/[Br.] swot for an exam

e. workbook

f. to inject (drug)/to shoot/to mainline

g. lecture

h. lecture hall

i. older children's playground

j. to hassle/[Br.] to rag a teacher/ [Br.] to take the Mickey/piss(?) out of a teacher

k. to fight/[Br.] scrap/brawl

l. to jump/skip rope

m. Student Information Service

n. student or graduate of the ENA

o. to take unauthorized time off/ [Br.] French leave

Emotions

See also "Sex."

ANGER

la rogne bad temper

mousser de rage (*lit.*, to froth/foam with anger) to blow a fuse, to hit the roof

piquer une crise (*lit.*, to fly into a crisis/fit) to throw a fit, to fly off the handle

faire mousser quelqu'un (*lit.*, to make someone foam/froth) to piss someone off, to get someone's back up

être de mauvais poil to be in a bad mood

NOTE: **Être de bon poil** means "to be in a good mood."

être en fumasse/en suif to be sore/steamed up

se mettre/se foutre en pétard to go ballistic, to fly off the handle (**pétard** [*lit.*, firecracker])

se mettre en renaud to blow a gasket/fuse, to lose one's temper

grimper au cocotier (*lit.*, to climb up the coconut tree) to fly off the handle

se foutre en rogne to blow one's top, to get one's dander up

se monter la tête/le bourrichon to get worked up, [Br.] to get het up

le pétardier grumpy person, quick-tempered bastard

«Il mousse de rage et elle, elle se fout en pétard parce que leur fille a le ballon/est en cloque.» "He's hit the roof and she's gone ballistic because their daughter's knocked up/[Br.] got a bun in the oven/[Br.] up the spout."

NOTE: **Avoir le ballon, être en cloque** (to be pregnant) should only be used in very informal situations; the standard phrase is **être enceinte.**

«Quel pétardier! Il est en suif parce que sa môme se fout en rogne chaque fois qu'il en parle.» "What a bad-tempered bastard! He's all steamed up because his kid/brat blows her top every time he mentions it."

CRYING

chialer to cry, to blubber

sniffer (int.) to cry

NOTE: **Sniffer** is more common in its transitive usage meaning "to sniff (drugs), to huff (solvents), to snort (cocaine)."

Snif! Boo-hoo!

pisser de l'œil (*lit.*, to piss through one's eyes) to cry, to burst into tears

le/la chialeur(-euse) whiner, crybaby

«Elle a chialé toute la journée et, snif! snif!, j'ai fini par verser des pleurs moi-même.» "She's been blubbering all day long and, boo-hoo!, I ended up shedding a few tears myself."

«Quelle chialeuse! Elle pisse de l'œil chaque fois que j'en parle.» "What a crybaby she is! She bursts into tears/starts blubbering every time I mention it."

EMBARRASSMENT

piquer un fard/un soleil (*lit.*, to hurriedly put on one's makeup/a sun) to go as red as a beet(root)

se sentir tout con(?) to feel like a dork/[Br.] (right) prick(?)

avoir l'air con(?) to look (bloody) stupid

se retrouver comme un con(?) to be left feeling like a complete asshole(?)/[Br.] prat/[Br.] plonker

l'andouille(?) (f) dork/jerk/[Br.] plonker/[Br.] wally

la tête de nœud(!) dickhead(?)/[Br.] wanker(?)

«Elle a piqué un fard et moi, je me sentais tout con!(?)**»** "She turned bright red/as red as a beet(root) and I felt like a dork/[Br.] a right prick(?)/[Br.] a real plonker."

«J'ai voulu la tchatcher mais elle s'est tirée. Tout le monde me regardait et moi, je me suis retrouvé comme un con.(?)**»** "I wanted to sweet-talk her/[Br.] chat her up, but she split/[Br.] scarpered. Everyone was looking at me, and I was left feeling like a complete dickhead(?)/[Br.] plonker."

«Quelle andouille!(?) **Elle a l'air con quand elle met ces fringues.»** "What a dork/[Br.] wally! She looks (bloody) stupid when she puts these clothes/[Br.] this gear on."

FEAR

NOTE: There are many slang words in French that indicate "fear": **la bloblote, la chiasse, la cliche, la pétoche, le taf, le trac, le tracos, le tracsir/traczir, la traquette, la tremblote, la trouille.**

NOTE: **La chiasse**(?), **la cliche**(?) literally mean "diarrhea" and are used in a verbal phrase with **avoir** meaning "to be scared shitless(?)/[Br.] shit-scared(?)": **j'ai la chiasse(?)/la cliche(?)**.

NOTE: There are also many verbs and verbal phrases meaning "to be afraid": **caner** (also used in the sense of "to die" and "to give up"), **chocotter** (to tremble with fear), **fouetter** (*lit.,* to whip, flog), **grelotter, moiter** (*lit.,* to be sweaty/clammy), **mouetter/mouiller (son froc)** (to wet oneself [with fear]), **taffer, traquer, trouilloter** (also means "to stink," [Br.] "to pong"), **avoir la bloblote, avoir les boules** (to shit(?) a brick, [Br.] to be shit-scared(?)), **avoir les chocottes/les colombins/les copeaux/les foies/les foies blancs/les fumerons/les grelots/les jetons/les miches à zéro/les miches qui font bravo, avoir/filer/foutre(!) les flubes, avoir le trouillomètre à zéro** (to be scared stiff), **les avoir à zéro, chier(?) dans son froc/sa culotte** (to shit(?) a brick, [Br.] to be shit-scared(?)), **les avoir moites(?)** (to wet oneself [with fear]), **ne bander que d'une(!), bander mou(!)** (*lit.,* to fail to have an erection), **serrer les fesses(?)**.

«Je me suis retrouvé seul devant quatre durs. Dès que le premier m'a regardé j'ai chié(?) dans mon froc.» "I found myself alone faced by four tough guys/[Br.] hard cases. As soon as the first one looked at me, I was scared shitless(?)/[Br.] shat(?) myself/[Br.] was shit-scared(?)."

«Elle a eu le trouillomètre à zéro quand il lui a dit qu'il avait flingué son gosse.» "She was scared stiff/scared to death when he said that he had shot her son/blown her son's brains out."

«Moi, avoir la bloblote dans une situation pareille? Tu déconnes!» "You're talking crap(?)/bullshit(?) if you think I'd be scared in such a situation!"

JOY

être verni(e) (*lit.,* to be varnished, shiny, glossy) to be lucky

avoir du cul(?) (*lit.,* ass(?), [Br.] bum, arse(?)) to be lucky, [Br.] to be a jammy bastard

être aux anges

avoir les pieds nickelés (*lit.,* to have nickel-plated feet) to have the luck of the devil, [Br.] to be jammy, to be lucky

être au septième ciel (*lit.,* to be in seventh heaven) to be on cloud nine

être aux anges (*lit.,* to be with the angels) to be in seventh heaven, [Br.] to be over the moon

s'emballer to get carried away, to get overexcited

planer (*lit.*, to glide, hover) to be high (as a kite), [Br.] to be over the moon

NOTE: **Planer** can mean "to be extremely happy" but also "to be stoned" (on drugs) and "to be cut off from reality."

avoir du bol to be in luck

avoir un coup de bol to have a stroke of luck

«Elle a toujours eu du cul et lui, il a les pieds nickelés. Ils sont tous les deux au septième ciel.» "She's always been a lucky/[Br.] jammy bastard, and he has the luck of the devil/leads a charmed life. They're both on cloud nine."

«Elle s'est emballée! Elle était aux anges quand il lui a fait un petit bisou.» "She really got carried away! She was over the moon when he gave her a peck (on the cheek)."

«Ils ont eu un coup de bol ou, comme dit l'autre, ils ont toujours du cul!» "They've had a stroke of luck or, as the saying goes, they're always lucky/jammy bastards!"

NOTE: With the exception of the mildly vulgar phrase **avoir du cul**⚠, the above expressions concerning joy are inoffensive and can be used in most situations. The verb **s'emballer** may be used with sarcastic overtones.

«Elle plane à quatre mille. C'est pas la peine de lui parler.» "She's got her head in the clouds. It's not worth talking to her."

See also "Sex."

THREATS AND VIOLENCE

Acts of violence: fights/fighting

casser la gueule⚠ **à quelqu'un** to beat somebody up, to smash somebody's face in

foutre⚠ **le poing sur la gueule de quelqu'un** to punch somebody's face in

chercher le rif/rififi to look for a fight

se castagner to have a fight/[Br.] punch-up

la castagne fighting/[Br.] punch-up

chercher des crosses (*lit.*, to look for butts [of rifles], grips [of revolvers]) to look for trouble

défoncer/abîmer/arranger le portrait à quelqu'un to bash somebody's face in, to rearrange someone's face/[Br.] features

«Y a de l'abus! Je vais te casser la gueule⚠ **si tu n'arrêtes pas de me taper sur les nerfs.» «Et ta sœur! T'es pas capable de me foutre**⚠ **les jetons!»** "That's going too far!/[Br.] That's OTT! I'll smash your face in if you don't stop getting on my nerves." "Get lost! You don't scare me!"

NOTE: Colloquial/slang register for threats of physical violence of a fairly intense nature.

NOTE: The expression **foutre**(?) **les jetons à quelqu'un** should not be used in polite company; a slightly milder variation is **ficher les jetons à quelqu'un**.

«Ferme-la, sinon moi, je vais te foutre(?) **mon poing sur la gueule**(?)**.»** "Shut your trap, otherwise I'm gonna/going to punch your face in."

«Il se castagne avec les flics tous les soirs.» «Oui, il a toujours aimé la castagne.» "He has a brawl/[Br.] punch-up with the cops every night." "Yes, he's always liked a good fight/[Br.] scrap."

NOTE: Colloquial register for a fight/[Br.] punch-up that is quite violent.

«Si tu me cherches des crosses, tu vas les avoir! Ferme ta gueule ou je te défonce/je t'arrange le portrait.» "If you're looking for trouble, you've come to the right place! Shut your trap/[Br.] gob, or I'll rearrange your face/[Br.] features."

Acts of violence: murder

buter quelqu'un; faire la peau à quelqu'un to bump somebody off, to kill somebody

flinguer to gun down ▪ **«Il a buté un flic après avoir fait la peau à sa femme. C'est le deuxième flic qui l'a flingué.»** "He bumped off a cop after killing his wife. The second cop gunned him down."

NOTE: **Le flingue** (gun, rifle); **le flingueur, la flingueuse** (contract killer); **se flinguer** (to blow one's brains out).

WISHES/DELUSIONS

mourir d'envie de faire quelque chose to be dying to do something

avoir une sacrée envie de faire quelque chose to really want/[Br.] to be (bloody) keen to do something

se berlurer to delude oneself

se faire du cinéma to imagine things, [Br.] to be pie in the sky

gambergeailler to daydream

avoir la berlue to be seeing things

«Elle meurt d'envie de devenir actrice de cinéma et passe son temps à gambergeailler. Mais elle se berlure si elle croit qu'elle va réussir.» "She's dying to become a movie star and spends all her time daydreaming. But she's kidding/deluding herself if she thinks she's going to succeed."

EXERCISES

C'est à vous maintenant!

A *Complete the following slang French expressions on the left and match them with their English translation on the right.*

____ 1. avoir l'air ____________

____ 2. avoir le ____________ à zéro

____ 3. avoir les pieds ____________

____ 4. foutre le ____________ sur la ____________ de quelqu'un

____ 5. faire la ____________ à quelqu'un

____ 6. se faire du ____________

____ 7. ____________ de rage

____ 8. être en ____________

____ 9. ____________ de l'œil

____ 10. piquer un ____________

a. to punch somebody's face in

b. to turn as red as a beet(root)

c. to bump somebody off

d. to imagine things

e. to be pregnant

f. to blow a fuse

g. to cry

h. to be afraid

i. to have the luck of the devil

j. to look (bloody) stupid

B *Translate the following slang French expressions into English.*

1. chier dans son froc ____________________
2. les avoir moites ____________________
3. planer à quatre mille ____________________
4. chercher le rififi ____________________
5. être aux anges ____________________

Entertainment

See also "Art," "Food and Eating," "The Movies," "Music."

BARS

le bistro(t), le bistroquet watering hole, bar, pub, local

la bistouille mixture of coffee and alcohol

NOTE: Coffee with calvados is common in Normandy; it is a kind of **bistouille** as the calvados is normally poured into the (dregs of the) coffee.

s'en jeter un derrière la cravate (*lit.*, to throw/[Br.] chuck one behind one's tie) to have a drink, to knock one back

l'alcoolo (m) alkie, lush, [Br.] dipso, souse

l'alcool blanc (m) colorless spirit(s)

le café-calva coffee with calvados

le bistrot du coin local (watering hole)

s'en jeter un derrière la cravate

l'apéro (m) aperitif

NOTE: **Apéro** is an abbreviation of the standard noun **apéritif**.

l'ardoise (f) credit (in a bar), tab, [Br.] slate

«C'est dans le bistrot du coin que cet alcoolo a laissé une ardoise.» "It was in the bar [local, pub] that this alkie/[Br.] dipso/lush left without paying."

«On pourra s'en jeter un derrière la cravate dans ce bistroquet. Toi, tu prendras ton apéro, et moi, je prendrai un café-calva.» "We can go and have a quick (swift) one in this bar/pub. You can have your aperitif, and I'll have a coffee and calvados."

BROTHELS

le bordel, le claque, le baisodrome brothel, whorehouse, [Br.] knocking-shop

la pute whore

le boui-boui brothel, cheap café, dive

«Ce quartier est plein de claques et de bouis-bouis; on voit des putes partout.» "This district is full of whorehouses and dives; there are hookers/whores to be seen everywhere."

See also "Sex" (Prostitution).

CIRCUS

le cirque d'hiver winter circus

NOTE: **Cirque** is used in slang French to mean "hassle" as in the expression **Quel cirque pour sortir du supermarché** ("What a hassle/drag getting out of the supermarket"). The expression **mener le petit/prosper au cirque** means "to make love" (referring to a man).

«J'ai emmené mon fiston au cirque d'hiver et on a bien rigolé.» "I took my kid to the winter circus and we had a really good laugh."

CLASSICAL MUSIC

la zicmu, la zizique music

NOTE: **Zizique** is also used to mean "tunes" or "elevator/[Br.] wallpaper music." See "Music."

le musico(s) musician

le zinzin (annoying) hum/buzz; violin; thingamajig

NOTE: **Zinzin** is used in different meanings in slang French; as an adjective, it means "bonkers," "loopy" as in the expression **il est complètement zinzin** ("he's completely bonkers").

«Ma gonzesse m'a obligé à aller écouter une symphonie de Beethoven en ville. Il y avait une centaine de musicos mais j'ai pas tellement apprécié cette zicmu et au bout de dix minutes j'en avais marre de ce zinzin.» "My chick/[Br.] bird made me go and listen to a Beethoven symphony in town. There were a hundred musicians, but I didn't really dig the music and after ten minutes the noise really bugged me."

JAZZ CLUBS

la carotte (*lit.*, carrot) (soprano) saxophone

le poireau (*lit.*, leek) clarinet

le saxo sax(ophone), sax player

le jazz jazz

le jazz-rock jazz-rock

le jazzman jazzman

le hot hot jazz

«On est allés dans une boîte où l'on jouait du hot et du jazz-rock. Le saxo était formidable mais le mec qui jouait du poireau n'était pas terrible.» "We went to a nightclub where they played hot jazz and jazz-rock. The sax player was great but the guy who played the clarinet wasn't all that good/[Br.] wasn't up to much."

NOTE: When **on** is used to mean "we," a plural agreement should be made in the perfect tenses when spelling verbs conjugated with **être** as in **on est allé(e)s/sorti(e)s.**

NIGHTCLUBS

le videur (*lit.*, a person who empties) bouncer

le/la noctambule night owl/reveler

la boîte de nuit, le night-club nightclub

sortir en boîte to go nightclubbing

la discothèque discotheque

le disco disco music

«Ils sont sortis en boîte, ces noctambules, mais à l'entrée de la deuxième boîte qu'ils ont visitée, un videur les a accusés d'avoir trop picolé.» "These night owls/[Br.] revelers went nightclubbing but as they went into their second club, a bouncer accused them of being boozed/lit up."

POPULAR MUSIC

les vieux routiers de la variété française old established stars/[Br.] stagers of (middle-of-the-road) French popular music (**les vieux routiers** [*lit.*, the old long-distance truck/[Br.] lorry drivers])

le rocke(u)r, la rockeuse rocker, rock musician, rock fan, headbanger

NOTE: **Rockeur** (which can also mean a "tough guy") has an alternate form, **le rockie** or **le rocky.**

le rock rock ('n' roll)

le rap rap

le rappeur, la rappeuse rapper

rapper to rap, to play rap, to dance to rap music

le funk funk

le ragga ragga(muffin)

le raï rai

le reggae reggae

la techno techno

«Nos amis vont souvent à l'Olympia pour voir les vieux routiers de la variété française mais avec nos copains, nous, on préfère écouter le rock et le rap et aller dans les boîtes de nuit pour danser et pour écouter le reggae et la techno.» "Our friends often go to the Olympia to see the old stars of French pop(ular music), but with our buddies/[Br.] mates we prefer to listen to rock and rap and to go to nightclubs to dance and to listen to reggae and techno."

THEATER

jouer devant les banquettes (*lit.*, to play in front of [empty] seats) to play to an almost empty house

jouer à guichets fermés (*lit.*, to play with the ticket office closed) to play to a full house

NOTE: The expression **jouer à guichets fermés** is also used in sports.

le cachetonneur, la cachetonneuse pick-up/[Br.] jobbing actor/actress

NOTE: **Cachetonneur** means an actor **qui court le cachet** (who is chasing after any sort of work); **le cachet** (the takings).

courir les théâtres to do the rounds of the theaters

le frimant walk-on, bit-part player

la star star

le théâtre de boulevard light comedies (performed in the theaters of the Paris boulevards)

«Mon mec est un cachetonneur qui joue d'habitude devant les banquettes. Il ne sera jamais une star mais il a des chances de trouver du boulot comme frimant au TNP.» "My guy/[Br.] bloke is a pick-up/[Br.] jobbing actor who usually plays in front of nearly empty houses. He'll never be a star, but he has a chance of getting bit parts at the TNP."

NOTE: **TNP [Théâtre National Populaire]** is France's state-funded theater.

PLACES AND SOURCES OF ENTERTAINMENT

l'appart[ement] (m) apartment, [Br.] flat

le baloche local dance

la (fête) bamboula wild party

NOTE: Care is needed here since **un bamboula**(!) refers to **un homme de race noire** and the wrong gender could cause great offense.

la boîte de nuit nightclub

le bordel brothel

NOTE: **«C'est le bordel!»** "It's a shambles/[Br.] tip!"

la boum (young people's) party

la casbah place, pad ■ **«Ta casbah ou la mienne?»** "Your place or mine?"

la chouille party, bash

le cinoche movies

la colo [colonie de vacances] children's summer camp

NOTE: **Colo** is not to be confused with **colon** (colonel), as in **«Ben, mon colon!»** (Gee whiz!/[Br.] Blimey [Charlie]!)

la crémerie somewhere else ■ **«Changeons de crémerie!»** "Let's move on/go somewhere else!"

NOTE: **Crémerie** literally means a dairy. The expression has come about because dairies are very common shops in France.

un endroit glauque, un endroit louche a shady dive

le nanar rotten/lousy film

la partie carrée (*lit.*, squared game [originally a cardplayers' term]) foursome ■ **«Je n'ai rien contre une partie carrée, pourvu que ce soit simplement le cinoche!»** "I've got nothing against a foursome, provided it's just the movies!"

la partouse orgy

le/la partousard(e), le/la partouzard(e) person taking part in an orgy

la piaule (crash) pad ■ **«Il s'est déniché une petite piaule dans un quartier chic!»** "He's found himself a little (crash) pad in a hip/[Br.] smart/trendy district!"

le pogo dance

le soft soft porn ■ **«Je ne sors pas avec lui—il est accro du soft!»** "I'm not going out with him—he's into soft porn!"

la téloche TV, tube, [Br.] telly

la touzepar [*verlan*: **partouze**] orgy ▪ **«Chez lui, c'est toujours la touze-par!»** "At his place there's always an orgy (going on)!"

le troquet small café, joint ▪ **«Je connais un petit troquet sympa où on peut s'amuser.»** "I know a nice little joint where we can have a good time."

ENTERTAINING ONESELF

faire la bamboula to live it up, [Br.] to go on the razzle

(se) baquer to go for a dip ▪ **«Si on se baquait?»** "How about a dip?"

faire un bœuf (*lit.*, to do a steer) to have a jam session

faire la bombe (*lit.*, to do a bomb) to party

faire la bringue to party, [Br.] to go on the razzle ▪ **«Pour elle, tout prétexte est bon pour faire la bringue!»** "For her, any old excuse to party!"

casquer to cough up, to fork out ▪ **«C'est toujours les gosses qui font la bombe et papa qui casque!»** "It's always the kids who (have the) party and dad who coughs up!"

chouiller to party

faire une fiesta to have a party

NOTE: Compare **faire une fiesta à tout casser** (to have a hell of a party).

guincher to dance, to bop

faire la java (*lit.*, to do a java) to have a (party) bash

faire la noce (*lit.*, to do a wedding party) to live it up, to boogie ▪ **«J'ai déjà dépassé la quarantaine—je suis trop vieille pour faire la noce!»** "I'm already past forty—I'm too old to live it up/boogie!"

être à la noce (*lit.*, to be at the wedding party) to have a whale/hell of a time ▪ **«À d'autres! Regarde cette octogénaire—elle est bien à la noce!»** "Nonsense! Look at that eighty-year-old—she's having a hell/whale of a time!"

faire la nouba to party

partouser to take part in an orgy ▪ **«Je ne peux rien faire ce matin, j'ai partousé tout le week-end!»** "I'm no use at all this morning, I was orgying all (the) weekend!"

pogoter to dance

HOW THE ENTERTAINMENT GOES

astap [à se taper le cul par terre] (*lit.*, to bang your butt on the ground) hysterical, sidesplitting

la barbe drag

bidonnant hysterical(ly funny), sidesplitting

casser la baraque (*lit.*, to smash the joint) to bring the house down

la Bérézina disaster ■ **«C'est la Bérézina!»** "It's a disaster!"

> NOTE: Napoleon's armies were decimated at Bérézina during the retreat from Moscow.

ne pas casser des briques (*lit.*, not to break any bricks) not to do much ■ **«Pour moi, ce film ne casse pas des briques.»** "This film doesn't do much for me."

> NOTE: The correct grammar would be **pas de briques**, but this expression is always used as indicated above.

coûter bonbon (*lit.*, to cost a candy) to cost an arm and a leg ■ **«On peut bien y aller, mais ça te coûtera bonbon!»** "We can go there alright, but it'll cost you an arm and a leg!"

chébran [*verlan*: **branché**] trendy

chiant(e) dead (utterly) boring

la chienlit (*lit.*, the dog's litter) utter shambles ■ **«C'est la chienlit!»** "It's a real mess!"

écroulé(e) doubled up ■ **«Elle a été écroulée de rire!»** "She was doubled up with laughter!"

enquiquinant(e) deadly dull ■ **«Normalement, j'aime bien ses pièces, mais celle-ci est enquiquinante!»** "Normally, I like his plays, but this one is deadly dull!"

> NOTE: **Enquiquinant** can also mean a pain (in the neck). The verb **enquiquiner** itself is either to bore stiff or to bug, [Br.] get up someone's nose.

folklo[rique] weird (and wonderful) ■ **«T'as vu le décor?—Très folklo!»** "Have you seen the scenery?—Pretty weird!"

lâcher son fou (*lit.*, to let one's gun off) to have a great time

> NOTE: **Fou** is a corruption of **fusil**.

«Même s'il est fou, il sait bien lâcher son fou!» "Even if he is mad, he knows how to have a great time!"

gégène great, terrific

se gondoler (*lit.*, to go warped) to crack up, fall over/[Br.] fall about laughing ■ **«À l'arrivée de Robin Williams tout le monde s'est gondolé!»** "When Robin Williams came on, everyone cracked up!"

hyper, hypra mega ■ **«On s'est hyper bien régalé!»** "We had a mega feast!"

impec [impeccable] perfect!, [Br.] great (stuff)! ■ **«Tu vas avec? —Impec!»** "You're coming with us? —Perfect!"

jouissif barrel of laughs ■ **«Subir cette mise en scène, c'est pas jouissif!»** "Having to watch this production is not exactly a barrel of laughs!"

NOTE: **Jouissif** is a colloquial adjective derived from **jouir**, to enjoy. One should normally be cautious using this verb, as it also means to enjoy sexually.

marrant(e) funny ■ **«Il me dit quelque chose—il est très marrant!»** "He does something for me—he's very funny!"

NOTE: Nowadays, **marrant** is probably more commonly used than **comique** and **drôle**, because it is an affectionate term, indicating that the person or circumstance has touched the speaker.

mélo[dramatique] over-the-top, [Br.] OTT

le must must, must-see ■ **«C'est un must!»** "It's a must/not to be missed!"

pas net(te) (*lit.*, not straight) shady, [Br.] dodgy ■ **«Gagner du fric comme ça, c'est pas net!»** "Earning money like that, it's shady/[Br.] dodgy!"

planant(e) mellow [music]

rasant(e) deathly (deadly) dull, a real drag

ringard(e), ringardos tacky, [Br.] naff ■ **«Plus c'est ringardos, plus ça plaît au public!»** "The more tacky/naff it is, the more the public like(s) it!"

la ringardise tackiness ■ **«La mise en scène a été d'une ringardise incroyable!»** "The production was unbelievably tacky!"

sympa [sympathique] nice, friendly, pleasant

super super, great

super (marrant[e]) mega (funny)

tarte thick, ridiculous, [Br.] dim, [Br.] naff

tartignol(e) ridiculous, [Br.] naff

se faire tartir to be bored to death/shitless⑦/[Br.] witless ■ **«Avec toute cette musique des années 50, je me suis fait tartir là!»** "With all that music from the Fifties, they had me bored to death/[Br.] witless!"

top great, magic, [Br.] fab

tordant(e) sidesplitting

se tordre (de rire) (*lit.*, to writhe [with laughter]) to be doubled up with laughter ■ **«J'ai mal au ventre, pour m'être tordu!»** "My stomach hurts from laughing!"

vulgos vulgar, coarse, gross

EXERCISES

C'est à vous maintenant!

A *Where would you be if you found yourself at the following?*

1. une bamboula ______________________________
2. une boîte de nuit ______________________________
3. une chouille ______________________________
4. une boum ______________________________
5. une touzepar ______________________________
6. un baloche ______________________________
7. une colo ______________________________
8. un nanar ______________________________

B *Put a ✓, ✗, or — next to each expression to indicate whether it is positive, negative, or neutral.*

____ 1. enquiquinant

____ 2. chébran

____ 3. la Bérézina

____ 4. impec

____ 5. mélo

____ 6. casquer

____ 7. gégène

____ 8. astap

____ 9. guincher

____ 10. pas net

C *You are at another party, this time in Tours, known as le petit Paris. People are discussing their reactions to various types of entertainment. Give an English version of each comment.*

1. On a fait la noce!

____

2. Ça a cassé la baraque!

____

3. Ca n'a pas cassé des briques!

____

4. **Ce que j'en pense? Hyper jouissif!**

____

5. **Comme toujours, vulgos et tartignol!**

____

6. **C'était la barbe!**

____

D *Give the slang or idiomatic French equivalent of the following English words and phrases.*

1. to play to an almost empty house _______________
2. bit-part player _______________
3. the established stars of (middle-of-the-road) French popular music _______________
4. mixture of coffee and alcohol _______________
5. whorehouse/[Br.] knocking-shop _______________
6. saxophone, sax player _______________
7. to go nightclubbing _______________
8. to do the rounds of the theaters _______________
9. to play to a full house _______________
10. to have a drink/[Br.] to knock one back _______________

E *Translate the following French sentences into English. The preceding explanations in English will give you a context.*

1. You are in a watering hole/bar with a friend and can't resist making this comment: **Dans ce bistroquet, il n'y a que des alcoolos. J'ai pas envie de prendre mon apéro ici.**

____

____

2. You and your fiancée had a problem in a jazz club. You tell a friend what happened: **Dans la boîte où on est allés, on voulait rapper mais un jazzman et le videur nous ont dit d'aller ailleurs.**

___

___

3. You write to a pen pal/[Br.] pen friend about your experiences in Paris: **J'ai voulu courir les théâtres parisiens et voir les grandes stars mais mon frangin a dit qu'il préférait sortir en boîte.**

___

___

Food and Eating

See also "Entertainment."

NAMES FOR AND QUALITIES OF FOOD

la bouffeⓉ chow, food, grub, [Br.] tucker

la petite bouffe feast/[Br.] (bit of a) nosh-up ■ **«Nous nous sommes fait une petite bouffe.»** "We chowed down./[Br.] We had a bit of a nosh-up."

la boustifⓉ lousy/poor/nasty grub ■ **«Chez elle, la boustif c'est la règle!»** "At her place, lousy/poor/nasty grub is what you get!"

la boustifailleⓉ lousy/poor grub

NOTE: When **-aille** is added to a word, it is almost always pejorative.

le casse-croûte (*lit.*, crust break) snack

NOTE: **Casser la croûte** means "to have a bite to eat, to snack, [Br.] to bridge the gap."

«Normalement, je casse la croûte à cette heure-ci.» "Normally, I have a bite to eat at this time."

le casse-graine (*lit.*, grain/seed break) snack

cramé(e) burned to death, burned to cinder(s)

le (petit) déj breakfast ■ **«Le déj, le déca, les jeunes de nos jours ne parlent que par des abréviations!»** "Brekkie, decaf, young people nowadays only talk in abbreviations!"

le frichti cooked meal ■ **«Je te prépare un frichti?»** "Shall I make you/[Br.] do you a cooked meal?"

le fricot chow, food, grub, [Br.] tucker

du gâteau piece of cake ■ **«On n'aura pas de problèmes pour y pénétrer. C'est du gâteau!»** "We won't have any problems getting in. It's a piece of cake!"

la grailleⓉ nasty grub, [Br.] duff ■ **«Chez mon corres, c'était toujours la graille!»** "At my pen pal's/[Br.] pen friend's, it was always nasty grub/[Br.] duff!"

NOTE: Compare **le graillon** (burned fat).

le gueuleton feast, blowout ■ **«C'est la fin du carême, je te promets un vrai gueuleton!»** "It's the end of Lent, so I promise you a real blowout!"

le poiscaille fish ■ **«Ce Chardonnay va bien avec le poiscaille.»** "That Chardonnay goes well with the fish."

le rata chow, food, grub, [Br.] tucker

> NOTE: Compare **ne pas se dormir sur le rata**, "not to fall asleep on the job." The French expression can also have a similar sexual connotation to its English equivalent.

la tambouille chow, food, grub, [Br.] tucker

faire la tambouille (*lit.*, to do the grub) to do the cooking

les rogatons (mpl) leftovers ■ **«C'est pas un gourmet—on lui donne les rogatons!»** "He's no gourmet—we'll give him the leftovers!"

la ragougnasse swill, pig swill ■ **«Les fermiers mangent bien. Ce sont les BCBG qui mangent de la ragougnasse!»** "Farmers eat well. It's the preppies who eat (pig) swill!"

TYPES OF FOOD

la barbaque tough meat

la bidoche meat

> NOTE: **Un(e) bidochon**, a stereotypical blue-collar worker, is named after the characters in Binet's cartoon-strip *Les Bidochon*. Compare "They're a meat-and-potatoes/[Br.] meat-and-two-veg family."

le bricheton bread

le calendos Camembert

la carne (tough) meat

le casse-dalle sandwich, [Br.] butty, [Br.] sarny

les fayots (mpl) beans

le frome/le frometon cheese

> NOTE: **-ton** is always an amusing or pejorative suffix.

le gueuleton feast, [Br.] slap-up meal

la lavasse (*lit.*, "the water left over from the dishwashing/[Br.] washing [-up]) dishwater, [Br.] watery, piddly soup

les patates (f) potatoes ■ **«Chez lui on ne bouffe que des patates à la sauce cailloux!»** "All they live on at his place is bread and water!"

NOTE: This colorful and common expression is used when someone has a reputation for very poor cooking, lacking in both taste and quantity.

le sauciflard salami

STAGES OF HUNGER

avoir un appétit d'oiseau to eat like a bird ▪ **«Elle a l'air d'un oiseau et l'appétit d'un oiseau!»** "She looks like a bird and eats like a bird!"

manger trois fois rien (*lit.*, to eat three times nothing) to eat next to nothing ▪ **«Elle a gardé la ligne pour avoir toujours mangé trois fois rien!»** "She's trim because she always eats next to nothing!"

Ça creuse! (*lit.*, It's digging away.) My stomach's growling/[Br.] playing tunes! ▪ **«Ça creuse! Il est temps de manger!»** "My stomach's growling/[Br.] playing tunes! It's time to eat!"

avoir un bon coup de fourchette (*lit.*, to have a way with a fork) to have a hearty appetite ▪ **«Il faut y mettre tout le paquet, Charlot a un bon coup de fourchette!»** "You'd better put the whole packet in; Charlie's got a hearty appetite!"

avoir un creux (*lit.*, to have a hollow), **avoir la dalle** (*lit.*, to have a flagstone/paving stone) to be hungry ▪ **«J'ai toujours un creux à onze heures!»** "I'm always hungry at eleven!"

avoir la fringale⑦ to be hungry, to have the munchies ▪ **«Ce parfum glorieux! J'ai la fringale maintenant!»** "That wonderful smell! I'm hungry now!"

avoir une faim de loup (*lit.*, to have a wolf's hunger) to be as hungry as a bear ▪ **«Je pourrais manger n'importe quoi—j'ai une faim de loup!»** "I could eat any old thing—I'm as hungry as a bear!"

crever de faim to be dying of hunger ▪ **«Si je ne crève pas de froid, je vais certainement crever de faim!»** "If I don't die of the cold, I'll certainly die of hunger!"

Charlot a un bon coup de fourchette.

NAMING THE EATERS

le bâfreur, une bâfreuse hog, glutton, pig, [Br.] greedy guts ■ **«Toute famille a son bâfreur!»** "Every family has its hog/pig!"

le bouffeur pig/[Br.] guzzler ■ **«Avec son visage joufflu, on sait bien que c'est un bouffeur!»** "With his chubby face, you know he's a pig/[Br.] guzzler alright!"

le/la difficile picky eater/[Br.] faddy ■ **«Il est vraiment difficile sur la nourriture!»** "He's really picky/[Br.] faddy about his food!"

la fine-gueule (*lit.*, fine mouth) gourmet ■ **«Elle se croit une fine-gueule!»** "She fancies herself (as) a gourmet!"

le goinfre hog, glutton ■ **«Il est goinfre, c'est vrai, mais pas seulement sur le plan de la nourriture!»** "It's true he's a hog, but not just for food!"

le glouton, la gloutonne hog, glutton

le gourmand glutton, [Br.] greedy guts ■ **«Il est plutôt gourmand que gourmet!»** "He's more greedy than gourmet!"

le gourmet gourmet, discerning eater

le mangeur, la mangeuse (good) eater ■ **«C'est un grand mangeur, que lui!»** "He can certainly pack it away!"

THE ACT OF EATING

attaquer to start ■ **«Alors, on l'attaque?»** "Shall we start, then?"

bâfrer to feed one's face, to pig out, [Br.] to pig oneself ■ **«On a toujours l'ocas de bâfrer chez elle!»** "There's always the opportunity of feeding your face at her place!"

becqueter, becter to eat, [Br.] to nosh ■ **«À quelle heure tu bectes?»** "What time do you eat?"

Il n'y a rien à becqueter. There's nothing to eat.

bouffer to eat ■ **«On bouffe à huit heures?»** "Shall we eat at eight?"

NOTE: Compare **Ça me bouffe!**, It really gets me!

se faire une bouffe (*lit.*, to make oneself a feed) to eat together, to have a meal together ■ **«C'est mon anniversaire! Si on se faisait une bouffe?»** "It's my birthday! How about having a meal together?"

bouffer comme un chancre (*lit.*, to eat like a canker) to eat like a horse ■ **«Il ne mange rien de la semaine, puis il bouffe comme un chancre quand il arrive chez nous!»** "He eats nothing all week, then eats like a horse when he comes here!"

avoir les dents du fond qui baignent (*lit.*, to have your back teeth steeped in it) to have pigged out, to be full to bursting ■ **«Qu'est-ce qu'on a bien mangé! J'ai les dents de fond qui baignent!»** "Didn't we eat well! I'm full to bursting!"

graillerⓉ to eat ■ **«On graille ensemble?»** "Shall we eat together?"

bouffer à la pelle (*lit.*, to eat with a shovel) to shovel it down ■ **«C'est comme ça qu'on se tient à table à Berkeley? Ce jeune gentleman bouffe à la pelle!»** "Is that what they call table manners at Berkeley? This young guy/[Br.] toff is just shoveling it down!"

s'empiffrerⓉ to stuff oneself, to feed one's face ■ **«Qu'est-ce que tu attends? Si on s'empiffre comme lui, on prend du poids!»** "What do you expect? If you feed your face like he does, you put on weight!"

se farcirⓉ to stuff oneself ■ **«On dirait de la façon dont il se farcit, qu'on avait bien un dindon chez nous!»** "From the way he's stuffing himself, you'd say we had a turkey with us!"

se payerⓉ to be full [up], full to bursting, [Br.] full as an egg ■ **«Ça c'était excellent! Nous nous sommes vraiment payés!»** "That was excellent! We're full!"

caler to be full ■ **«Rien de plus, merci! Je cale déjà!»** "Nothing more, thanks! I'm already full!"

> NOTE: This colorful expression has nautical roots, **la cale** being the hold of the ship. So, **caler** originally meant "to fill the hold of the ship."

casser la graine (*lit.*, to break the grain/seed) to have a bite to eat ■ **«On n'a rien mangé de la journée, cassons la graine!»** "We've eaten nothing all day, let's have a bite to eat!"

s'en mettre plein la lampe (*lit.*, to fill one's lamp with it) to feed one's face, [Br.] to have a slap-up/first-rate meal

picorer to pick at one's food ■ **«Tu ne vas jamais être grand, si tu continues à picorer comme ça!»** "You'll never be tall if you go on picking at your food like that!"

se taper la cloche (*lit.*, to ring one's bell) to feed one's face, [Br.] to have a slap-up/first-rate meal ■ **«C'est la fin des examens et ce soir on se tape la cloche!»** "It's the end of the exams and tonight we're having a [Br.] slap-up/first-rate meal!"

EXERCISES

C'est à vous maintenant!

A *Before each of the words for food, put a ✓, ✗, or — to show whether the food is good, bad, or neutral.*

____ 1. les rogatons

____ 2. un casse-graine

____ 3. la boustifaille

____ 4. un gueuleton

____ 5. la tambouille

____ 6. la bouffe

____ 7. la ragougnasse

____ 8. le boustif

____ 9. un casse-croûte

____ 10. le rata

____ 11. la graille

____ 12. le déj

B *You have a French-speaking friend who is fond of using colloquial language. When invited to a meal, you decide to impress your friend by answering all her/his questions about food in streetwise French. In the following conversation, write out a colloquial version of all the English answers.*

1. AMI(E) En principe, tu manges beaucoup de pain?
   VOUS Say you stuff yourself on bread.

   ____

2. AMI(E) Très bien et qu'est-ce que tu aimes comme soupe?
   VOUS Say you like onion soup but don't like watery soup.

   ____

3. AMI(E) Je ne vais pas t'en servir, je t'assure! Et quant au frome?
   VOUS Say you'd like to eat some Camembert.

   ____

4. AMI(E) Il y en a toujours chez moi! Et comme légumes avec les côtelettes que je te prépare?
   VOUS Say you like potatoes and beans.

   ____

C *Along with your American friend, Alex, who speaks no French, you have been invited to a dinner party at the home of some friends in Québec. Interpret your Québécois friends' comments for Alex.*

1. Monsieur Alex, il a le fringale?

 ____

2. Très bien, alors, on attaque!

 ____

3. Normalement, on graille à quelle heure chez vous?

 ____

4. Ne faites pas attention à notre fille! Elle bouffe comme un chancre!

 ____

 ____

5. Oui, et il y a notre fils qui picore par contraste! Il est tombé amoureux!

 ____

 ____

6. Alors, Monsieur Alex, on bâfre ici, n'est-ce pas?

 ____

Foreigners

NAMES FOR FOREIGNERS

NOTE: French, like English, has a number of terms for foreigners, which are for the most part deeply insulting, but some of them may be used humorously, depending on the context. Here is a list:

Aussie, Australian **un kangourou**(?) (*lit.*, kangaroo)

Brit, Englishman ([Br.] limey, [Br.] sasanach, [Br.] pommy) **un rosbif** (*lit.*, a roast beef), **un bifteck** (*lit.*, a steak)

Chink(!), Chinkie(!), Chinaman(!) **un chinetoque**(!)**, un bridé**(!)**, un noiche**

NOTE: **Noiche** is an example of *verlan* and is based on **chinois**.

dago(!), Hispanic, South American **un espingouin**(!)**, un latino**(?)**, un rastaquouère**(!)

Kiwi, New Zealander **un kiwi**

kraut(!), Jerry(!), Hun(!) **un boche**(!)**, un chleuh**(!)**, un fritz**(!)**, un frisé**(!)**, un fridolin**(!)

nip(!), Jap(?) **un jap**(!)

Portuguese **un porto**(!) (*lit.*, port [the drink]), **un portos**(!)

Russian, Russki(!) **un ruski**(!)**, un ruskof**(!)**, un popof**(!)

wop(!) (Italian), [Br.] eyetie(!) **un rital**(!)**, un macaroni**(!)

Yank(?), Yankee(?) **un amerloque**(!)**, un amerluche**(!)**, un ricain**(?)**, un yankee**(?)

Names for races/foreigners (not country-specific)

Arab **Maghrébin(e)** (standard term for anyone from the **Maghreb**, that part of North Africa composed of Algeria, Morocco, and Tunisia); **un raton**(!)**, un bic**(!)**, un bicot**(!)**, un crouille**(!)**, un bougnoule**(!) (used of any dark-skinned foreigner in France but is often used as a term of abuse for Arabs)

Second-generation Arab born in France **un beur, une beurette** (the latter designates a young girl of Arab descent but born in France, often torn culturally between the French way of life and that of her [immigrant] parents)

Jew, hebe(!), kike(!) **un youpin(!), un youtre(!), un feuj(!)**

nigger(!!), nig-nog(!!) **un négro(!), un nègre(?), un bamboula(!), un moricaud(!), un kebla/keubla**

NOTE: **Un kebla/keubla** is an example of *verlan* and is based on the English word "black."

wog(!) **un bougnoule(!), un bamboula(!)**

wop(!) (someone of "Mediterranean" appearance) **un métèque(?);** (Italian) **un rital(!), un macaroni(!)**

EXPRESSIONS INVOLVING NAMES OF FOREIGNERS

NOTE: Some of these expressions are extremely offensive, as indicated by our normal symbols. The others should be used with discretion and only in very informal circumstances.

«Elle travaille comme un nègre(?).» "She works like a slave/a nigger(!)."

«Lui, il parle petit-nègre et même son patron parle français comme une vache espagnole.» "He speaks broken French and even his boss speaks pidgin French/lousy French."

«Ça fait une demi-heure que je ne l'ai pas vue. Elle a dû filer à l'anglaise.» "I haven't seen her for half an hour. She must have taken French leave/slinked off."

«Quel bazar! C'est comme un combat de nègres(?) dans un tunnel.» "What a shambles/mess! It's (all) as clear as mud/shit(?)."

«Vous cherchez l'Hôtel de Ville? Pour y aller, c'est plutôt chinois.» "You're trying to find the Town Hall? It's pretty difficult to get there."

«Alors ce soir, on va tous faire la bamboula(?).» "This evening, we're all gonna/going to paint the town red."

NOTE: An alternative slang expression for **faire la bamboula** is **faire la bringue**.

EXERCISES

C'est à vous maintenant!

A *Match the offensive French names for foreigners listed on the left with their acceptable French alternative on the right.*

_____	1. un youtre(!)	a. un(e) italien(ne)
_____	2. un bridé(!)	b. un(e) américain(e)
_____	3. un jap(!)	c. un(e) arab(e)
_____	4. un ricain(?)	d. un(e) juif(-ve)
_____	5. un chleuh(!)	e. un(e) noir(e)
_____	6. un moricaud(!)	f. un(e) japonais(e)
_____	7. un bic(!)	g. un(e) allemand(e)
_____	8. un macaroni(!)	h. un(e) chinois(e)

B *Fill in the blanks in the following sentences with the slang French or standard French term referring to a foreigner.*

1. Elle n'est pas allée à l'école aujourd'hui. Ce qui m'inquiète, c'est que très souvent son frangin file à ________________.
2. Il est né au Maroc; il est donc ________________.
3. Ce ________________ est né à Auckland.
4. Ils sont anglais, mais pour moi ce sont des ________________.
5. Né à Lisbonne, ce ________________ parle français comme une vache ________________.
6. Elle est crevée! Ça fait douze heures qu'elle travaille comme un ________________.

Health

See also "Conversations and Invitations," "The Human Body."

HOW ARE YOU FEELING?

aller tout doux (*lit.*, to go quite gently) to be so-so/fair/middling ■ **«Je ne vais que tout doux après mon intervention.»** "I'm only so-so after my operation."

comme ci comme ça (*lit.*, like this, like that) so-so, fair to middling ■ **«C'est toujours comme ci comme ça avec lui!»** "He's always fair to middling!"

ne pas se sentir très vaillant (*lit.*, not to feel very valiant) to be a bit under the weather/[Br.] off form/off it/off ■ **«Après la grippe, je ne me sens toujours pas très vaillant!»** "After my flu, I'm still a bit under the weather/[Br.] off form!"

> NOTE: **Vaillant** also retains its original meaning of "valiant, brave, stout-hearted." In the jousting arenas in the age of chivalry, someone who was unwell was often perceived as not very stout-hearted!

ne pas être dans son assiette to be under the weather/[Br.] not up to the mark ■ **«Elle n'est pas dans son assiette à cause de ce sacré virus!»** "She's under the weather thanks to this darned virus!"

> NOTE: Originally, **assiette** meant a person's sitting position, so the expression meant that you were lying down, not sitting.

se sentir un peu chose (*lit.*, to feel a bit thingy) to feel funny/peculiar

avoir l'air tout chose (*lit.*, to look all thingy) to look really peculiar

se sentir patraque to be under the weather/[Br.] off color

ne pas se sentir d'attaque to be under the weather, [Br.] to not be up to the mark ■ **«Il ne se sent jamais d'attaque, quand il s'agit de bosser un peu!»** "He's never all there/[Br.] up to the mark, when it's a question of doing a bit of hard work!"

> NOTE: This was originally a military expression. In Western European wars, you had to be really ill not to take part in an attack on the enemy. There were no doctor's notes in those days!

se faire choper (*lit.*, to get oneself caught/[Br.] nicked) to come down with, [Br.] to catch a dose of, [Br.] to get laid down (low) by ■ **«Elle s'est chopé une bronchite pendant les pluies.»** "She came down with bronchitis during the rains."

être mal en point (*lit.*, to be badly placed) to be in a poor/bad way

filer un mauvais coton to be (in) a sorry state ■ **«Rien qu'à regarder son visage, on voit qu'elle file un mauvais coton!»** "Just looking at her face, you can see the sorry state she's in!"

NOTE: Literally "to spin a bad cotton," this expression gives a faint hint of just how hard our ancestors once had to work in order to scratch out a living. In the old cottage industries and even in the factories that later developed, you would work until you were in such a bad way that you could not spin your cotton properly.

péter le feu to be full of energy, there is no stopping him/her ■ **«Même si elle a soixante-cinq ans, elle pète le feu!»** "She may be sixty-five, but there's no stopping her!"

NOTE: Literally "to fart fire," i.e., having so much energy that one's guns are fully primed and ready for battle.

être en pleine forme to be on (in) (top) form

avoir la forme to be in great shape

tenir la forme to keep in shape/trim/one's figure

être bien en point to be fit, healthy

se porter comme un charme (*lit.*, to carry oneself like a charm) to be as fit as a fiddle/[Br.] flea

retrouver la forme to get fit/in shape

garder la ligne (*lit.*, to keep the line) to keep trim ■ **«Il faut qu'il fasse de la gymnastique, s'il veut garder la ligne!»** "He needs to get to the gym, if he wants to keep trim!"

se sentir ___ ans de moins to feel ___ years younger ■ **«Grâce à cette crème, je me sens quinze ans de moins!»** "Thanks to that cream, I feel fifteen years younger!"

péter le feu

faire jeune/vieux (vieille) (*lit.*, to make young/old) to look young/old ■ **«Elle fait plus vieille qu'elle ne l'est!»** "She looks older than she is!"

prendre de la bouteille, prendre du bouchon to be getting on, [Br.] to be knocking on a bit

NOTE: Both these expressions relate to the corking of the wine as it gradually loses its contents through an imperfect cork, a metaphor for life's spirit. Nowadays, it is also argued that the first of these two expressions refers to the bottle-like shape many people develop as they grow older.

être dans les vapes(?) (*lit.*, to be in the vapors) to be out for the count (with drink, drugs, etc.), to be out cold

être sur le flanc (*lit.*, to be on one's side [in bed]) to be laid up

SPECIFIC SYMPTOMS AND COMPLAINTS

le bobo hurt, sore (to/from small children) ■ **«Ça te fait bobo?»** "Does that hurt you?"

tomber dans les pommes(?) to pass out, [Br.] to flake out ■ **«Il est tombé dans les pommes à cause de la chaleur.»** "He passed out because of the heat."

NOTE: This is a pleasant picture of someone falling among the apples from an apple tree in the orchard.

tourner de l'œil (*lit.*, to turn your eye) to pass out, [Br.] to flake out

avoir un sérieux mal de crâne to have a nasty headache

avoir l'œil au beurre noir/avoir l'œil poché/avoir le cocard to have a black eye

NOTE: All these expressions have colorful origins, like the state they describe. Butter was put on a black eye to reduce the swelling, or it could look like a poached egg, or it was a mixture of blue, white, and red, looking like the cockade on the three-cornered hat worn at the time of the French Revolution.

se crever(?) to ruin one's health, to wreck oneself ■ **«Il s'est crevé pour avoir bu tant de gnole!»** "He's wrecked his health, drinking all that firewater!"

NOTE: The basic meaning of **crever** is "to burst/split," so all expressions involving **crever** and degenerating health hark back to the original idea of the body splitting open, as it does when full of pus.

attraper la crève(?) (*lit.*, to catch the split) to catch one's death/a cold

avoir la crève(?) to be ill

déconner to cause trouble, to act up, [Br.] to play up ■ **«Elle a le foie qui déconne!»** "Her liver's acting up/[Br.] playing her up!"

dégobillerⓘ, **dégueuler**ⓘ to vomit, puke

NOTE: The literal meaning of **dégobiller/dégueuler** would be "to dis-swallow/ [Br.] dis-chops," if such words existed.

ça sent le sapin (s)he doesn't have long/[Br.] (s)he's not long to go now
■ **«Quant à elle, ça sent le sapin depuis déjà dix ans!»** "As for her, she hasn't had long to go for ten years already!"

NOTE: **Ça sent le sapin** (there's a smell of pine); coffins were traditionally made of pinewood, with its powerful-smelling sap.

PSEUDOMEDICAL VOCABULARY

le billard operating table

canerⓘ, **claquer**ⓘ, **crever**ⓘ, **clamecer, casser sa pipe** to die, to kick the bucket

NOTE: There was a tradition, which still existed into the nineteenth century, whereby a man was buried with his broken clay pipe, his pipe normally being one of his treasured possessions.

l'hosto (m) hospital

le macab corpse, stiff

le macchabée corpse, stiff

la muscu [musculation] bodybuilding

séropo [séropositif(-ive)] HIV-positive (person)

le toubibⓘ doc(tor), quack

EXERCISES

C'est à vous maintenant!

A *Put the following statements about health into the correct order, from very poor to very good.*

1. être bien en point ___, ___, ___, ___, ___, ___, ___, ___
2. ne pas se sentir très vaillant
3. être sur le flanc
4. péter le feu
5. retrouver sa forme
6. filer un mauvais coton
7. aller tout doux
8. ne pas être dans son assiette

B *Find the matching pairs of statements, one from each column.*

___	1. prendre de la bouteille	a. être bien en point
___	2. avoir l'œil poché	b. tomber dans les pommes
___	3. tourner de l'œil	c. claquer
___	4. dégueuler	d. aller comme ci comme ça
___	5. caner	e. prendre du bouchon
___	6. être en pleine forme	f. avoir le cocard
___	7. aller tout doux	g. dégobiller

C *In Paris, you have a French acquaintance who constantly talks streetwise! She is telling you about her health and your friend Alex is nonplussed. Interpret for Alex.*

1. J'suis allée voir le toubib.

   ____

2. Puis, j'suis allée à l'hosto.

   ____

3. Je croyais que je crevais!

   ____

4. Le chirurgien m'a mise sur le billard.

   ____

5. Et ça sentait le sapin!

   ____

6. Mais, maintenant, je pète le feu!

   ____

Hobbies and Pastimes

See also "Entertainment," "Land and Countryside," "Sports."

VARIOUS ENTHUSIASTS

l'accro [accroché] (m) nut, fanatic

l'accro du rap rap fanatic, [Br.] raphead

être accro à to be hooked on, to be a fan of ■ **«Il ne va certainement pas sortir avec nous—il est accro aux vieux films de John Wayne et il y en a un à la Une ce soir!»** "You certainly won't get him to come out with us—he's hooked on old John Wayne movies, and there's one on Channel 1 this evening!"

NOTE: This group of expressions originates from the verb **accrocher** (to hook [onto]) and can be used to suggest that someone is either hooked on a particular pastime or on drugs.

l'amateur (m) **de** fan of/into

l'amateur de jazz jazz fan

être grand amateur de (*lit.*, to be a great fan of) to be into . . . in a big way ■ **«Tu sais, c'est un grand amateur du théâtre expérimental.»** "You know, (s)he's into experimental theater in a big way."

le bricoleur, la bricoleuse home-improvement/do-it-yourself/[Br.] DIY enthusiast

être bricoleur(-euse) to be good with your hands, to be a do-it-yourselfer ■ **«Il est bricoleur pendant ses moments perdus.»** "He's a do-it-yourselfer in his spare time."

NOTE: **Bricoler** (to go in for do-it-yourself, [Br.] DIY); **(se) bricoler** has the secondary meaning **se masturber**.

le/la cinéphile film buff

le/la fana de jazz jazz freak

le fana de football soccer, [Br.] football fan

le/la mélomane music lover

le/la mordu(e) d'informatique computer buff

le/la mordu(e) de lecture bookworm

HOBBIES AND PASTIMES

le bricolage home improvement, do-it-yourself/[Br.] DIY ■ **«Elle est très pour le bricolage!»** "She's really into/[Br.] keen on do-it-yourself!"

le lèche-vitrines (*lit.*, window-licking) window-shopping ■ **«Elle n'arrête jamais de faire du lèche-vitrines!»** "She never stops (her) window-shopping!"

le potager vegetable garden, [Br.] allotment ■ **«Il est toujours au potager avec ces tubes de bière.»** "He's always out in the garden/[Br.] in his allotment with his cans of beer."

SHOWING YOUR TALENTS OR OTHERWISE

s'accrocher à (*lit.*, to hook onto) to keep at, to stick at/to/with ■ **«Il n'a pas de vrai talent, mais il s'y accroche!»** "He's got no real talent, but he sticks with it!"

être adroit/habile de ses mains to be good with one's hands ■ **«Il est bête comme ses pieds, mais il est très habile de ses mains!»** "He's as dumb as a post/[Br.] thick as two short planks, but very good with his hands."

être doué(e) pour (*lit.*, to be gifted at) to be gifted in, [Br.] to be a dab hand at ■ **«Elle est douée pour le dessin.»** "She's gifted in/[Br.] a dab hand at drawing."

avoir du talent pour to have a talent for ■ **«Elle n'a pas de vrai talent pour ce qu'elle fait!»** "She's got no real talent for what she does!"

Elle n'arrête jamais de faire du lèche-vitrines!

avoir un don naturel pour to have a gift for, to be cut out for ■ **«Je n'ai pas de don naturel pour ce boulot.»** "I'm not cut out for this job."

avoir la main verte (*lit.*, to have a green hand) to have a green thumb/[Br.] green fingers ■ **«Si elle a la main verte! Tout ce qu'elle touche, pousse!»** "Has she got a green thumb! Everything she touches, grows!"

être monsieur/madame je-sais-tout (*lit.*, to be Mr./Mrs. I-Know-It-All) to be a bit of a know-it-all/[Br.] know-all ■ **«Pour les films noirs, il est un peu monsieur je-sais-tout!»** "As far as *films noirs* are concerned, he's a bit of a know-it-all/[Br.] know-all!"

se débrouiller (tout seul[e]) to get by, to manage (on one's own) ▪ **«Laisse-moi faire! Je me débrouille tout seul!»** "Let me get on with it! I can manage on my own!"

> NOTE: Care is needed with this expression, since those looking for double meanings can and will interpret it as **se masturber**.

être hanté(e) (*lit.*, to be haunted by), **être obsédé(e) par** to be obsessed with ▪ **«Il est hanté par le jazz traditionnel!»** "He's obsessed with trad(itional) jazz/straight-ahead jazz!"

prendre son pied avec (*lit.*, to take one's foot with) to get off on ▪ **«Elle est très intello—elle prend son pied avec les romans de Marcel Proust!»** "She's quite an egghead—she gets off on the novels of Marcel Proust!"

> NOTE: Although this expression has obvious sexual implications, it can be used, as in the example, to suggest a person sublimates her/his sexual drive with other hobbies.

ne savoir rien de rien (*lit.*, not to know anything about anything) to be clueless ▪ **«Il fait de son mieux avec le moteur, mais, il n'en sait rien de rien!»** "He does his best with the engine, but he hasn't got a clue!"

LETTING ONE'S HAIR DOWN

s'éclater to freak out ▪ **«C'est gênant la façon dont il s'éclate toujours à la disco.»** "It's embarrassing, the way he always freaks out at the disco!"

s'en payer une tranche (*lit.*, to pay for a slice) to have a great time ▪ **«Si tu le fais, je te paie une tranche!»** "If you'll do it, I'll show you a great time!"

faire la bringue㊋ (*lit.*, to go on a binge) to go out on the town/[Br.] razzle ▪ **«Quand l'équipe joue à l'extérieur, tous les joueurs font la bringue!»** "When the team plays away (from home), all the players go out on the town."

faire la tournée des grands ducs (*lit.*, to do the Grand Dukes' tour) to have a night out, to paint the town red, to hit the high spots ▪ **«Il s'est fait une crise de cœur, en faisant la tournée des grands ducs!»** "He gave himself a heart attack, painting the town red!"

guincher㊋ to dance, to shake a leg, [Br.] to have a spin ▪ **«Avec ces grosses cuisses, elle a des problèmes pour guincher!»** "With those thunder/[Br.] elephant thighs, she has problems dancing!"

en guincher une㊋ (*lit.*, to dance a good one) to dance, to shake a leg, [Br.] to have a spin ▪ **«Il l'a pelotée, après en avoir guinché une!»** "He made out with her after they shook a leg/[Br.] had a little spin!"

faire du ski-bar (*lit.*, to do some ski-barring) to play the nineteenth hole ■ **«Un bon skieur, lui? Tu voudrais rire! Il n'est bon que pour faire du ski-bar!»** "Him, a good skier? You have to be joking! The only thing he's good for is the nineteenth hole!"

faire de l'après-ski (*lit.*, to do some after-ski) to play the nineteenth hole ■ **«Si seulement elle jouait au golf comme elle fait de l'après-ski!»** "If only she played golf like she plays the nineteenth hole!"

EXERCISES

C'est à vous maintenant!

A *How would you say the following phrases in streetwise French?*

1. a computer buff ______________________
2. a film buff ______________________
3. a home-improvement/DIY enthusiast ______________________
4. a rap fanatic/[Br.] raphead ______________________
5. a soccer fan ______________________
6. a bookworm ______________________
7. a jazz fan ______________________
8. a music lover ______________________

B *How good are people at their various hobbies? Arrange these descriptions in the correct order, going from very poor to very good.*

1. **Elle est habile.** ___, ___, ___, ___, ___, ___
2. **Il se débrouille!**
3. **Elle a du talent.**
4. **Il ne sait rien de rien!**
5. **Elle a un don naturel.**
6. **Il s'y accroche.**

C *Find the matching pairs, taking one expression from each column.*

____	1. être doué	a. être obsédé
____	2. être au potager	b. faire la tournée des grands ducs
____	3. être hanté	c. faire de l'après-ski
____	4. faire la bringue	d. avoir la main verte
____	5. faire du ski-bar	e. avoir du talent

The Human Body

See also "Sex."

PARTS OF THE BODY

The male body

NOTE: Many of the expressions listed here (the exceptions are fairly obvious!) apply to the female body too.

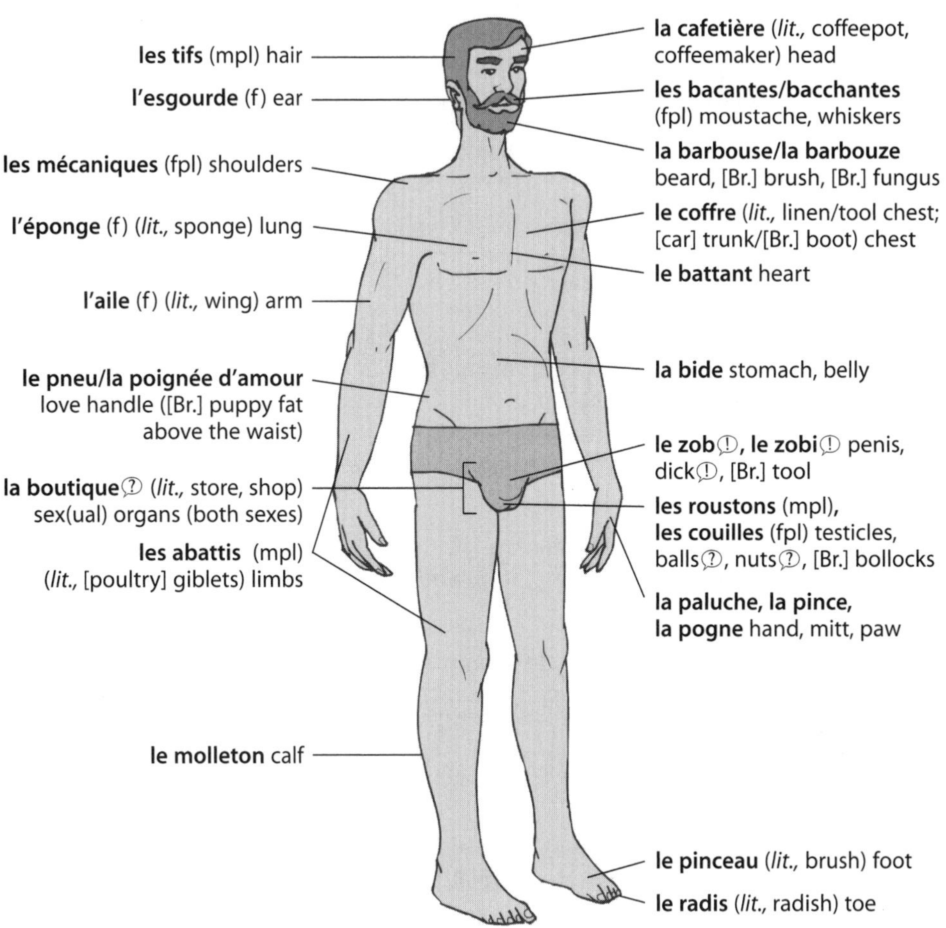

Alternative slang expressions for parts of the male (and in many cases female) body

Head: **la bille** (*lit.*, marble, [billiard] ball), **la binette** (mug, block), **la caboche, le caillou** (*lit.*, stone, pebble), **la caisse** (*lit.*, box, crate; cash register; drum), **le caisson** (*lit.*, box, case, crate), **le carafon** (*lit.*, small decanter/carafe), **le cassis** (*lit.*, black currant), **le citron** (*lit.*, lemon), **la citrouille** (*lit.*, pumpkin), **la coloquinte** (*lit.*, colocynth, bitter apple), **le gadin, la mansarde** (*lit.*, garret, attic), **le melon** (*lit.*, melon), **le plafond** (*lit.*, ceiling), **la poire** (*lit.*, pear), **la pomme** (*lit.*, apple), **le sinoquet, la sorbonne** (*lit.*, Sorbonne University), **la terrine** (*lit.*, earthenware vessel), **la théière** (*lit.*, teapot), **la toiture** (*lit.*, roof, roofing), **la trogne** (mug, [Br.] dial), **la trompette** (*lit.*, trumpet), **la tronche**.

Hair: **l'alfa** (m) (*lit.*, Esparto grass), **les baguettes** (fpl) (*lit.*, sticks, chopsticks, [bread] baguettes), **les crayons** (mpl) (*lit.*, pencils, crayons), **le cresson** (*lit.*, watercress), **les douilles** (fpl) (*lit.*, cartridge cases, cartridges, sockets), **le gazon** (*lit.*, lawn, grass), **les marguerites** (fpl) (*lit.*, daisies = white hairs), **les plumes** (fpl) (*lit.*, feathers), **les roseaux** (mpl) (*lit.*, reeds), **la tignasse, les vermicelles** (fpl) (*lit.*, vermicelli, angel-hair pasta).

Moustache: **la baffi, le balai à chiottes** (*lit.*, [Br.] john/bog/brush), **les charmeuses** (fpl) (*lit.*, charmers), **la moustagache**.

> NOTE: **Moustagache** is an example of *javanais* or "av" slang, where "ag" is inserted in the middle of the original word "moustache," rather than the more normal "av."

Ear(s): **les écoutilles** (fpl) (*lit.*, hatchways), **les escalopes** (fpl) (*lit.*, escalopes; also means "feet"), **les étiquettes** (fpl) (*lit.*, labels), **les feuilles** (fpl) (*lit.*, leaves), **les loches** (fpl) (*lit.*, loach [fish], gray slugs), **les manettes** (fpl) (*lit.*, levers, taps), **les portugaises** (fpl) (*lit.*, Portuguese oysters), **les zozores** (fpl), **l'étagère** (f) **à mégots** (*lit.*, the shelf for one's cigarette butts).

Arm(s): **les abattis** (mpl), **l'aileron** (m) (*lit.*, aerofoil), **les allonges** (fpl) (*lit.*, extensions, leaves [of table]), **le brandillon, la manivelle** (*lit.*, crank, starting handle).

Hand: **la cuiller** (*lit.*, spoon), **le grappin** (*lit.*, grapnel; drag [of crane], grab) (used in the phrase on page 129 which is preceded by an *), **la louche** (*lit.*, ladle), **la patte** (*lit.*, [dog's] paw, [bird's] foot).

> NOTE: **La patte** can refer to either the hand or the foot in slang French and is found in a large number of set expressions (see page 129 for some of them).

Finger(s): **les francforts** (mpl) (*lit.*, frankfurters), **les salsifis** (mpl) (*lit.*, oyster plants), **la fourchette du père Adam** (when used for eating) (*lit.*, old Adam's fork).

Beard: **le piège** (*lit.*, trap), **le piège à macaronis, le piège à poux**.

NOTE: These expressions literally mean "macaroni/louse trap."

Shoulder(s): **les endosses** (fpl), **les épahules** (fpl), **le porte-manteau** (*lit.*, coat hanger).

Lung: **le soufflet** (*lit.*, bellows), **la soupape** (*lit.*, valve).

NOTE: In slang, the word **éponge** (see illustration on page 125) is also used for an alcoholic (**C'est une vieille éponge.**) and also for a nymphomaniac.

Heart: **le palpitant, le trembleur**.

Stomach: **le baquet** (*lit.*, tub), **la boîte à ragoût** (*lit.*, stew can/[Br.] tin), **le bidon** (*lit.*, can, [Br.] tin), **la brioche** (*lit.*, brioche), **le buffet** (*lit.*, sideboard, buffet), **le cornet** (*lit.*, paper cone; by extension "bag of candy/sweets," "bag of French fries/[Br.] chips"), **l'estom'** (m), **le fusil** (*lit.*, rifle, gun), **le gésier** (*lit.*, gizzard), **le gras-double** (*lit.*, tripe), **la lampe** (*lit.*, lamp, light, bulb), **le lampion** (*lit.*, Chinese lantern), **le tiroir** (*lit.*, drawer).

Penis (all of these words will cause offense): (!)**l'arbalète** (f) (*lit.*, crossbow), **l'ardillon** (m) (*lit.*, prong, tongue [of buckle]), **l'asperge** (f) (*lit.*, asparagus), **la balayette** (*lit.*, [hand]brush), **la biroute, la bistouquette, la bite** (*lit.*, mooring post, bollard), **le bonhomme** (*lit.*, guy, fellow, [husband] old man), **le bout** (*lit.*, end, tip), **le brandon** (*lit.*, firebrand), **le braquemart** (*lit.*, double-bladed sword), **le chinois** (*lit.*, Chinese man), **la chipolata** (*lit.*, chipolata), **la clarinette** (*lit.*, clarinet), **la coquette** (*lit.*, flirt), **le dard** (*lit.*, javelin, spear), **le darrac, la défonceuse** (*lit.*, powerful plow/[Br.] plough used for breaking up the soil), **l'engin** (m) (*lit.*, machine, instrument, tool), **le flageolet** (*lit.*, flageolet [small flute]), **le gland** (*lit.*, acorn), **le gourdin** (*lit.*, club, bludgeon), **le guise, le guizot, le jacquot** (*lit.*, "Polly" [of parrot]), **le jean nu-tête** (*lit.*, bare-headed John), **le macaroni** (*lit.*, macaroni), **la matraque** (*lit.*, baton, truncheon, billy [club]), **le nœud** (*lit.*, knot, bow), **l'outil** (m) (*lit.*, tool), **le paf** (*lit.*, bam!/wham!/slam!), **la pine, le polard, le Popaul, la quéquette, la queue** (*lit.*, tail, handle, stalk), **le sabre** (*lit.*, saber/[Br.] sabre), **le tébi, le teube, la tige** (*lit.*, stem, stalk), **la trique** (*lit.*, cudgel), **le zeb, le zébi, le zib, le zibar, le zigouigoui, le zizi, le chauve à col roulé** (*lit.*, the bald-headed man wearing a turtleneck/polo neck), **le cigare à moustaches** (*lit.*, the cigar with a mustache/moustache), **le manche (à balai/à couilles)** (*lit.*, broomstick, broomshaft); **les couilles** [fpl] = nuts(!), balls(!)), **l'os à moelle** (*lit.*, marrowbone), **le papillon du Sénégal** (*lit.*, Senegal butterfly), **le petit frère** (*lit.*, little/kid brother), **le robinet d'amour** (*lit.*, love faucet/tap).

NOTE: **Tébi/teube** are examples of *verlan* and derive from **bite**; **quéquette** places the emphasis on smallness while **zizi** is used mainly by small boys (compare [Br.] "willy").

Sex(ual) organs: **les bijoux** (mpl) **de famille** (*lit.*, family jewels), **le service trois-pièces** (*lit.*, three-piece service).

Testicles (all of these words will cause offense): ⓘ**les agobilles** (fpl), **les balloches** (fpl), **les bonbons** (mpl) (*lit.*, pieces of candy, sweets), **les burettes** (fpl), **les burnes** (fpl), **les couilles** (fpl), **les coucougnettes** (fpl), **les douillettes** (fpl) (*lit.*, [clerical] overcoats; [babies'] quilted coats), **les figues** (fpl) (*lit.*, figs), **les grelots** (mpl) (*lit.*, [small spherical] bells), **les joyeuses** (fpl) (*lit.*, joyful/merry ones), **les noisettes** (fpl) (*lit.*, hazelnuts), **les olives** (fpl) (*lit.*, olives), **les orphelines** (fpl) (*lit.*, [female] orphans), **les pelotes** (fpl) (*lit.*, balls [of wool]), **les précieuses** (fpl) (*lit.*, precious ones/things), **les prunes** (fpl) (*lit.*, plums), **les rognons** (mpl) (*lit.*, kidneys), **les roubignolles** (fpl), **les rouleaux** (mpl) (*lit.*, rolls/rollers), **les roupettes** (fpl), **les roustons** (mpl), **les valseuses** (fpl) (*lit.*, [female] waltzers).

Calf: **le molletegomme, le molleton** (*lit.*, cotton fleece, swansdown), **le molltegonne, le moltogon**.

Foot/feet: **l'arpion** (m), **l'escalope** (f) (*lit.*, escalope), **le fromage** (*lit.*, cheese), **les fumerons** (mpl), **la latte** (*lit.*, lath, board, slat), **le nougat** (*lit.*, nougat), **les oignes** (mpl), **les oignons** (mpl) (*lit.*, onions), **le panard, la patte** (*lit.*, leg, paw [of animal]), **le paturon** (*lit.*, pastern [horse, animals]), **le pilon** (*lit.*, pestle, wooden leg), **le pinglot, le pingouin** (*lit.*, penguin), **la raquette** (*lit.*, racket, [table tennis] bat), **les ripatons** (mpl), **les targettes** (fpl) (*lit.*, bolts), **la tige** (*lit.*, stem, stalk), **le trottinet**.

Toe: **le radis** (*lit.*, radish).

Expressions involving slang words for parts of the male (and in most cases female) body

«Il s'est fait sauter le caisson.» "He's blown his brains out./He's shot himself in the head."

«Il se creuse le citron mais il ne trouve pas la réponse.» "He's racking his brains, but he can't think of the answer."

«Elle a pris une pêche en pleine poire.» "She got a smack on the kisser."

«Il faut pas la prendre pour une poire.» "She's no patsy/[Br.] mug."

«Moi, j'ai refusé mais lui, bonne poire, il a accepté.» "I refused but, like the patsy/[Br.] mug he is, he accepted."

«Arrête de faire la tronche!» "Stop moping/sulking!"

«Il s'est fait tailler les crayons.» "He got a haircut/[Br.] had his lawn mowed."

«Tous les deux, ils ont le cresson clairsemé/ils perdent leurs plumes.» "Both of them are thinning on top./Neither of them has got much hair."

«Ce pépère est dur de la feuille.» "This old guy is hard of hearing."

«Je lui ai serré la cuiller/la louche et ça m'a flanqué la trouille.» "I shook his hand/[Br.] shook paws with him, and it gave me the willies/scared me stiff."

***«Elle a mis le grappin sur une vache à lait.»** "She's hooked a real sucker/[Br.] mug/cash cow."

«Eh ben! Tu as vraiment le coup de patte.» "Well, you've really got the knack/the magic touch."

«Elle est retombée sur ses pattes.» "She really landed/fell on her feet."

«Je lui ai graissé la patte.» "I bribed him/her./I greased his/her palm."

«Ça ne casse pas trois pattes à un canard.» "It's no great shakes."

«Il a toujours porté des pattes d'éléphant/des pattes d'eph.» "He's always worn bell-bottoms/[Br.] flares/flared trousers."

«Cet accident, il l'a mis sur les endosses de son frangin.» "He made his brother/[Br.] brud take the rap/[Br.] carry the can for this accident."

«Ils n'ont rien dans le buffet.» "They've got no guts/balls(?)."

«Je m'en suis mis/collé/foutu(!) plein la lampe.» "I pigged out./I stuffed myself with food."

«Elle a un polichinelle dans le tiroir.» "She's knocked up./[Br.] She has a bun in the oven./She's in the club."

«Il faut pas le regarder. Il a le gourdin(!) et il se polit le chinois(?)/il s'allonge le macaroni(!).» "You mustn't look at him. He's got a hard-on(?) and he's jerking/[Br.] wanking himself off(?)/[Br.] banging the bishop(?)."

«Quand je les ai trouvés dans ma piaule, ils étaient en train de faire zizi-panpan(?).» "When I found them in my pad, they were getting it on/[Br.] having a shag(?)/[Br.] having it off(?)."

The female body

NOTE: Many of the expressions listed here (the exceptions are fairly obvious!) apply to the male body, too.

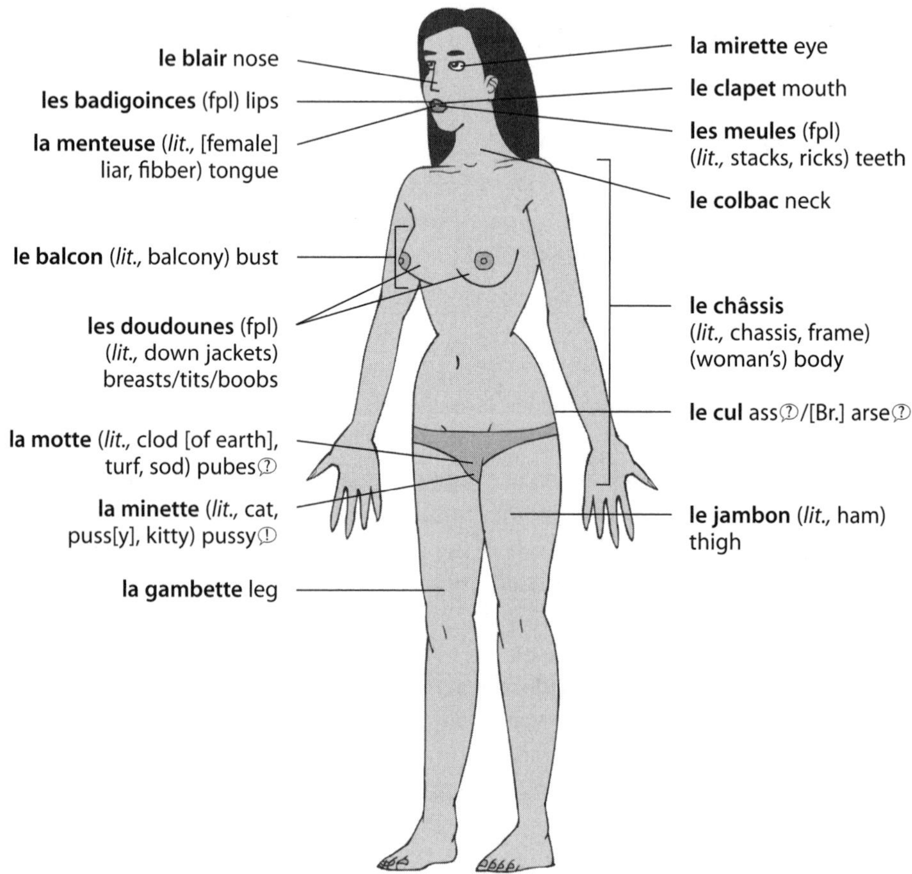

Alternative slang expressions for parts of the female (and in many cases male) body

Hairstyles: **l'afro, la balayeuse** (long hair; *lit.*, streetsweeper, road-sweeper), **la banane** (French plait/braid, quiff; [of man] teddy-boy haircut; *lit.*, banana), **la choupette** (tuft), **la choucroute** (curly hairdo, beehive; *lit.*, sauerkraut), **l'iroquoise** (f) (Mohican haircut), **la queue de cheval** (pony-tail), **la queue de canard** (DA, duck's ass(?)/[Br.] arse(?)).

Eye(s): **les agates** (fpl), **les boules** (fpl) **de loto** (round eyes; *lit.*, lottery balls), **le calot** (*lit.*, [large] marble), **les carreaux** (m) (*lit.*, window panes), **le châsse, le nœil, le neunœil, le quinquet** (*lit.*, oil lamp).

Nose: **l'aubergine** (f) (red nose; *lit.*, eggplant, aubergine), **le blase/blaze, le fer à souder** (big nose; *lit.*, soldering iron), **la lampe à souder** (big nose; *lit.*, blowtorch, [Br.] blowlamp), **le nase, la patate** (flat nose; *lit.*, [sweet] potato), **le pif, le quart de brie** (big nose; *lit.*, 250 g of Brie cheese), **la ruche** (*lit.*, beehive), **le step, le tarbouif, le tarin, le tasseau** (*lit.*, length of wood), **la tomate** (red nose; *lit.*, tomato), **la trompette** (*lit.*, trumpet), **la truffe** (flat nose; *lit.*, truffle).

> NOTE: **Aubergine** also means "female meter maid, traffic warden" in slang French. **Patate** is more widely used in slang for a "potato."

Mouth: **le babin, la boîte à mensonges** (*lit.*, box of lies), **la dalle** (*lit.*, paving stone, slab), **le dégueuloir** (*lit.*, the spew hole), **la gargue, le gicleur** (*lit.*, jet), **la goule** (*lit.*, ghoul), **la gueule, la margoulette, le micro** (*lit.*, microphone), **le porte-pipe** (*lit.*, pipe holder), **le saladier** (*lit.*, salad bowl), **la salle à manger** (*lit.*, dining room), **la tirelire** (*lit.*, money box, piggy bank).

Lips: **les babines** (fpl) (*lit.*, [animal] chops), **les babouines** (fpl), **les bagougnasses** (fpl), **les limaces** (fpl) (*lit.*, [zool.] slugs), **les pompeuses** (fpl) (*lit.*, the pompous ones).

Tongue: **la bavarde** (*lit.*, chatterbox, blabbermouth), **la calpette** (with the emphasis on gossip), **l'escalope** (f) (*lit.*, escalope), **la langouse, la languetouse, la languette, la mouillette** (*lit.*, finger of bread), **la tapette** (*lit.*, little tap; flyswatter).

Tooth/teeth: **la chaille, le croc** (*lit.*, fang), **le crochet** (*lit.*, hook), **les dominos** (*lit.*, dominoes), **la grille d'égout** (set of teeth; *lit.*, sewer grate), **le piano** (set of teeth; *lit.*, piano), **les quenottes** (fpl) (baby teeth), **la ratiche, les tabourets** (mpl) (*lit.*, stools), **la touche de piano** (*lit.*, piano key).

Neck: **le colas, le kiki/quiqui, le lampion** (*lit.*, Chinese lantern), **le porte-cravate** (*lit.*, tie holder).

Bust: **l'avant-scène** (f) (*lit.*, [theater] apron, proscenium, box), **le balcon** (*lit.*, [theater] dress/lower circle).

Breasts/tits (these words may well cause offense if used in the wrong context or situation): **les airbags** (mpl) (*lit.*, airbags), **les amortisseurs** (mpl) (*lit.*, shock absorbers), **les avantages** (mpl) (*lit.*, advantages), **les ballochards** (mpl), **les blagues** (fpl) **à tabac** (drooping breasts; *lit.*, tobacco pouches), **les boîtes** (fpl) **à lait** (*lit.*, milk boxes/cartons), **les lolos** (mpl) (also mean "milk" in children's language), **les mandarines** (fpl) (small breasts; *lit.*, mandarin oranges, tangerines), **les miches** (fpl) (*lit.*, round loaves, [Br.] cobs), **les nénés** (mpl), **les nibards** (mpl), **les niches** (fpl) (*lit.*, niches, recesses, kennels), **les nichons** (mpl), **les œufs sur le plat** (*lit.*, fried eggs), **les oranges** (fpl) (small breasts; *lit.*, oranges), **les parechocs** (mpl) (*lit.*, fender, [Br.] bumper), **les roberts** (mpl), **les rondins** (mpl) (*lit.*, logs), **les roploplots** (mpl), **les rotoplots** (mpl), **les tétasses** (fpl) (withered breasts).

Bottom/ass/[Br.] arse (these words are very likely to cause offense): **l'arche** (f) (*lit.*, arch), **l'arrière-train** (m) (*lit.*, [animal] hindquarters), **l'artiche** (m), **le baba, le baigneur** (*lit.*, swimmer, bather), **le bavard** (*lit.*, chatterbox, blabbermouth), **le bol** (*lit.*, bowl), **le dargeot, le dargif, l'entremichon** (m)**, le faubourg** (*lit.*, suburb), **le foiron, le père Fouettard, le gagne-pain** (*lit.*, breadwinner), **le joufflu** (*lit.*, chubby-cheeked person), **les jumelles** (fpl) (*lit.*, [female] twins, buttocks), **la lune** (*lit.*, moon), **les meules** (fpl) (buttocks; *lit.*, millstones), **les miches** (mpl) (buttocks; *lit.*, round loaf, [Br.] cob), **la noix** (*lit.*, walnut), **le panier** (*lit.*, basket), **les petits pains** (mpl) (buttocks; *lit.*, bread rolls), **le pétard** (*lit.*, firecracker, [Br.] banger), **le pétoulet, le pétrousquin, le pétrus, le pont-arrière** (*lit.*, rear bridge), **le popotin, le postère [postérieur], le pot** (*lit.*, pot, potty), **le prose/proze, le prosinard, le tafanard, le train** (*lit.*, train), **le troussequin** (*lit.*, [horseriding] cantle), **la turbine** (*lit.*, turbine), **le valseur** (*lit.*, waltzer), **le vase** (*lit.*, vase).

Anus (these words and phrases are offensive): **l'as** (m) **de trèfle** (*lit.*, the ace of clubs), **la bagouse** (*lit.*, ring), **la bague** (*lit.*, ring), **la chouette** (*lit.*, owl), **le couloir aux lentilles** (*lit.*, lentil passage), **le dé à coudre** (*lit.*, thimble), **le dix** (*lit.*, ten), **l'échalote** (f) (*lit.*, shallot), **l'entrée** (f) **des artistes** (*lit.*, stage door), **l'entrée** (f) **de service** (*lit.*, service/tradesmen's entrance), **le fignard, le fignolet, le fion, la lucarne enchantée** (*lit.*, the magic/enchanted skylight), **le moutardier** (*lit.*, the mustard pot), **l'œil de bronze** (*lit.*, bronze eye), **l'œillet** (m) (*lit.*, eyelet), **la pièce de dix ronds** (*lit.*, ten cent coin), **le point noir** (*lit.*, blackhead, problem, [Br.] blackspot), **le pot** (*lit.*, pot, potty), **la turbine à chocolat** (*lit.*, chocolate turbine).

Pubic hair/pubes (these words should be used with great discretion and only in the most informal situations): **le barbu** (*lit.*, bearded man), **le cresson** (*lit.*, watercress), **le gazon** (*lit.*, lawn), **la laitue** (*lit.*, lettuce), **le tablier de sapeur** (*lit.*, [Br.] sapper's apron; [cul.] tripe in breadcrumbs), **la touffe** (*lit.*, tuft).

Vagina/genitals/pussy (these words are offensive and should be used with great discretion, if at all): **l'abricot** (*lit.*, apricot), **le baba** ([cul.] baba; also, [Br.] bum), **le bénitier** (*lit.*, stoup, font), **le berlingot** (*lit.*, piece of hard candy), **le berlingue, la boîte à ouvrage** (*lit.*, sewing box, workbox), **la boîte aux lettres** (*lit.*, letter box), **la boutique** (*lit.*, shop, boutique), **le centre** (*lit.*, center/[Br.] centre), **la chagatte** (an example of *javanais* slang and derived from **chatte**), **le chat** (*lit.*, cat, tomcat), **la chatte** (*lit.*, [female] cat, pussy), **la choune, le con, la cramouille, la craquette, la fente** (*lit.*, crack, slit), **la figue** (*lit.*, fig), **la foufoune, le frifri, la greffière** (*lit.*, [jur.] clerk of the court), **la grip(p)ette, le lac** (*lit.*, lake), **la laitue** (*lit.*, lettuce), **le mille-feuille** (*lit.*, cream/vanilla slice, napoleon), **le minet** (*lit.*, puss, pussy), **la moniche, la moule** (*lit.*, mussel), **la pâquerette** (*lit.*, daisy), **la teuche** [*verlan*: **chatte**], **le turlu**.

Clitoris (these words are offensive and should be used with great discretion, if at all): (!)**le bonbon** (*lit.*, piece of candy, sweet, [Br.] sweetie), **le bouton** (*lit.*, button), **le clicli, la cliquette, le clito, la framboise** (*lit.*, raspberry), **le grain de café** (*lit.*, coffee bean), **la praline** (*lit.*, sugared almond).

Thigh: **le gigot** (*lit.*, leg of lamb), **le jambonneau** (*lit.*, knuckle of lamb; also means "guitar," "mandolin," or "banjo" in slang).

Leg(s): **la badine** (*lit.*, rod), **les baguettes** (fpl) (*lit.*, sticks, chopsticks, [Br.] French sticks), **les brancards** (mpl) (*lit.*, [cart] shafts, poles), **la calouse, la canne** (*lit.*, [walking] stick, cane), **le compas** (*lit.*, [pair of] compasses), **l'échalas** (m) (thin leg; *lit.*, stake, pole), **la flûte** (*lit.*, flute, [Br.] French stick), **les fusains** (mpl) (in the singular, "priest in his cassock"), **la guibolle, les manivelles** (fpl) (*lit.*, cranks, [Br.] starting handles), **le poteau** (fat leg; *lit.*, post, [execution] stake), **la quille** (*lit.*, skittle).

Expressions involving parts of the female (and in most cases male) body

«Elle m'en met plein les mirettes! Mais quand je lui ai dit ça, elle m'a crié ‹Ferme ton clapet›.» "She blows me away!/She really slays me! But when I told her that, she shouted, 'Shut your face/[Br.] gob.'"

«Il est très doué de la menteuse mais quand il a le feu au cul(!), c'est une tête de nœud.» "He's a good talker/He's got the gift of the gab, but when he's feeling horny/randy, he's a real dickhead(!)."

NOTE: **Quand il a le feu au cul** literally means "when he has a fire up his ass(!)/ [Br.] arse(!)."

«J'en ai plein/ras le cul(!) parce que ma gonzesse m'a ordonné de foutre(!) le camp.» "I'm really pissed off(!)/[Br.] I'm fed up to the back teeth because my old lady has told me to clear out/[Br.] bugger(!) off."

NOTE: **J'en ai plein/ras le cul** literally means "my ass(!)/[Br.] arse(!) is full of it"; **gonzesse** means "chick," "babe," [Br.] "bird" in addition to meaning "wife," "old lady."

«Il pète plus haut que son cul(!).» "He's full of himself./He has a really high opinion of himself."

«Il adore brouter la motte(!)/brouter le cresson(!)/faire minette(!)/faire une descente au barbu(!) et ensuite il lui demande de lui tailler une pipe(!)/ une plume(!)/un pompier(!).» "He just loves to go muff-diving(!)/He just loves to eat hair-pie(!), and afterwards he asks her to suck him off(!)/to give him a blow-job(!)."

«Elle en a gros sur la patate car quand elle avait fini de se pourlécher les babines, il lui a dit qu'il n'y avait plus rien à bouffer.» "She's really peeved/ She's really pissed off(?) because when she'd finished licking her lips, he told her that there was no grub/chow left."

«Y a du monde au balcon(?). Je suis tellement impressionné que je ne tiens pas sur les guibolles.» "She's got really big/great tits(?). I'm so impressed that I'm a bit shaky on the old pins/[Br.] timbers."

«Il s'est fait taper dans la lune(!).» "He got [Br.] buggered(!)./He took it up the back passage/the ass(?)/[Br.] arse(?)."

«Quel con(!)! Il a trop bu et il ne tient plus sur ses quilles.» "What a dickhead(!)/ prize idiot! He's had too much to drink and he can no longer stand up/ he's wobbly on the old pins."

See also "Sex," "Beauty" (Hair).

EXERCISES

C'est à vous maintenant!

A *The following words for parts of the body are examples of* verlan *or* javanais. *Give the standard or slang French word they derive from.*

1. **la moustagache** ____________________
2. **le teube**(!) ____________________
3. **la chagatte**(!) ____________________

B *Give the* **one** *slang French word (or phrase) for a part of the body that has* **both** *the meanings given.*

1. head/coffee pot ____________________
2. chest/trunk or [Br.] boot of a car ____________________
3. arm/wing ____________________
4. lung/sponge ____________________
5. head/lemon ____________________
6. head/teapot ____________________
7. hair/feathers ____________________
8. beard/trap ____________________

9. lung/bellows ______________________
10. testicles/plums ______________________
11. toe/radish ______________________
12. breasts/fried eggs ______________________
13. anus/ace of clubs ______________________

C *Your friend has translated literally, or word for word, a number of slang French expressions involving parts of the body. You need to work out what were the original phrases he translated so badly. When you have done that, give the idiomatic English translation of the original slang French expression.*

1. There are people on the balcony.

____

2. My bottom is full.

____

3. They have nothing in the dresser/sideboard.

____

4. He has always carried elephants' feet.

____

5. She has put grappling irons on a dairy cow.

____

6. He is drilling a hole in his lemon.

____

7. He is very gifted with the lady liar.

____

Immigrants and Immigration

ETHNIC GROUPS (NAMES)

See "Foreigners" (Names for Foreigners).

IMMIGRANTS

le clandestin illegal worker/immigrant

l'immigré (m)/**l'ouvrier** (m) **(qui est) en situation irrégulière** immigrant/worker whose papers are not in order

NOTE: Standard French distinguishes between **l'immigrant(e)** (m/f) (one who has recently arrived) and **l'immigré(e)** (m/f) (one who is more established in France).

l'immigré de la deuxième génération second-generation immigrant

le/la beur second-generation North African born in France

travailler au noir to work illegally

SOS Racisme anti-racist organization

touche pas à mon pote anti-racist slogan meaning "leave my pal/[Br.] mate alone"

NOTE: All the words and phrases listed above are standard French expressions except for **touche pas à mon pote**, which is familiar.

«Ces clandestins travaillent au noir depuis très longtemps: ils sont tous en situation irrégulière.» "All of these illegal immigrants have been working illegally for a very long time; their papers are not in order."

«Ces beurs sont allés à la manif de SOS Racisme et ils ont crié à tue-tête, ‹Touche pas à mon pote!›» "These second-generation North Africans (who were born in France) went to the SOS Racisme demo(nstration) and shouted at the top of their voices, 'Get your hands off my buddy/[Br.] mate!' "

NOTE: **Manif** is a familiar abbreviation of the standard noun **manifestation.**

CLOTHING

NOTE: The terms marked (ok) are standard French expressions.

la djellaba(ok) (d)jellaba

le foulard islamique(ok) chador

le fez(ok) fez

le turban(ok) turban

NOTE: **La djellaba** is a loose, hooded woolen cloak worn by Arab men. **Le foulard islamique** is a more familiar (journalistic) expression for **le tchador**—an Islamic veil covering a woman's head but not the face—which became controversial during the 1990s in France when it was considered to be an "ostentatious" religious symbol when worn in French secular state schools.

«Dans ce quartier on voit énormément de djellabas et de foulards islamiques mais pas beaucoup de fez et de turbans.» "In this district, you see a lot of jellabas and chadors but not a lot of fezzes and turbans."

HOUSING

NOTE: The terms marked (ok) are standard French expressions.

le/la HLM(ok) public housing, low rent, subsidized apartment, (low rent) apartment building, [Br.] (block of) council flat(s)

le loyer(ok) rent

le/la locataire(ok) tenant

le cloporte, le concepige, le pipelet, la pipelette janitor/concierge/caretaker

NOTE: **Un(e) HLM (Habitation à Loyer Modéré)** and **le loyer** are both standard French expressions; the standard French noun for "janitor" is **concierge** (m/f).

«Dans ce HLM personne ne paie le loyer et les cloportes se foutent(!) **de la gueule des locataires.»** "In this apartment block/[Br.] block of council flats, nobody pays their rent and the caretakers/janitors don't give a damn about/[Br.] take the piss(?) out of the tenants."

RELIGION

NOTE: The terms marked (ok) are standard French expressions.

la mosquée(ok) mosque

le tapis de prière(ok) prayer mat/rug

le mullah/mollah mulla(h) (elder)

les moudjahiddin mujahedin, mujahedeen (militant)

l'intégrisme (m) fundamentalism

l'intégriste (m/f) fundamentalist

«Dans la mosquée, les mullahs rangeaient leurs tapis de prière.» "In the mosque, the mullahs were putting away their prayer mats."

«Les moudjahiddin sont des intégristes.» "The mujahedin are (Islamic) fundamentalists."

EXERCISE

C'est à vous maintenant!

Translate the following sentences into French.

1. This illegal immigrant's papers are not in order.

   ____

2. "Get your hands off my buddy/[Br.] mate," shouted the young North Africans (who were born in France).

   ____

3. The mullah left his cheap apartment/[Br.] council flat to go to the mosque.

   ____

4. Fundamentalists always have a prayer mat.

   ____

5. The janitor/caretaker says that many tenants work illegally but always pay their rent.

   ____

   ____

Information Technology

COMPUTERS

NOTE: The terms marked ⓞⓚ are standard French expressions.

le PC personal computer

le clavierⓞⓚ keyboard

la sourisⓞⓚ mouse

le cédérom (CD Romⓞⓚ**)** CD-ROM

NOTE: The standard French term for a PC is **un ordinateur (personnel/individuel)**. French vocabulary in the realm of computer science is heavily anglicized and many "French" expressions are literal translations or transliterations from the English.

le tapis de sourisⓞⓚ mousepad, [Br.] mousemat

l'informatiqueⓞⓚ (f) computer science, [Br.] informatics

l'informaticien(-ienne)ⓞⓚ (m/f) computer scientist

le fichierⓞⓚ file

la disquetteⓞⓚ floppy disk

le lecteur de disquettesⓞⓚ disk drive

le disque durⓞⓚ hard drive

l'écran (m) **d'ordinateur**ⓞⓚ computer screen

être balaise/balèze/balèse en informatique to be a computer whiz kid/whiz

«Mon beauf s'est payé un PC mais il ne sait pas la différence entre une disquette et un disque dur. Quel connard!» "My brother-in-law bought himself a PC but he doesn't know the difference between a floppy disk and a hard drive. What an asshole⑦/[Br.] a plonker!"

NOTE: **Beauf**, in addition to meaning "brother-in-law" (an abbreviation of **beau-frère**), also refers to an average, middle-class, somewhat reactionary Frenchman or a "redneck," a "square."

«Ma frangine est vraiment balaise en informatique.» "My sister is a real computer whiz kid/whiz."

E-MAIL

l'e-mail (m) e-mail

NOTE: The standard French expression for "e-mail" is **courrier** (m) **électronique.**

envoyer un e-mail à quelqu'un to e-mail someone

l'adresse(ok) (f) address

«**J'ai voulu lui envoyer un e-mail mais je ne connais pas son adresse.**» "I wanted to send him an e-mail but I don't know his (e-mail) address."

SOFTWARE

NOTE: The terms marked by (ok) have become standard expressions in French.

le software software

l'ingénieur (m) **(en) logiciel**(ok) software engineer

la logithèque(ok) software library

NOTE: The standard French noun for "software" is **logiciel** (m).

le progiciel(ok) software package

le piratage de logiciels(ok) software piracy

le fabricant de logiciels(ok) software manufacturer

«**On n'a pas le software qu'il faut: j'ai emprunté tout ce qu'il y a dans notre logithèque mais notre ingénieur logiciel m'a expliqué que ça ne marchera pas.**» "We don't have the necessary software; I borrowed everything we have in our software library, but our software engineer explained to me that it's no good."

le piratage de logiciels

INTERNET

Internet Internet

surfer sur Internet/sur le net to surf the net

l'internaute (m/f) net surfer, Internet user

NOTE: **Internet** tends to be used without the definite article in French.

le modem modem

le site site

«Dès qu'il a installé un modem, j'ai pu surfer sur Internet. Tiens, je serai bientôt un internaute superclasse.» "As soon as he installed a modem, I was able to surf the net. Wow, I'll soon be a brilliant net surfer."

NOTE: **Super** often precedes an adjective or a noun in slang French to intensify it and often forms a single word as in **supernana** (great chick) or **superchiant(e)** (deadly/[Br.] bloody boring).

EXERCISE

C'est à vous maintenant!

Fill in the blanks in the following sentences with one of the words listed below.

disque	disquette	écran	e-mail	fichier
internaute	lecteur	logiciel	logithèque	modem
PC	piratage	surfer		

1. Le ________________ de logiciels est un crime.
2. Cet ingénieur ________________ travaille dans la ________________ au deuxième étage.
3. Cette ________________ passe des heures à ________________ sur Internet.
4. Je n'ai pas encore fait installer un ________________ et, par conséquent, je ne pourrai pas vous envoyer un ________________.
5. Mon ________________ dur est en panne mais heureusement le ________________ dont vous avez besoin se trouve aussi sur cette ________________.

Land and Countryside

See also "Animals."

la cambrousse countryside ■ **«Si on décampait pour la cambrousse?»** "How's about taking off/[Br.] skedaddling off to the country(side)?"

le bled village, small town, dump ■ **«Il est vrai que j'habite Paris, mais Billancourt est mon bled.»** "It's true I live in Paris, but Billancourt is my village."

le patelin place, dump

au bout du monde (*lit.*, at the end of the world) out in the boonies, [Br.] at the back of beyond ■ **«Ils ont choisi de vivre au bout du monde.»** "They've chosen to live out in the boonies/[Br.] in the back of beyond."

au diable vauvert (*lit.*, with the devil in Vauvert [in the Gard region]) stuck out in the sticks, miles from anywhere ■ **«Tu sais, celle-là a tendance à se rendre au diable vauvert n'importe quand!»** "You know, that one has a tendency to take off to the sticks (at) any old time!"

la brousse sticks, boonies, [Br.] the back of beyond ■ **«Faut pas essayer de la contacter—elle vit dans la brousse!»** "Don't bother to try and contact her—she lives in the sticks!"

le trou perdu (*lit.*, lost hole) sticks, [Br.] the back of beyond ■ **«La Renaudié? Ça, c'est un trou perdu!»** "La Renaudié? That's out in the boonies/[Br.] [in] the back of beyond!"

pays de cocagne (*lit.*, the land of [Old] Cockayne) land of milk and honey, one's dream place ■ **«Pour eux, Paris-Plage est pays de cocagne!»** "For them, Paris-Plage is a dream come true!"

dans une merde noire(!) (*lit.*, in a pile of black shit(?)) up shit creek (without a paddle)(?) ■ **«Nous sommes vraiment dans une merde noire cette fois-ci!»** "We're really up shit creek this time!"(?)

dans le secteur in the area; [Br.] roundabouts ■ **«T'as vu l'hélicoptère de police qui fouillait dans le secteur cette nuit?»** "Did you see the police helicopter sniffing around here/[Br.] roundabouts last night?"

dans les parages in the vicinity ■ **«Depuis sa promotion, on ne le voit plus jamais dans les parages. Il faut le chercher dans les quartiers chic!»** "Since he got promoted, you never see him (a)round here anymore. You need to look for him in the upscale/[Br.] smart parts of town!"

NOTE: **Les parages** is of nautical origin and is the sea distance from a nearby landmass.

l'enfer (m) hell ■ **«C'est l'enfer pour vivre ici!»** It's hell living here!"

être du coin (*lit.*, to be of the corner) to be local, from (a)round here ■ **«La mairie? Je suis désolée, je ne suis pas du coin.»** "The town hall? I'm sorry, I'm not from (a)round here."

des contrées lointaines distant parts ■ **«Après le divorce, elle est partie pour des contrées lointaines.»** "After the divorce, she left for distant parts."

villageois(e), rustaud(e) hillbilly ■ **«On ne peut pas utiliser son visage. Il n'est pas très photogénique—trop rustaud pour les téléspectateurs!»** "We can't use his face. He's not very photogenic—too hillbilly for the viewers!"

le/la cousin(e) de province (*lit.*, cousin from the provinces) country cousin ■ **«T'as vu ses fringues? Elle fait toujours la cousine de province!»** "Have you seen her get-up? She always looks like the country cousin!"

le/la country country and western music ■ **«Hank Williams était beaucoup plus qu'un chanteur de country! Il était une idole pour plusieurs générations.»** "Hank Williams was a lot more than just a country and western singer. He was an idol for many generations."

la country musique country music

le cul-terreux (pl: **des culs-terreux**)⑦ country bumpkin, hick, someone from the sticks

NOTE: This expression is a less polite variant on the idea of a man/woman of the soil. The image is of someone so near to the soil that it gets up his/her backside.

terre à terre down-to-earth, matter-of-fact ■ **«Moi, je suis très terre à terre.»** "I'm very down-to-earth."

NOTE: It is an interesting reflection on human nature and on language, that, in French, just like in English, the people who use this expression tend to be the opposite of what they claim.

revenir sur terre to come back down to earth ■ **«D'accord, vieux, Demi Moore t'a souri—maintenant, il faut revenir sur terre! On a du travail!»** "Okay, pal, so Demi Moore gave you a smile—now, you come back down to earth! We've got work to do!"

ne pas toucher terre (*lit.*, not to touch the ground) to walk on air ■ **«J'ai l'impression de ne pas toucher terre depuis son arrivée!»** "I feel as if I've been walking on air since he came!"

avoir la nostalgie de la terre natale (*lit.*, to have nostalgia for the land of one's birth), **avoir la nostalgie du pays** to be homesick ■ **«Je n'arrive pas à m'habituer à cette ville. J'ai trop de nostalgie du pays.»** "I can't settle down in this town. I'm too homesick."

me-lèche-les-prunes(!) Sticksville, [Br.] Much-Binding-in-the-Marsh ■ **«Tu vois, elle nous envoie une lettre de me-lèche-les prunes!»** "See, she's sent us a letter from Sticksville!"

> NOTE: This expression can be taken as highly humorous or as very crude, depending on the company. It is a typical piece of French mockery of sexual parts and practices, put together to look like one of the thousands of innocuous, compound names that have been given to country villages over the centuries.

le paradis paradise ■ **«Ici, c'est un paradis sur terre!»** "It's paradise on earth here!"

le plancher des vaches (*lit.*, the cows' ground) dry land, terra firma ■ **«Jean-Louis est très nerveux—il ne quitterait jamais le plancher des vaches pour voler en avion!»** "Jean-Louis is the nervous type—he'd never leave dry land for a plane trip!"

terre ferme dry land, terra firma ■ **«Je resterai plutôt sur terre ferme—je n'ai pas encore le pied marin!»** "I'll just stay on terra firma—I haven't found my sea legs yet!"

être encore sur terre (*lit.*, to be still on the ground) to be still in the land of the living ■ **«Mais, c'est bien toi! Je ne te croyais pas encore sur terre!»** "But, it's you! I didn't think you were still in the land of the living!"

Il ne quitterait jamais le plancher des vaches pour voler en avion.

foutreⓅ **par terre** to mess up, to screw up ■ **«Tu vas voir, ça va tout foutre par terre!»** "You just see, that'll screw everything up!"

NOTE: This expression originally developed from the idea of spilling everything out of a sack or box onto the ground.

se terrer (*lit.*, to earth oneself) to hide, [Br.] to go to earth/ground ■ **«Ah, tu ressors maintenant—où tu t'es terré?»** "Ah, you're back among us now—where've you been hiding?"

être terré(e) dans to be holed up in, [Br.] to go to earth (ground) in ■ **«Elle est terrée dans cette baraque avec un jeune zonard.»** "She's holed up in that dump with a young dropout."

marquer son territoire to mark out one's territory ■ **«Il est bizarre, notre nouveau voisin! Remarque-le, qui marque son territoire, tout comme un cabot!»** "He's odd, our new neighbor! Look at him, marking out his territory, just like a pooch!"

EXERCISES

C'est à vous maintenant!

A *A detective is quizzing an informant about suspects implicated in a large gold bullion robbery. Determine which suspect(s) is/are (1) supposed to be in the village itself, (2) somewhere in the vicinity, (3) not local, (4) in the place of their dreams, or (5) out in the sticks.*

a. Thierry Tomalin, il est où? —Difficile à dire... dans la brousse sans doute.

b. Et Benjamin Lecadet? —La même chose... dans un trou perdu!

c. Et Frou-Frou Beljambe? —Ah, elle... elle est dans les parages?

d. Quant à Colin Maillard? —Lui, il est toujours dans ce bled.

e. Et sa cousine, Colette? —Dans son pays de cocagne, St-Tropez.

f. Et Boris Finegueule? —Je ne sais pas. Il n'est pas du coin.

1. ______________________________

2. ______________________________

3. ______________________________

4. ______________________________

5. ______________________________

B *Without using any of the expressions in Exercise A, render the following statements in French.*

1. You need to come down to earth.

 ____

2. I am very down to earth!

 ____

3. She's walking on air.

 ____

4. I'll stay on terra firma!

 ____

5. That'll screw everything up!

 ____

6. It's a paradise on earth!

 ____

The Movies

See also "Entertainment."

GENERAL

l'amateur (m)**, le grand amateur de cinéma, le/la cinéphile** moviegoer, filmgoer, cinema goer

la bédé [bande dessinée] (strip-)cartoon

le bide (complet) (total) flop

la boîte the can ■ **«On ne peut rien changer. Le film est déjà dans la boîte!»** "We can't change anything. The film is already in the can!"

NOTE: Traditionally, the master reels of film were and are still kept in metal boxes, to guard against deterioration.

le cabotin, une cabotine ham actor ■ **«Il a tous les gestes d'un cabotin—on dirait une marionnette!»** "He's got all the gestures of a ham actor—you'd say he was a puppet!"

le clip clip, videoclip

le ciné, le cinoche, l'écran (m) movies, flicks, cinema, pictures, screen

la comédie musicale musical

la daube pits, end ■ **«J'ai vu des films atroces, mais ça c'est la daube!»** "I've seen some atrocious films, but that really is the pits!"

le délire great success

le grand écran the big screen

NOTE: Compare **le petit écran** (the small screen, television).

«Cet acteur du petit écran n'a pas su faire la transition au grand écran.» "This TV actor wasn't able to make the move to the big screen."

l'adaptation (f) **à l'écran** screen adaptation

l'image (f) **à l'écran** screen image

les épreuves (fpl) rushes

le film de cul/de fesse(s) (*lit.*, bottom film) porn movie, skin flick ■ **«Il ne faut pas de talent pour tourner un film de cul!»** "You don't need any talent to make a porn movie! "

NOTE: **Le magazine de fesses** (a porn magazine/[Br.] porny mag).

«Pour lui, la littérature, c'est les magazines de fesses!» "For him, the word 'literature' means porn magazines/[Br.] porny mags!"

ne pas faire de films (*lit.*, to not make any films) to really mean it, to mean it for real ■ **«Tu peux compter sur elle. Elle ne fait pas de films!»** "You can count on her. She's for real!"

gnangnan (adj. inv.) corny, [Br.] twee

le court métrage short (film)

le long métrage feature film

le programme à deux longs métrages double-feature program

long métrage (inv.) feature-length (movie/film)

minable pathetic, useless, wretched

le nanar⑦ rotten/lousy film

nase rock-bottom (adj.), as bad as it gets ■ **«C'était gênant, le scénario était nase!»** "It was embarrassing; the screenplay was as bad as it gets!"

le navet bomb, turkey

le polar thriller

le policier thriller

la première premiere

projeter, passer à l'écran to screen, to show ■ **«Cela lui a fait plaisir de voir le film passer à l'écran dans sa ville natale.»** "It gave her pleasure to see the film screened in her native town."

avoir un succès fou to be a smash hit ■ **«Les films de Tom Hanks ont toujours un succès fou!»** "Tom Hanks's films are always a smash hit!"

passer un test d'écran to do/take a screen test ■ **«Quand elle passe un test d'écran, elle fait toujours plus vieille!»** "When she does a screen test, she always looks older!"

tourner un film to make a film

le tournage making of a film

faire du cinéma (*lit.*, to do a bit of cinema) to do a song and dance (see also "Art") ■ **«N'en faites pas de cinéma!»** "Don't do a song and dance about it!"

STARDOM

la vedette top-billing star

NOTE: Originally from printers' language: **en vedette** "bold type."

la vedette, la star star

avoir la vedette (*lit.*, to have the bold print) to get top billing, [Br.] to top the bill ■ **«Dans ce film, Nicole Kidman va avoir la vedette.»** "In this film Nicole Kidman will get top billing."

être en vedette (*lit.*, to be in bold print) to be in the limelight ■ **«Elle est différente de la plupart des stars. Elle n'aime pas être en vedette.»** "She's different from most stars. She doesn't like being in the limelight."

mettre en vedette (*lit.*, to put in bold print) to give someone star billing, to highlight

accaparer la vedette (*lit.*, to corner the bold print) to hog the limelight ■ **«C'est un mauvais acteur qui accapare toujours la vedette!»** "He's a bad actor, always hogging the limelight!"

la rampe footlights (see also "Entertainment" [*Theater*]) ■ **«Elle est toujours bien dans sa peau devant la rampe.»** "She's always in tune with herself in front of the footlights."

NOTE: Originally a theatrical expression (the limelights were held in a wooden ramp at the edge of the stage), which extended into the world of the cinema.

passer bien (*lit.*, to pass well) to be/look good on film/camera

passer la rampe (*lit.*, to get over the footlights) to come/get across ■ **«Cette interprétation ne passe pas la rampe.»** "This bit of acting doesn't come/get across."

EXERCISES

C'est à vous maintenant!

A *Match the film titles with the right definitions.*

____	1. L'Inspecteur et l'assassin unijambe	a. un court métrage
____	2. Maxine, fille des rues	b. une comédie musicale
____	3. Astérix et les jeux Olympiques	c. un polar
____	4. Les pingouins de l'Arctique (15 minutes)	d. un film de fesse
____	5. *Singing in the Rain*	e. un long métrage
____	6. *American Beauty* (110 minutes)	f. une bédé

B *Find the pairs or groups of words that go together.*

1. un policier
2. l'écran
3. un cinéphile
4. un film de cul
5. un court métrage
6. un polar
7. le cinoche
8. un long métrage
9. un film de fesse
10. un amateur de cinéma
11. le ciné

____, ____

____, ____

____, ____

____, ____, ____

____, ____

C *Francine Froufrou is a young film actress. Below is the sequence of events leading to her first success. Put them in the order in which they occurred.*

____, ____, ____, ____, ____, ____, ____

1. Elle a un succès fou.
2. Elle voit les épreuves.
3. Le film a sa première.
4. Elle passe un test d'écran.
5. On montre des clips publicitaires.
6. Elle commence à tourner le film.
7. Le film est dans la boîte.

Music

GENERAL VOCABULARY

un[e] accro du jazz jazz freak

NOTE: **Accro** (from **accroché**, hooked on to) can be used to describe someone who is mad about (on) almost anything.

un amphi[théâtre] a music hall, stadium

un baladeur a Walkman

destroy blaring, loud, violent [music] ■ **«Sa musique est trop destroy pour ses parents!»** "His music is too loud [and aggressive] for his parents!"

un disque noir/vinyle an LP, a long-playing record

un 33 tours [also **un 30 cm**] an LP, a long-playing record

esgourder to hear, listen ■ **«Esgourde-moi ça—ça passe pour de la musique!»** "Just listen to that—and they call that music!"

exploser to explode ■ **«Ce groupe a explosé sur la scène il y a quelques mois.»** "This group exploded onto the scene a few months ago."

un flyer a rave [evening]

NOTE: As the name implies, this is the sort of rave where publicity spreads by word of mouth, to avoid the attention of the authorities.

folklo (adj. inv.) loopy, weird (and wonderful)

un ghetto-blaster a ghetto-blaster

une gratte a guitar

gratter les cordes (*lit.,* to scratch the strings) to play the guitar ■ **«Qu'est-ce qu'il fait comme métier? Il gratte les cordes un peu quand ça le prend!»** "What does he do for a job? He plays the guitar a bit when the mood takes/comes over him!"

NOTE: This expression can be misinterpreted by those with a lavatorial sense of humor. See also **cordes** on pages 57 and 216.

un gig a gig, concert

NOTE: **Un gig** also = **un boulot** "a job."

un hardeur/une hardeuse a rocker, rock chick

K7 a cassette [audio or video]

faire la manche (*lit.*, to do a sleeve) to perform in the streets, [Br.] to busk/ go busking

NOTE: **Faire la manche** also means "to beg."

un/une mélomane a music buff, music fanatic

les musiciens (mpl) [haricot] beans

le musicos musician, [Br.] muso ■ **«Je n'aime pas le musicos avec mes repas!»** "I don't like [Br.] muso with my meals!"

piailler to screech (out) ■ **«Elle ne chante pas—elle piaille!»** "She doesn't sing—she screeches!"

un piano du pauvre (*lit.*, poor man's piano), **un piano à bretelles** (*lit.*, piano with suspenders/straps/braces) accordion, a squeeze-box

le rap rap

NOTE: Compare **rapiste** (m/f).

«Je ne suis pas rapiste, moi!» "I'm not one for rap!"

la rasta rasta

une soirée rave a rave [evening]

la sono [la sonorisation] sound system ■ **«La sono a mal fonctionné au repas des noces.»** "The sound system malfunctioned/[Br.] played up at the wedding reception."

la techno techno

top great, awesome; [Br.] fab ■ **«Pour moi, sa nouvelle chanson est top!»** "For me, his new song is awesome!"

la variétoche middle-of-the-road music ■ **«Il y a trop de variétoche à la télé!»** "There's too much middle-of-the-road stuff on TV/[Br.] the telly!"

la zizique tunes, schmalzy/elevator ([Br.] wallpaper) music ■ **«Je ne sais pas pourquoi un musicien avec tant de talent passe son temps à jouer de la zizique!»** "I don't know why such a talented musician spends his time playing elevator/[Br.] wallpaper music."

GENERAL EXPRESSIONS

un bémol flat [mus.], damper, downer, [Br.] dampener ■ **«Ça va mettre le bémol à leur concert.»** "That'll put a damper on their concert!"

un disque d'or a gold record, [Br.] golden disc ■ **«Elvis a obtenu un disque d'or pour la majorité de ses chansons.»** "Elvis got a gold record/[Br.] golden disc for most of his songs."

la même chanson the same old song/tune/story ■ **«Chez lui, c'est toujours la même chanson!»** "With him, it's always the same old story!"

changer de disque to change the record ■ **«Pour une fois, change de disque, je t'en supplie!»** "Just for once, change the record, I beg you!"

au feeling by intuition ■ **«C'est un naturel, il joue au feeling!»** "He's a natural—he plays by intuition!"

NTM [nique ta mère⦸]

NOTE: **NTM** is a rap group that became famous overnight for the overturning of a judgment against them for incitement to disorder. The group's name is currently synonymous among right-wingers with rabble-rousing.

«Ce sont de véritables NTM!» "They're a bunch/[Br.] right lot of rabble-rousers!"

le palmarès the winners, honors list, prizewinners ■ **«Elle a gagné le prix du palmarès de la chanson européenne.»** "She's topped the hit parade of European singers."

piane-piane slowly [slowly]/softly, softly ■ **«Sa musique n'est pas pour moi, c'est trop piane-piane!»** "Her music's not for me, it's too pokey/slow/[Br.] slowly, slowly!"

piano-piano slowly ■ **«Allons-y piano-piano!»** "Let's not rush this!"

le vedettariat the stars (those who have attained stardom) ■ **«Tu sais, tous les membres du vedettariat sont très fiers d'eux!»** "You know, all those stars are really egotistical/[Br.] really fancy themselves!"

MUSICAL VENUES

Bobino a major concert hall in Paris that tends to specialize in popular singers and concerts ■ **«J'ai vu Barbara chez Bobino.»** "I saw Barbara [sing] at Bobino's."

Olympia the major concert hall in Paris ■ **«Elle a déjà fait l'Olympia.»** "She's already done the Olympia."

L'Opéra Bastille the modern Paris opera house (built 1989) where most of the capital's opera is performed

le Palais Garnier = L'Opéra the old Paris opera house. Nowadays it provides mostly ballet, with some opera. ■ **«Depuis sa promotion on ne le voit guère à l'Olympia. Maintenant, c'est plutôt le Palais Garnier!»** "Since he got promoted, you hardly see him at the Olympia. Nowadays, it's more likely to be the Palais Garnier!"

La Villette the La Villette performing arts center ▪ **«Elle, étant pour la musique expérimentale, elle s'est décampée pour La Villette!»** "Her being one for experimental music, she's gone and left us for La Villette!"

NOTE: La Villette was once a cattle market and slaughterhouse in the northeast of Paris. It now houses a large arts center, specializing in experimental music and dance, as well as a science and technology center and museum.

CHILDREN'S MUSIC

la comptine(ok) nursery rhyme

faire dodo to go to sleep, to be asleep

aller faire dodo to go beddy-bye, [Br.] to go to beddy-byes

le bobo sore, cut

«Maman a guéri le gros bobo, alors va faire dodo et je te chanterai une comptine.» "Mommy's/[Br.] Mummy's made you better, so go beddy-bye/ [Br.] to beddy-byes and I'll sing you a nursery rhyme."

CLASSICAL MUSIC

See "Entertainment" (Classical Music).

ETHNIC MUSIC

See "Entertainment" (Popular Music).

POPULAR DANCES

NOTE: The terms marked (ok) are standard French expressions.

la java(ok) popular waltz

NOTE: **Faire la java** means, metaphorically, "to be out on the town," "to live it up."

la tarentelle(ok) tarantella

le tango(ok) tango

le swing(ok) (dance) jive, (music) swing

le slow slow dance, fox-trot

danser un slow to do a slow dance

danser le swing to jive, to swing dance ▪ **«Ces couples adorent danser la java mais leurs gosses préfèrent danser le swing et ensuite un slow.»** "These couples love doing a popular waltz but their kids prefer to jive and then to do a slow dance/dance a slow number."

POPULAR MUSIC

NOTE: The terms marked (ok) are standard French expressions.

le hit parade(ok) hit parade

le skeud platter

NOTE: **Skeud** (also written **squeud**) is *verlan* for **disque**; in addition to meaning a "vinyl" disk, it is also used to refer to a CD in slang French.

le tube(ok) hit record, smash hit

le CD(ok) CD, compact disk

la K7(ok) **(cassette)** cassette

chanter en play-back(ok) to lip-sync, to mime

faire une tournée(ok) to go on tour

changer de boîte to change labels/record company

le vidéoclip(ok) promo(tional) video

le walkman Walkman

NOTE: The standard French noun for a "Walkman" is **un baladeur**.

le top cinquante(ok) top fifty

l'agent(ok) (m) agent

la vedette américaine(ok) (*lit.*, American star) support act

être à l'affiche(ok) to be on the bill

être en tête d'affiche(ok) to be top of the bill ■ **«Il n'avait jamais eu un seul tube avant de changer de boîte mais son dernier CD et le vidéoclip qui va avec ont fait un tabac. Il va faire une tournée et dans un mois il sera en tête d'affiche à Bercy.»** "He hadn't had a single hit before he changed labels/record companies, but his latest CD and promo video were a huge hit. He's going on tour, and in a month he'll top the bill at Bercy."

NOTE: **Faire un tabac** can be used for almost anything in the world of show business that is a resounding success. It is also used to refer to best-selling novels.

See also "Entertainment" (Popular Music).

RAP

NOTE: French rap tends to be more "committed" than its Anglo-Saxon counterpart and often concerns itself with social, racial, and political issues, and the problems connected with the *banlieues*, the suburbs of large towns and cities that often have high unemployment and large ethnic communities, often housed in **HLM [Habitations à Loyers Modérés]** (cheap apartments or [Br.] council flats in large tenement blocks).

See "Entertainment" (Popular Music).

REGIONAL MUSIC

Brittany

le bagad Breton (pipe) band

la bombarde type of Breton oboe

le biniou Breton bagpipe

NOTE: **Le bagad** is composed of drums, bagpipes, and **bombardes**. The Breton plural of **bagad** is **bagadou**. The standard French noun for "bagpipe" is **la cornemuse**. Breton music has had a resurgence of popularity in France, doubtless helped by a popular song by Alain Souchon (music by Laurent Voulzy) entitled *Le bagad de Lann Bihoué* (1978).

«J'adore écouter la musique bretonne et surtout un bon bagad avec ses bombardes et ses binious.» "I love listening to Breton music, especially a good pipe band with its Breton bagpipes and oboes."

See also "Entertainment."

EXERCISES

C'est à vous maintenant!

A *Find the five matching pairs.*

1. un baladeur	5. la zizique	9. Bobino
2. un disque noir	6. le Palais Royal	10. L'Opéra Bastille
3. le Palais Garnier	7. un 30 cm	11. la variétoche
4. un piano à bretelles	8. Olympia	12. un ghetto-blaster

____—____

____—____

____—____

____—____

____—____

B *You are with an English-speaking friend at a party in Bordeaux. Interpret these sarcastic comments for your friend, who is feeling a bit left out.*

1. Cette chanteuse mérite un disque noir et non pas un disque d'or!

 ____

2. Il ne faut pas de ghetto-blaster pour cette musique destroy!

 ____

3. Il appartient à la Villette avec sa musique folklo!

 ____

4. Ils vous obligent d'esgourder le musicos dans leur sacré restaurant!

 ____

5. Ce n'est pas l'Opéra Bastille! C'est plutôt un gig pour les hardeurs!

 ____

6. Il va trop piane-piane avec son piano à bretelles!

 ____

7. Eux, des membres du vedettariat! —Bah, non, ce sont plutôt de vrais NTM!

 ____

C *Use the expressions in the box below to help you find the missing word in each statement.*

bémol	feeling	explosé	arrivé
accro	palmarès	amphi	chanson

1. Rien qu'à la voir, tu sais qu'elle joue au ________________!
2. L'acoustique est mauvaise, on n'entend pas le groupe au fond de l'________________!
3. Ce n'est pas un vrai ________________ du jazz. Il vient pour chercher les filles!
4. L'ambiance froide là-bas met le ________________ sur tous les gigs!
5. Il ne va pas gagner le prix du ________________ avec cette chanson-là!

6. **Il ne parle que du football! Chez lui, c'est toujours la même ________________!**

7. **On l'a pris pour une terroriste, la façon dont elle a ________________ sur la scène!**

D *Give an appropriate French word or phrase for a dance that allows you to . . .*

1. smooch ________________
2. move to the rhythm of rock 'n' roll ________________
3. imitate an Argentinian model ________________
4. imitate an Italian model ________________

E *You wish to tell a French friend that it's not a good idea to lip-sync to a recording if she is top of the bill in a concert, even if it's her latest smash hit she is singing. Fill in the blanks below in order to get across your message.*

Quand on est ________________ et qu'on va chanter son dernier ________________, il ne faut pas ________________.

F *Give a slang or familiar French equivalent of the following standard French words and phrases.*

1. **un baladeur** ________________
2. **un disque** ________________
3. **aller au lit** ________________
4. **sa maison de disque** ________________
5. **une petite plaie** ________________

Names

See also "Entertainment."

NOTE: As in English, colloquial French uses a lot of names (for example, Peter, John, John Doe), often with a humorous intent. The following are among the most common such names, a knowledge of which will help you to be more streetwise.

Alphonse: téléphoner à Alphonse (humorous, old-fashioned) to go to the john, [Br.] to spend a penny, [Br.] to see a man about a dog ■ **«Excusez-moi, je vais téléphoner à Alphonse!»** "Excuse me, I'm going to the john/[Br.] I'm off to see a man about a dog!"

Arthur: se faire appeler Arthur to get bawled out, to get your head bitten off

les Athéniens: «C'est là que les Athéniens s'atteignirent!» "That's when things started to go downhill!"

la Bastoche Bastille area of Paris

la bécane computer

NOTE: This term derives from the name of a popular motorbike (**mobylette**), which also serves as a general word for machine. **Bécane** has a humorously anarchic feel when it refers to computers, typical of the French disrespect for authority. Many find it a welcome antidote to the often excessive respect accorded to the computers that run so many people's lives. The use of **bécane** for **ordinateur** will undoubtedly bring a smile to your audience!

la Bérézina: «C'est la Bérézina!» "It's an out-and-out disaster/shambles!"

NOTE: It was at Bérézina that Napoleon's troops were decimated under appalling conditions during the retreat from Moscow, a retreat that is engraved on the French psyche. (See pages 99 and 203.)

le/la Blanche-Neige(!) coon(!), nigger(!!), wog(!)

NOTE: The reference to a well-loved mythical (and Disney) figure is intentionally cynical. This is a form of sarcastic humor, which says far more about the unpleasantness of the user than it does about the intended target. The great majority of French speakers find this sort of expression rightly and deeply offensive, whatever their color.

le Boul' Mich trendy Boulevard St-Michel on the Left Bank of the River Seine in Paris

la Brésilienne(?) transvestite or transsexual Brazilian prostitute

le Bronx: «Il a mis le Bronx là-dedans!» "He's made a (right) mess of it!"

Byzance: «C'est Byzance!» "It's the last word in luxury!"

NOTE: This is a reference to the heyday of the Byzantine empire and all its riches.

la Camarde: «La Camarde l'attend!» "Death/The Grim Reaper is waiting for him!"

NOTE: The origin of this name is disputed. There are those who say that the Grim Reaper's most distinguishing feature is its **camard** (flat nose). Others claim that the name is a shortened form of **camarade** (buddy, pal, [Br.] mate). Both groups may be right and we may find ourselves escorted on our final journey by our flat-nosed old friend!

les Champs (m) Les Champs-Élysées

le Château-la-Pompe (tap) water ■ **«Donne-moi du Château-la-Pompe!»** "Give me some water!"

NOTE: Castle-Pump is a humorous sideswipe at the names of château-bottled wines. As **pompe** can have sexual connotations, the expression may cause hilarity among those with a rather crude sense of humor.

Duchnoque (m) bud(dy), pal, [Br.] mate, [Br.] His Nibs ■ **«On ne sait jamais avec Duchnoque, là-bas!»** "You never know with buddy-boy over there!"

Ducon(?) dickhead(!), shit-head(?), shit-for-brains(?)

NOTE: An obvious play on **con**.

Étienne: «À la tienne, Étienne!» "Cheers!"

NOTE: This expression derives from the response to the toast **Bonne santé!**, which is **à la tienne!** "to yours!"

la Faucheuse Grim Reaper (Death) ■ **«Plutôt fauché que la Faucheuse!»** "Better broke than dead!"

le Fridolin(!) Kraut(!)

le Frisé(!) Kraut(!)

NOTE: Both these terms may be offensive or humorous, depending on the tone of voice and the relationship between the people concerned.

les Grecs: «Va te faire enculer(!)/faire chez les Grecs!» "Fuck off(!)!/[Br.] Eat it!/[Br.] Go and get stuffed(!)!/[Br.] Sod off(!)!/[Br.] Bugger off(!)!"

NOTE: This expression derives from classical Greece. At certain periods in this civilization, it was acceptable for distinguished citizens to have a beautiful boy as an intimate companion. This was in keeping with a democracy built on a slave underclass.

l'internauteⓞⓚ (m/f) Web surfer

NOTE: This neat term is a play on **Argonaute** and **astronaute**. It gives a picture of the heroes and heroines of the Internet navigating undiscovered realms of cyberspace.

Jacques: faire le Jacques to spaz out, to play the fool, to clown around

le Jules man, boyfriend, [Br.] squeeze

la Julie girlfriend, [Br.] squeeze, [Br.] bird

Lutèce Paris

NOTE: This is a humorous hark back to the Roman occupation.

le macchabée stiff, corpse

le grand manitou big white chief, big shot, big enchilada ▪ **«Il fait toujours le grand manitou!»** "He's always playing the big shot!"

NOTE: Among the Algonquin Indians the manitou was a good or evil spirit. The name came by extension to mean someone with great, supernatural powers (like the CEO in the United States or the MD in the United Kingdom).

le marcel vest

la Marie-Chantal preppy, [Br.] Sloane-ranger

NOTE: The name Marie-Chantal was unfairly associated with unimaginative girls from traditional, well-off families.

la Marie-couche-toi-là① slut, [Br.] slag, pro(stitute)

NOTE: Used more often of an easily available woman than of a working prostitute.

Me-Lèche-les-Prunes② humorous, fictitious name for a dull village in the sticks

NOTE: Since **prunes** has an obvious sexual connotation (see page 128), this expression may be best avoided in polite company.

le micky nobody, nonentity

Monsieur Machin(-Truc) Mr. Thingamabob ([Br.] Thingummibob)

le montesquieu 200 franc bill

NOTE: A picture of the writer, Montesquieu, figured on this banknote.

Paname Paris

NOTE: Like Lutèce, the name has a humorous, mock-learned ring to it.

le pascal 500 franc bill

NOTE: A picture of the mathematician, Pascal, figured on this banknote.

le pékin guy, [Br.] bloke

le Pérou: «Ce n'est pas le Pérou!» "It won't break the bank!"

Pétaouchrok humorous-sounding fictitious name for a place way out in the boonies/[Br.] in the back of beyond ■ **«Elle s'est fait envoyer à Pétaouchrok!»** "She got herself sent off to Timbuktu!"

le Rambo (Paris Railways) security officer

le raymond square (person) ■ **«C'est un vrai raymond, avec ses pantoufles et sa pipe!»** "He's a real square, with his slippers and his pipe!"

le/la richard swell, [Br.] off, [Br.] nob

des roberts⚠ (mpl) jugs, knockers, tits

romano⚠ (adj.) gypsy, [Br.] gippo

ruskof⚠ Russki⚠

sainte-nitouche Goody Two-shoes

Saint-Glinglin Doomsday

attendre jusqu'à la Saint-Glinglin to wait till Doomsday

Tartempion, Trucmuche what's her/his name, thingy

Tintin! No way, José!/[Br.] Not on your nelly!

Trifouillis-les-Oies fictional dull French village

la Valda bullet, a slug

NOTE: The name comes from a well-known bullet-shaped throat lozenge.

EXERCISES

C'est à vous maintenant!

A *Put each of the names in the box under the right heading in the table.*

Alphonse	Arthur	Bastoche	Blanche-Neige	la Camarde
Ducon	Étienne	Fridolin	Lutèce	Tintin

1. humorous ______________________
2. unpleasant ______________________
3. place name ______________________
4. racist ______________________
5. contrary ______________________

B *In the following lists of names there are eight pairs that go well together. Find the pairs, using one name from each list.*

_____	1. un Jules	a. Lutèce
_____	2. la Camarde	b. un montesquieu
_____	3. un Fridolin	c. Tartempion
_____	4. Me-Lèche-les-Prunes	d. une Julie
_____	5. Trucmuche	e. une Valda
_____	6. un pascal	f. la Faucheuse
_____	7. un macchabée	g. Trifouillis-les-Oies
_____	8. Paname	h. un Frisé

Press, Magazines, Books

Apostrophes the best-known literary talk show on French TV, whose format has been somewhat dumbed down in recent years ■ **«Il attend son élévation aux Apostrophes!»** "He's waiting for the call to the Charlie Rose/South Bank Show!"

le bouquin book

bouquiner to read; to frequent the **bouquiniste** stalls

le/la bouquiniste bookstall holder

> NOTE: You will find the **bouquinistes** along the banks of the Seine near the Île de la Cité, in what is referred to as the **quartier Latin** (Latin Quarter). The bookstalls are long wooden boxes attached to the walls, which open out into little covered stalls, providing an amazing variety of books, pictures, prints, etc.

le BVP [Bureau de Vérification de la Publicité] French advertising standards commission ■ **«Cette pub a bien choqué ma belle-mère! Elle va appeler le BVP!»** "That TV commercial did a good job of shocking my mother-in-law! She's going to phone the commission!"

la CAO [Conception Assistée par Ordinateur] CAD (computer-aided design) ■ **«Rien qu'à voir le dessin, on sent le style de la CAO!»** "You've only to look at the drawing to know it's CAD-based!"

l'édito (m) **[éditorial]** editorial, leading article

la fête de l'Huma *Huma(nité)* festival

> NOTE: A press and book festival organized by the *Humanité* newspaper.

Galligrasseuil ■ **«Qui va gagner cette fois-ci? —Sans doute la Maison Galligrasseuil!»** "Who's going to win this time? —It'll probably go to Galligrasseuil!"

> NOTE: Galligrasseuil is the satirical name of a fictitious publisher, combining the names of the three major publishing houses: Gallimard + Grasset + Éditions du Seuil. Most years, almost all the top literary prizes seem to be won by one of these three houses, to the general resentment of others.

(se) gargariser de mots (*lit.*, to gargle with words) to be taken in by one's own words ■ **«Les présentateurs à la Une ont tendance à se gargariser de mots.»** "The presenters on Channel One tend to believe what they're saying!"

l'IFOP [l'Institut Français d'Opinion Publique] a polling institute ▪ **«Selon l'IFOP ça sera encore une année difficile.»** "According to IFOP, it's going to be another difficult year!"

info ou intox information or intoxication ▪ **«Nous gavent-ils d'info ou d'intox?»** "Are they stuffing us with what we need to know or what they want us to hear?"

NOTE: This is a catchphrase originally coined in broadcasting.

IPSOS another French polling institute ▪ **«On va demander chez IPSOS!»** "Let's ask IPSOS!"

NOTE: **IPSOS** is named after the temple of the oracle in Ipsos in ancient Phrygia.

la PAO [Publication Assistée par Ordinateur] desktop publishing

le poche paperback, pocket edition

le roman de gare (*lit.*, [train] station novel) beach/weekend novel, potboiler

série noire (*lit.*, black series) ▪ **«Quand je pense à eux, je pense série noire!»** "When I think of them, I think of Agatha Christie/Hitchcock!"

NOTE: A famous whodunnit series, the name has now also come to stand for a constant series of problems, since the hallmark of the series was repeated deaths, attacks, robberies, financial scams.

la TAO [Traduction Assistée par Ordinateur] computer-assisted translation

(se) gargariser de mots

EXERCISES

C'est à vous maintenant!

A *Find among the names and acronyms in the box, the equivalent of:*

CAO	le BVP	l'IFOP	Galligrasseuil
la PAO	IPSOS	Apostrophes	la TAO

1. a literary talk show ______________________
2. a fictitious publisher ______________________
3. desktop publishing ______________________
4. a CAD drawing ______________________
5. computer-assisted translation ______________________
6. an advertising standards body ______________________
7. two polling institutes ______________________

B *Now for a piece of lateral thinking! Work out the links in the following string. Our friend Guy is walking along the Left Bank of the Seine in and around the student quarter. Explain where Guy ends up and the series of small discoveries that take him there. There is no such thing as one correct answer. Any interpretation that makes sense is right!*

bouquiner
bouquin
un poche
la série noire
un édito
publicitaire
la fête de l'Huma

____

____

____

____

____

Regions and Francophone Countries

l'Arlésienne (*lit.*, the woman of Arles) the invisible man or woman, character ■ **«Nelly? Elle fait toujours l'Arlésienne!»** "Nelly? You never see her!"

NOTE: In Bizet's opera, **l'Arlésienne** never appears.

l'Armor (ancient Celtic name for) coastal Brittany ■ **«Il a la nostalgie du vieil Armor.»** "He yearns for Ancient Armor."

la banlieue suburbs ■ **«Qu'est-ce que tu attends? Ils habitent la banlieue!»** "What do you expect? They live in the suburbs/the outskirts!"

NOTE: France seems to suffer even more than other Western European countries from a degradation of the old, comfortable city suburbs, which are increasingly and unfairly perceived as dumping grounds for undesirables.

les Belges Belgians ■ **«Cet Américain parle bien le français, mais il a l'accent belge!»** "That American speaks good French, but he's got a real Belgian accent!"

NOTE: Unfortunately certain French use the Belgians as a butt of their humor (compare the English and the Irish, the Americans and the Canadians). See also page 170.

beur Arab (*verlan*: **arabe**)

black, blanc, beur(!) (*lit.*, black, white, Arab) ■ **«À bas le black, blanc, beur!»** "Down with the new French tricolor!" (roughly)

NOTE: For ultra-right-wingers, these should be the updated colors of the French tricolor (**bleu, blanc, rouge**). This expression has heavy, unpleasant racist connotations.

les Caldoches white New Caledonians

les Canaques, les Kanaks indigenous, Melanesian population of **Nouvelle Calédonie**

les CRS [les Compagnies Républicaines de Sécurité] French state security police

NOTE: Often referred to as the riot squad. This is only one of their duties, albeit the most high profile. Sometimes mockingly referred to by students as the **centres de rattrapage scolaire** (remedial schools).

la DATAR [la Délégation à l'Aménagement du Territoire] government agency whose task is to help develop the regions of metropolitan France via internal and foreign investment

le DOM [Département d'Outre-Mer] overseas *département* ■ **«Il n'y a pas d'argent pour ça. Nous ne sommes pas un DOM, tu sais!»** "There's no money for that. We're not a DOM, you know!"

NOTE: Four overseas ex-colonies (**la Guadeloupe, la Guyane, la Martinique, la Réunion**) are now fully independent territories with the status of full *départements*. Many mainland French people are under the illusion that these *départements* receive unfairly large grants and subsidies, whereas the inhabitants claim the opposite, with some justification.

les DOM-TOM (m) the *départements d'outre-mer* and the *territoires d'outre-mer* (see page 170)

[Le Palais de] l'Élysée Élysée palace

NOTE: The French equivalent of the White House, [Br.] 10 Downing Street.

l'ETA Basque separatist movement

l'Europe passoire (*lit.*, sieve, colander) Europe open house (roughly)

NOTE: The expression refers to the Maastricht treaty, which many believe has led to an upsurge in illegal immigration, particularly into France.

Euzkadi (see **ETA**) Basque

la France profonde (*lit.*, deep France) the real heart of France; backward-looking France

Francilien(-ienne) belonging to or an inhabitant of the Île de France (the prosperous Paris outreaches); compare suburbanites, [Br.] Home Counties ■ **«Tu sais, ces Franciliens, ils sont tous un peu BCBG!»** "You know, these Île-de-France people are all a bit preppy/[Br.] Sloany!"

la Francilienne expressway/[Br.] motorway that encircles the Paris region

la grande bleue (*lit.*, the great [big] blue) Mediterranean Sea

l'Hexagone (m) metropolitan France ■ **«Moi, je suis hexagonaliste!»** "Me, I'm pushing for (metropolitan) France!"

NOTE: So-called because of France's approximately hexagonal shape. The expression has an inward-looking, nationalistic feel to it.

Moi, je suis hexagonaliste!

l'intégrisme (m) (*lit.*, integrationism) fundamentalism ▪ **«Il y a trop d'intégrisme dans notre pays!»** "There's too much fundamentalism in our country!"

NOTE: The term refers to religious fundamentalism of any sort. However, many French people use it as a euphemism for Muslim fundamentalism, partly because of the large number of North Africans in France, partly also as a consequence of the fear engendered by Islamic fundamentalism in Algeria. Because of their shared history, Algeria is always felt to be very close to France.

(en) Lutèce (in/to) Paris

NOTE: A humorous, antique name for Paris.

le Maghreb, un Maghrébin, une Maghrébine⑦

NOTE: Originally a term for that part of North Africa governed by France until the 1950s and 1960s, **le Maghreb** now has racist undertones. It is directed at recent immigrants, particularly from Algeria and Morocco, who are perceived by the Far Right as having taken jobs and homes from the **Français de souche** (native-born French) and to have threatened the Judeo-Christian basis of the country.

le maquis (*lit.*, the scrub) Resistance (World War II)

le maquisard, une maquisarde member of the French Resistance

NOTE: The extremely brave French resistance movement during World War II. The term developed from the expression **prendre le maquis** (to take to the [scrub-covered] hills of the South of France [where the Resistance started]).

Marianne symbol of France; compare Uncle Sam, Britannia, John Bull ▪ **«C'est une vraie Marianne à la barricade!»** "She's a regular Marianne, storming the barricades!"

NOTE: This expression is often used, with an acknowledgment to Géricault's painting, as a reminder of the Commune and the Siege of Paris in 1870–71.

le/la métèqueⒹ foreigner, usually of mixed French and foreign blood

NOTE: This expression used to be very offensive, but since Georges Moustaki's phenomenal success with his song *Le métèque,* the term is often used quite affectionately. It therefore needs to be used with extreme care, as it is not easy to guess how it will be taken.

la métropole (*lit.*, the metropolis) continental France, including Corsica

Monsieur Bons Offices (*lit.*, Mr. Good-Offices) ombudsman, troubleshooter, mediator

le MRAP [Mouvement contre le Racisme et pour l'Amitié entre les Peuples] anti-racism group

NOTE: This movement grew up as a counter to growing ultra-right-wing activity in France in the 1990s.

Muroroa atoll in French Polynesia, notorious for atomic tests

noctambus Parisian nighttime bus service

l'Orsec [le Plan pour l'organisation des secours] national system of disaster relief, put into action on occasions such as the great floods of 1999

outre Quiévrain Belgium ■ **«D'où il vient? Autant que je sache, il habite le monde outre Quiévrain.»** "Where does he come from? As far as I know, he lives somewhere on the other side of Quiévrain."

> NOTE: Quiévrain is a small Belgian town sharing a border with France. This is a somewhat condescending confirmation of some French people's view of Belgium as a small country with small-minded people. (See also page 167.)

Paname humorous nickname for Paris

le Parigot, une Parigote Parisian

> NOTE: A sometimes affectionate, sometimes condescending name given to Parisians by the rest of France. See also **les soixante-quinze** below.

le Paris-Dakar controversial car race from France via the African desert to Senegal

la cité phocéenne Marseille

> NOTE: Marseille was originally named after Massilia, a city founded by Phocaean traders.

le quai de Javel location of the famous Citroën car factory

Ras l'Front! Down with the National Front!

> NOTE: A corruption of **à bas le Front**, this is a battle cry of the anti-racist movement.

les 75 [les soixante-quinze] Parisians ■ **«Voilà les soixante-quinze qui arrivent!»** "Here they come from Paris!"

> NOTE: 75 was the original license plate code for Paris. The only people who will be upset by this term are the Parisians themselves. Like the inhabitants of most, if not all capital cities, they are seen as overbearing, overloud, and overprivileged by the rest of the nation.

SOS Racisme popular, broad-based anti-racist organization

de souche (*lit.*, by stock/roots) native-born (often with certain racist connotations)

le TER [le Train Express Régional] local/regional/cross-country train

les TOM [les Territoires d'Outre-Mer]

> NOTE: **Les îles Kerguelen, la Nouvelle-Calédonie, Mayotte,** and **Saint-Pierre-et-Miquelon** are mostly island territories from the days of the French empire. Like

the **DOM** (see pages 168 and 208), they are often assumed by mainland French people to obtain an unfair share of government handouts, whereas they themselves feel underassisted, again with some justification.

EXERCISES

C'est à vous maintenant!

A *Which place/person or persons among those named in the box . . .*

les Canaques	les Belges	Marianne
le quai de Javel	France	Monsieur Bons Offices
Franciliens	l'Élysée	l'Arlésienne

1. might you call in to settle a dispute with your insurance company? ____________
2. is the French equivalent of Uncle Sam? ____________
3. is never seen? ____________
4. are the butt of French people's humor? ____________
5. live in **la Nouvelle-Calédonie?** ____________
6. is the French equivalent of the White House? ____________
7. is nicknamed the Hexagon? ____________

B *Taking one expression from each column, find the pairs that have a connection.*

____	1. **le Maghreb**	a. **les 75**
____	2. **les Belges**	b. **la cité phocéenne**
____	3. **les Parigots**	c. **les TOM**
____	4. **la grande bleue**	d. **le quai de Javel**
____	5. **Citroën**	e. **ETA**
____	6. **la Bretagne**	f. **l'intégrisme**
____	7. **les DOM**	g. **l'Armor**
____	8. **Euzkadi**	h. **outre Quiévrain**

C *Replace the italicized phrase in each statement with a more streetwise expression.*

1. Ils proviennent *du nord de l'Afrique.* ________________
2. Ce n'est pas *la France continentale*! ________________
3. Tu peux prendre *le bus après minuit.* ________________
4. Elle est *née à Paris.* ________________
5. Je crois qu'elle a été *membre de la Résistance.*
   ____
6. Tu ne connais pas *le système des trains régionaux*?
   ____
7. Je suis Française *de naissance.* ________________

Romance

See also "Sex."

LOVE'S GOOD SIDE

Stage 1

tomber sur quelqu'un (*lit.*, to fall on someone) to bump into someone

chercher de la fesse (*lit.*, to look for some ass(?)/bottom), **draguer** to go looking for some ass/[Br.] a bit of skirt/[Br.] the other/[Br.] crumpet ■ **«Il ne peut pas s'empêcher de draguer, c'est dans le sang!»** "He can't stop chasing the chicks/[Br.] birds; it's in his blood!"

la drague the chase, picking up women, womanizing ■ **«Tu sais son problème? Il ne pense qu'à la drague!»** "Do you know his problem? All he thinks of is the chase!"

le dragueur woman-chaser

baratiner quelqu'un/faire du baratin à quelqu'un/faire du gringue à (*lit.*, to do some sweet-talking to), **faire du plat à** (*lit.*, to do some [Br.] flat to) to come on to someone, [Br.] to chat someone up ■ **«Ne lui fais pas de plat—c'est ma frangine(?)!»** "Don't [Br.] chat her up—she's my sister!" ■ **«Venez voir mes estampes japonaises!»** "Come and see my (*lit.*, Japanese) etchings!" ■ **«Ah oui, tu fais un peu Toulouse-Lautrec!»** "Yes, you do look a bit like Toulouse-Lautrec!" (Or any other famous painter's name that comes to mind, providing he or she is old and none too pretty!)

> NOTE: A common humorous response to an invitation to an intimate art show. Can be positive or negative, depending on the tone!

faire de l'œil à quelqu'un/mater quelqu'un to give someone the eye/[Br.] to eye up ■ **«Si tu vas lui faire de l'œil comme ça, je te prête mon maquillage!»** "If you're going to give him the eye like that, I'll lend you my makeup!"

faire les yeux doux à quelqu'un (*lit.*, to make soft eyes) to make sheep's eyes at someone ■ **«Pas la peine de lui faire les yeux doux, il est sadique!»** "Don't waste your time making sheep's eyes at him, he's a sadist!"

manger quelqu'un des yeux (*lit.*, to eat someone with one's eyes) to devour someone with one's eyes

Rince-toi l'œil! Wash your eye out!

NOTE: Said with humorous aggression to someone who has been giving you the eye. It can be a brush-off or an invitation to further contact, depending on the tone!

faire du pied/genou à quelqu'un (*lit.*, to do some foot/knee to someone) to play footsie with someone

Stage 2

flirter to flirt

se laisser prendre to allow oneself to be taken in ■ **«Ne te laisse pas prendre par son smoking!»** "Don't let yourself be taken in by his tuxedo!"

taper dans l'œil de quelqu'un (*lit.*, to hit [into] someone's eye) to catch someone's fancy

le rencard date

filer un rencard (*lit.*, to spin a date) to make/to set up a date ■ **«Comment est-ce que je file un rencard avec Marie-Rose?»** "How do I set up a date with Marie-Rose?"

Stage 3

avoir un faible pour quelqu'un (*lit.*, to have a weakness for someone) to have a soft spot for someone ■ **«Tu ne sais pas la raison pour laquelle il est si gentil tout d'un coup? Il a un faible pour ta sœur!»** "Don't you know the reason why he's so nice all of a sudden? He's got a soft spot for your sister!"

avoir les atomes crochus (*lit.*, to have one's atoms hooked together) to hit it off

s'éclater (*lit.*, to blaze) to hit it off ■ **«On chante une vieille chanson ensemble et on s'éclate!»** "We sang an old song together and we really hit it off!"

avoir le/un ticket avec quelqu'un (*lit.*, to have a ticket with someone) to hit it off with someone ■ **«Je ne l'ai jamais vu comme ça! Il a clairement un ticket avec elle!»** "I've never seen him like that! He's obviously hit it off with her!"

faire une touche (*lit.*, to get a touch/nibble) to score (a hit), to make it

être dingue de quelqu'un to be mad about someone

avoir quelqu'un dans la peau (*lit.*, to have someone in your skin), **en pincer pour quelqu'un** (*lit.*, to catch it for someone) to be smitten by someone

subir le coup de foudre (*lit.*, to be hit by the thunderbolt) to fall in love at first sight

subir le coup de foudre

avoir le béguin pour quelqu'un to have a crush on someone

flasher sur quelqu'un (*lit.*, to flash on someone) to fall head over heels for someone ■ **«Il m'a souri et j'ai flashé sur lui, tout court!»** "He smiled at me and I fell head over heels for him, just like that!"

s'enamouracher de quelqu'un to fall head over heels for/[Br.] to be besotted by someone ■ **«Enamourache-toi de Céline après tes examens, pas avant!»** "Fall head over heels for Céline after your exams, not before!"

convoler to get hitched, to tie/[Br.] splice the knot ■ **«Elle a convolé en secondes noces avec un type formidable!»** "She got remarried to a great guy/[Br.] bloke!"

> NOTE: This humorous and affectionate word has its origins in the idea of the happy couple flying off together in blissful harmony.

passer devant monsieur le maire (*lit.*, to come in front of his honor the mayor) to get married ■ **«Tu ne vas pas porter cette vieille chemise pour passer devant monsieur le maire!»** "You're not going to wear that old shirt to get married!"

pacser to cohabit ■ **«Mariée? Non. Elle pacse avec un mec du quartier.»** "Married? No. She's living with a local guy/[Br.] lad."

> NOTE: The modern slang **pacser** derives from the 1999 Act, the **PACS [Pacte Civile de Solidarité]** establishing equal rights with those of married people for any couples cohabiting.

LOVE'S BAD SIDE

avoir le cafard (*lit.*, to have the [cock]roach) to have the blues ▪ **«Elle a toujours le cafard, quand elle joue du saxophone comme ça!»** "She's always got the blues, when she plays the saxophone like that!"

faire du cinéma/du cinoche (*lit.*, to do/make a bit of cinema) to cause a scene

être la douche écossaise (*lit.*, to be the Scottish shower) to blow hot and cold ▪ **«Avec lui, c'est toujours la douche écossaise!»** "He's always blowing hot and cold!"

NOTE: This colorful expression derives from the fact that Scottish showers have two separate faucets, one for hot water and one for cold. Blended warm water is not possible with such an arrangement.

faire marcher quelqu'un (*lit.*, to make someone walk) to lead (someone) on

mener quelqu'un en bateau (*lit.*, to lead someone in a walk) to lead someone up the garden path, to string someone along ▪ **«N'oublie pas ta pagaie! Elle va te mener en bateau!»** "Don't forget your paddle! She's going to take you for a ride (in her boat)!"

être de trop (*lit.*, to be superfluous) to be in the way/a fifth wheel, [Br.] to play gooseberry ▪ **«Je ne vais pas venir pour être de trop!»** "I'm not going to come to be the fifth wheel/[Br.] to play gooseberry!"

faire le poireau/poireauter (*lit.*, to do the leek) to hang around waiting ▪ **«Ça fait déjà une heure que je poireaute ici!»** "I've been standing waiting here for an hour!"

NOTE: **Poireauter** literally means "to stand looking like a leek."

cocufier⚠ to cheat on one's male partner

faire des infidélités to be unfaithful

lâcher, laisser choir, laisser tomber, plaquer (*lit.*, to flatten), **planter là** (*lit.*, to plant there) to ditch, to drop, to jilt someone ▪ **«Elle m'a planté là, pour avoir fait un peu de baratin à Louise! C'est pas fin!»** "She ditched me because I came on to/[Br.] chatted up Louise a bit! It's not fair!"

prendre un râteau (*lit.*, to take a rake) to be ditched/dumped/[Br.] John Doed

prendre une veste (*lit.*, to take a jacket)/**poser un lapin à quelqu'un** to stand someone up

avoir quelqu'un to take someone for a ride (normally used by the victim) ▪ **«Elle m'a bien eu!"»** "She took me for a real ride!"

se faire avoir to be had ■ **«Édouard aurait dû le voir venir! Il s'est fait avoir!»** "Edward should have seen it coming! He's been had!"

faire des ravages (*lit.*, to cause ravages) to break hearts ■ **«Avec cette figure elle a été faite pour faire des ravages!»** "With that face, she was made to break a few hearts!"

barboter (*lit.*, to paddle), **faucher** (*lit.*, to mow/cut down), **pincer, piquer, souffler** (*lit.*, to take a draft/[Br.] draught) **le copain/la copine à quelqu'un** to steal/swipe/[Br.] pinch someone's boyfriend/girlfriend ■ **«Ça, c'est la fin—il a fauché la copine à son meilleur ami!»** "That's the end—he's stolen/[Br.] pinched his best friend's girl!"

encloquer(!)**/mettre en cloque**(!) to put someone in the family way, to knock someone up, [Br.] to give someone a bun in the oven

avoir le ballon(?) (*lit.*, to have the [foot]ball) to be knocked up/pregnant/ [Br.] in the club, [Br.] to have a bun in the oven ■ **«C'était la première fois et elle en a le ballon!»** "It was the first time and she got knocked up from it!"

GENERAL VOCABULARY

une bise, un bécot, un bisou a kiss

se bécoter to neck

ma belle my beautiful

ma biche my darling [of a woman only]

mon chéri, ma chérie, mon chou, mon coco, ma cocotte, mon petit chou my darling, love, sweetie-pie

ma Dulcinée my darling [said of younger women only]

NOTE: Dulcinea was the young woman with whom the aged Don Quixote became so besotted.

faire des papouilles à quelqu'un (*lit.*, to give someone some cuddles) to feel someone up, [Br.] to touch someone up

peloter to feel (up), to grope, [Br.] to touch up

le pelotage groping, (heavy) petting

le rencard rendezvous, assignation

tripoter to paw

EXERCISES

C'est à vous maintenant!

A *You are driving in Montréal. By accident, you tune into a shortwave police radio transmission containing a report on some covert observation. Interpret what you hear for your fellow passenger.*

Le suspect, un certain Jean Dax, est arrivé au café Huron, chercher de la fesse. Dax fait du gringue à une fille de bar. Il lui fait de l'œil... elle lui fait les yeux doux! Ah! Il y a un problème maintenant... le patron du café n'est pas content. Dax fait du pied à la fille. Le patron crie «Rince-toi l'œil!» Le patron n'est pas content que la fille tape dans l'œil de Dax. Maintenant, il y a une bagarre!

____

____

____

____

____

____

B *Choose the French sentence in the column on the right that matches the English expression on the left.*

____	1. I've scored a hit!	a. **J'ai fait des ravages.**
____	2. I led him on.	b. **J'ai le ballon.**
____	3. I got married.	c. **Je l'ai fait marcher.**
____	4. I broke some hearts!	d. **J'ai fait une touche.**
____	5. I ditched him!	e. **Je lui ai posé un lapin.**
____	6. He touched/felt me up!	f. **Je l'ai planté là.**
____	7. I'm pregnant.	g. **Il m'a fait des papouilles.**
____	8. I stood him up!	h. **Je suis passé devant M. le maire.**

C *Place a ✓, ✗, or — next to each expression to show whether it is pleasant, unpleasant, or neutral.*

____	1. **baratiner**	____	6. **tripoter**
____	2. **ma Dulcinée**	____	7. **avoir un ticket**
____	3. **encloquer**	____	8. **subir le coup de foudre**
____	4. **peloter**	____	9. **convoler**
____	5. **flirter**	____	10. **en pincer pour quelqu'un**

Seaside and Mountains

See also "Travel and Transportation."

SUNBATHING

se rôtir le cuir (*lit.*, to roast one's leather)   to catch some rays, to sunbathe

se foutre(!)**, se mettre à poil**(?)   to strip (off), to peel (off)

topless   topless

faire du topless   to go topless

le transat [transatlantique]   deck chair

la pin up, la nana canon   pinup

le frimeur   poser, show-off

le maître nageur(ok)   lifeguard ■ **«Sur cette plage il est interdit de se foutre**(!) **à poil pour se rôtir le cuir mais j'ai vu une nana canon qui faisait du topless sur un transat.»** "You're not allowed to strip (off) completely on this beach to sunbathe/catch some rays, but I saw a real pinup/super babe who was topless on a deck chair."

SAILING

la baille   drink

le marsouin   sailor

le rafiot, le rafiau, le sabot (*lit.*, clog)   tub, bucket (boat)

> NOTE: **La Baille** (with capital letters) is slang French for **L'École navale** (the Naval College); **marsouin** can also mean a "marine" in slang French; **sabot** can also mean a "broken-down machine."

tomber à la baille   to fall into the water/[Br.] the drink

foutre(!) **quelqu'un à la baille**   to throw/[Br.] chuck someone into the water/[Br.] the drink

tous à la baille!   everyone into the water/[Br.] the drink! ■ **«On n'savait pas si les quatre marsouins étaient tombés à la baille ou si on les y avait foutus**(!)**! De toute façon, tout le monde voulait changer de rafiot et de capitaine.»**

"We didn't know if the four sailors had fallen into the water/[Br.] drink or if they'd been thrown/[Br.] chucked in! But in any case, everyone wanted a different tub/bucket and a different captain."

SKIING

NOTE: The terms marked (ok) are standard French expressions.

aller au ski to go skiing

NOTE: The standard French expression for "to go skiing" is **faire du ski.**

le ski acrobatique(ok) hotdogging, freestyling ▪ **«C'est un sacré lascar! C'est peut-être lui qui a inventé le ski acrobatique.»** "He's one helluva/hell of a guy! He could be the one who invented hotdogging/freestyling."

les lunettes (fpl) **de ski**(ok) ski goggles

le ski hors piste(ok) off-piste skiing

le ski alpin(ok) downhill skiing

les chaussures (fpl) **de ski**(ok) ski boots

la combinaison de ski(ok) ski suit

la station de ski(ok) ski resort

le/la skieur(-euse)(ok) skier

SWIMMING

le crawl(ok) crawl

crawler to swim the crawl

le crawler crawl swimmer

le dos crawlé(ok) backstroke

NOTE: The standard French for **crawler** is **nager le crawl**; **un crawler** in standard French is **un(e) nageur(-euse) de crawl.**

«Elle adore crawler dans la mer; moi, j'préfère le dos crawlé.» "She loves to swim the crawl in the sea. I prefer backstroke."

See also "Sports" (Swimming).

WATER SPORTS

le parapente(ok) paragliding

le pédalo(ok) pedal boat, [Br.] pedalo

faire du pédalo(ok) to go for a pedal boat ride

le ski nautiqueⓞⓚ waterskiing

le volley volleyball

le/la volleyeur(-euse)ⓞⓚ volleyball player

NOTE: The standard French expression for "volleyball" is **le volley-ball.**

«Ce frimeur joue au volley sur la plage tous les matins et ensuite il fait du parapente. Il dit qu'il n'y a que les gringalets qui font du pédalo.»
"This poser/show-off plays volleyball on the beach every morning and then he goes paragliding. He says that only weaklings/runts go for a pedal boat ride."

See also "Vacations" (Vacation Activities), *"Travel and Transportation."*

EXERCISES

C'est à vous maintenant!

A *You are on a beach on a very hot day with your boyfriend. All you want to do is a bit of topless sunbathing but you are inhibited by the lifeguard who obviously thinks you are a goddess; you think he is a show-off. Fill in the blanks below in order to say this to your partner.*

J'ai tellement envie de me ____________________ afin de me ____________________. Mais quand le ____________________ me fait de l'œil, j'ai pas envie de faire du ____________________. Quel ____________________!

B *You are going skiing. What would you wear on the following?*

1. your eyes ____________________
2. your feet ____________________
3. your body ____________________

C *The following French words have more than one meaning. Give at least two English translations.*

1. un marsouin ____________________
2. la baille ____________________
3. un sabot ____________________

D *Give the name of a person who practices the following sports or activities.*

1. le ski ______________________
2. le crawl ______________________
3. le volley ______________________

Sex

See also "The Human Body," "Romance."

GAY SEX

NOTE: There are many slang words and phrases in French for a "homosexual": **le caroline** (bottom man[?], butt boy[!], transvestite); **la Caroline du Nord/du Sud** = "North/South Carolina" in standard French), **le castor** (*lit.*, beaver; in police slang: male prostitute, homosexual), **l'empaffé** (m), **l'enculé** (m), **la folle** (*lit.*, madwoman = fairy, queen[?]), **le gay, le giton** (young, passive homosexual), **l'homo** (m), **la lopaille, la lope, la lopette, la pédale** (*lit.*, pedal), **le pédé, le pédoque, le pétanqueur, le rasdep** (this is *verlan* and based on **pédéraste**), **la sœur** (*lit.*, sister, nun = effeminate young man), **la tante** (*lit.*, aunt, auntie), **la tantouse, la tantouze, la tapette** (*lit.*, little tap; carpet beater; flyswatter; mousetrap), **la tata** (familiar word for "aunt, auntie"), **l'amateur** (m) **de rosette** (*lit.*, **rosette** means "asshole[!], arsehole[!]" in slang French), **l'amateur de terre jaune (terre jaune** [*lit.*, yellow soil/earth] is "sodomy" in slang French), **le bilboquet merdeux** (homosexual suffering from venereal disease), **bique et bouc** (passive and active homosexual; *lit.*, nanny goat and billy goat).

Bande (f) **d'enculés!**[!] means "What a load of fucking dickheads[!]/wankers[!]!"

L'enfoiré (m) means a "queer" or [Br.] "poofter," but **les enfoirés (du cœur)** are the singers and show business personalities who support the late comic Coluche's **restaurants du cœurs**, a charitable organization that feeds the homeless and the needy. **Les enfoirés**, who include some of France's top performers, give an annual, televised concert in support of the charity.

Most of the words for a homosexual listed above are very likely to cause offense, but members of the gay community in France refer to themselves as **gays.**

virer homo to become/turn gay

enculer, endauffer, endoffer[!] to buttfuck[!], [Br.] to bugger[!]

l'enculage[!] (m) buttfucking[!], [Br.] buggery[!]

la jaquette[?] (*lit.*, morning coat, [woman's] jacket; [dust]jacket/cover) (male) homosexuality

être/filer/refiler de la jaquette (flottante)[?] to be gay/queer/[Br.] bent

sortir du placard to come out (of the closet)

NOTE: The standard French expression for **sortir du placard** is **annoncer qu'on est homosexuel.**

le mouvement de libération des homosexuels gay lib(eration)

casser/bouffer du pédé(?) to gay-bash, to go queer-bashing(?)

emmancher (quelqu'un)(!) (**emmancher [quelque chose]** [*lit.*, to put a handle on (something)]) to buttfuck(!)/[Br.] bugger(!) (someone), [Br.] to go up the old dirt road(!)

se faire péter l'anneau/la rondelle(!) to get buttfucked(!)/[Br.] to get buggered(!)

(!)**«À trente balais, il a viré homo et depuis il endoffe**(!) **tous les pédoques**(?) **du quartier.** (!)"He turned gay when he was thirty, and since then he's been buttfucking(!) all the queers in the neighborhood."

(!)**«Il se fait péter la rondelle**(!) **tous les soirs mais les durs de sa banlieue détestent l'enculage**(!)**; ils adorent bouffer du pédé.**(?) (!)"He gets buttfucked(!) every night but the tough guys/[Br.] hard nuts in his suburb can't stand sodomy/[Br.] buggery(!); they just love to go queer-bashing(?)."

LESBIAN SEX

NOTE: There are many slang words and phrases in French for a lesbian, which are offensive: **la brouteuse, la gavousse** (an example of *javanais* and based on **gousse**), **la goudou, la gougnot(t)e, la gouine, la gousse** (*lit.*, [pea] pod; **une gousse d'ail** = clove of garlic; in slang French also = nymphomaniac), **la vrille** (*lit.*, tendril; gimlet; spiral), and **la puce travailleuse** (*lit.*, hardworking flea).

Brouteuse(!) is a derivative of the verb **brouter**, used in the verbal locutions **brouter le cresson/la motte**(!) (to perform cunnilingus) and **brouter la tige**(!) (to perform fellatio).

The words for lesbian listed above should be used with great discretion as they will cause offense in most contexts.

sentir/taper l'ail, manger de l'ail(?) (*lit.*, to smell of/eat garlic) to be/to appear to be a lesbian

faire les puces, faire la puce travailleuse(?) to simulate a lesbian relationship for the benefit of a voyeur

(!)**«Je crois qu'elle tape l'ail**(?) **mais d'après ces deux gouines**(!)**, elle fait la puce travailleuse**(!)**.»** (!)"I think she's a lesbian, but according to these two dykes(?)/dikes(?), she just puts on a show/puts it on (for the benefit of others)."

(!)**«Cette gavousse**(!) **adore brouter la motte**(!) **mais elle refuse de brouter la tige**(!)**.»** (!)"This dyke(?)/lesbo(?) just loves to eat hair pie(!)/[Br.] to go muff-diving(!), but she refuses to suck off a man(!)/to give a man a blow-job(!)."

MAKING LOVE

baiser ("to kiss" in standard French)/**calcer**/**fourrer** (*lit.*, to fill, stuff)/**tringler** (*lit.*, to mark with a line)/**trombonner quelqu'un** to bang/fuck/screw/shaft/[Br.] shag someone

la baise fucking, screwing

NOTE: "Sexual intercourse" in standard French is **rapports sexuels** (mpl).

en mouiller pour quelqu'un (*lit.*, to get wet for somebody) to be turned on by someone

baiser à la papa (*lit.*, to fuck like dad/the old man), **limer** to have a slow screw, to have the hots for someone

baiser en épicier (*lit.*, to fuck like a grocer) not to enjoy screwing/a screw

baiser en hussard/à la hussarde (*lit.*, to fuck like a hussar) to have a quick fuck/screw

baiser en levrette/en canard (*lit.*, to fuck like a greyhound bitch/duck) to fuck/[Br.] shag in doggie fashion

baiser en cygne (*lit.*, to fuck like a swan) to fuck/[Br.] shag with the woman's legs on the man's shoulders

baiser à la riche (*lit.*, to fuck like the rich) to have anal sex, to butt-fuck

le baiseur, la baiseuse horndog, [Br.] shag-happy person; horny/[Br.] randy bugger

jouir, prendre son pied, arracher son copeau, venir to come, to get it off, [Br.] to come off, to go over the mountain

tailler une branlette à quelqu'un, arracher le copeau (à quelqu'un) to get/[Br.] bring someone off, to ring someone's bell

avoir la trique (*lit.*, to have the cudgel), **bander, marquer midi** (*lit.*, to mark/indicate/register midday/noon), **avoir la gaule** (*lit.*, to have the pole/fishing rod) to have an erection, to have/get a hard-on

gauler (une femme) (*lit.*, to beat [a woman] with a pole; the verb is used in standard French meaning "to bring/shake down [fruit/nuts] with a pole) to have sex/get it on/[Br.] have it off (with a woman)

le cinq-à-sept (*lit.*, a five-to-seven) quick screw during the day

le jute sperm, spunk, cum

juter(!) (*lit.*, to be juicy, to drip with juice)   to come(?), [Br.] to cream(?), to pop one's cork(?)

l'extase(?) (f) (*lit.*, ecstasy)   climax

faire un soixante-neuf(!)   to sixty-nine(!)

le chaud-lapin(?) (*lit.*, hot rabbit), **un tringlomane**(!)   sex maniac

avoir le sang chaud(?) (*lit.*, to be hot-blooded, to be hotheaded)   to be a sex maniac

le puceau   virgin

le Sida   AIDS

le phallocrate   male chauvinist pig

le coureur   womanizer

être séropositif(-ive)   to be HIV positive

avoir les cuisses légères(?) (*lit.*, to have light thighs)   to be an easy lay

la mangeuse d'hommes   man-eater

la pouffiasse(!), **la roulure**(!)   slut(?), [Br.] scrubber(?)

le vieux garçon (*lit.*, old boy/young man/fellow)   confirmed bachelor

le pantouflard (*lit.*, slipper wearer)   stay-at-home

le tombeur (*lit.*, thrower)   casanova

le dragueur   ladies' man, womanizer (someone who goes out to pick up women)

draguer   to cruise, [Br.] to go on the pick-up/the pull

le satyre (*lit.*, satyr), **l'exhib** (m)   flasher

> NOTE: **Exhib** is an abbreviation of **exhibitionniste**, the standard French term for a "flasher"; **s'exhiber** is the corresponding verb.

montrer son artillerie(?) (*lit.*, to show/display one's artillery)   to flash

avoir la main baladeuse   to be a groper, to have roving hands

le cocu   cuckold

avoir le démon de midi (*lit.*, to have the midday devil)   to be suffering from the male menopause/midlife crisis

cochon, cochonne (adj.) (*lit.*, piggish)   dirty-minded, horny/[Br.] randy

vicelard (adj.) (*lit.*, depraved), **viceloque**   kinky, dirty

le vicelard   dirty old man, perv

être porté(e) sur la chose (*lit.*, to be partial to the thing) to be obsessed with sex, to have a one-track mind

papouiller (*lit.*, to tickle), **faire des papouilles à quelqu'un** to grope/paw someone, to feel someone up

se foutre à poil to strip (off)

s'envoyer quelqu'un (*lit.*, to get stuck with someone), **se farcir quelqu'un** (*lit.*, to get stuck with someone, to stuff oneself with someone) to get/[Br.] have it off with someone

culbuter une femme (*lit.*, to knock a woman over), **sauter une femme** (*lit.*, to jump over a woman) to bang/[Br.] to have it off with a woman

le baisodrome bedroom

NOTE: **Baisodrome** also means "whorehouse," [Br.] "knocking-shop" in slang French.

l'allumeuse (f) cock-teaser, prick-teaser

la vamp seductress

les prendre au berceau to be a cradle snatcher

marcher à la voile et à la vapeur (*lit.*, to run on sails and steam) to be bisexual, to be AC/DC

être jazz-tango (*lit.*, to be jazz-tango) to be bisexual, to be AC/DC

le diaphragme diaphragm, [Br.] Dutch cap

la capote anglaise (*lit.*, English hood) rubber, condom, [Br.] French letter, [Br.] Frenchie

le gode, le godemiché dildo

les prendre au berceau

le vibromasseur(!) vibrator(?)

chercher un peu de fesse(?) (*lit.*, to look for a bit of buttock) to look/go looking for a piece of ass(?)/[Br.] bit of skirt/[Br.] some crumpet

le travelot transvestite

astiquer(!) (*lit.*, to polish)/**branler**(!) (*lit.*, to shake)/**pignoler**(!) **quelqu'un** to get/[Br.] bring(!)/toss(!)/wank(!) someone off, to play with(!) someone

NOTE: French has a lot of slang words and expressions for "to masturbate," many of which may cause offense: **se branler** (**s'en branler** means "not to give a damn"; **se branler les couilles** means "[Br.] to do sweet FA(?)/bugger-all(!)"), **se finir (à la manivelle)** (*lit.*, to finish oneself off with a starting handle; meaning to reach orgasm through masturbating), **se fréquenter** (*lit.*, to frequent oneself, to keep oneself company), **se griffer** (*lit.*, to scratch oneself), **se palucher** (*lit.*, to shake hands with oneself), **se taper une pignole** (**la pignole** means "masturbation"), **se pogner, se taper une pogne** (**la pogne** means "masturbation"), **se toucher, se tripoter** (*lit.*, to fiddle with oneself, to finger oneself), **agacer le sous-préfet** (*lit.*, to irritate the sub-prefect), **amuser Charlot, s'amuser comme Charlot** (*lit.*, to entertain oneself like Charlie), **étrangler le borgne/Popaul** (*lit.*, to strangle the one-eyed man/Popaul), **jouer de la mandoline** (*lit.*, to play the mandolin; used of women, meaning "to finger(!) oneself [off]"), **s'allonger le macaroni** (*lit.*, to lengthen one's macaroni), **s'astiquer** (*lit.*, to polish oneself), **s'astiquer/se polir la colonne** (*lit.*, to polish one's column), **se taper la colonne, se mettre à cinq contre un** (*lit.*, to go five against one), **se coller/se taper un rassis, secouer le petit homme** (*lit.*, to shake the little man), **se faire boum** (*lit.*, to make oneself go bang/wallop), and **se faire une pogne/une touche.**

(!)**«Il en mouille**(!) **pour moi mais j'ai pas envie de le baiser**(!)**.»** (!)"He has the hots for me, but I don't fancy screwing him."

(!)**«Comme elle baise en épicier**(!) **j'aime mieux qu'elle me taille une branlette**(!)**/m'arrache le copeau**(!)**.»** (!)"As she doesn't enjoy a screw(?), I prefer her to give me a hand job(!)."

(!)**«J'ai eu la trique**(!) **dès qu'elle est entrée dans le baisodrome**(!) **et en un rien de temps j'ai juté**(!) **partout sur les draps.»** (!)"I got a hard-on(!) as soon as she came into the bedroom and in a few secs I came(!)/spunked(!) all over the sheets."

(!)**«Ce tringlomane**(!) **est persuadé que cette gonze**(?) **là-bas a les cuisses légères**(?) **et qu'elle sera d'accord pour faire un soixante-neuf**(!)**.»** (!)"This sex maniac is convinced that that chick over there is an easy lay(?) and that she will agree to do a sixty-nine(!)."

(!)**«Ce puceau est une véritable allumeuse**(?) **mais elle ne saurait pas quoi faire avec une capote anglaise**(?) **et encore moins avec un gode**(!)**.»** (!)"This virgin is a real prick-teaser(!), but she wouldn't know what to do with a rubber(?) and even less how to use a dildo(?)."

(!)«Il est vraiment porté sur la chose et passe ses soirées à chercher un peu de fesse(?); quand il ne trouve que dalle il finit par se branler(!).» (!)"He's really obsessed with sex and spends his evenings looking for a piece of ass(?)/[Br.] bit of skirt; when he doesn't find any, he ends up jerking himself off(!)/[Br.] having a wank(!)."

(!)«Ce travelot marche à la voile et à la vapeur mais il ne pourrait pas vous dire quand c'était la dernière fois qu'il a sauté(!) une femme.» (!)"This transvestite is AC/DC(?), but he couldn't tell you when he last screwed(?) a woman."

PROSTITUTION

le bordel, le claque(?) whorehouse/[Br.] knocking-shop(?)

le maquereau (*lit.*, mackerel) pimp

la maquerelle, la taulière (*lit.*, hotel boss) madam(e)

NOTE: A more literary alternative to **bordel** is **lupanar** (m); **une maison close** is the standard, neutral term.

NOTE: There are many other slang words for "pimp" in French, examples being **le barbeau** (*lit.*, barbel), **le barbillon** (*lit.*, barb, barbel; with the emphasis on a "small-time" or "young" pimp), **le bidochard, le hareng** (*lit.*, herring; also used to mean a "gendarme"), **le mac, le maquereautin** (with the emphasis on "small-time"), **le marlou, le merlan** (*lit.*, whiting), **le pescale, le poisson** (*lit.*, fish), **le proxo, le sauret**, and **le souteneur**. It will be noted that many of these terms refer to types of fish, as do many slang expressions for other aspects of prostitution. "Procuring" in standard French is **le proxénétisme**, a "procurer" is **le proxénète**, and "to pimp" is **faire du proxénétisme**.

la pute(?), **la morue**(?) (*lit.*, cod) whore, hooker

le baisodrome(!) brothel, whorehouse

la gagneuse (*lit.*, go-getter) whore earning good money

l'amazone (f) (*lit.*, horsewoman) prostitute working from a car

faire le trottoir (*lit.*, to do/walk the sidewalk/pavement) to be a street-walker, [Br.] to be on the game

faire le mac/le maquereau/le marlou to pimp

la chaude-lance(!) (*lit.*, hot lance/spear), **la chaude-pince**(!) (*lit.*, hot pliers/tongs), **la chaude-pisse**(!) (*lit.*, hot piss), **la chtouille**(!) VD/the clap(?)/ the pox(?)

choper la chtouille(!) to get a dose of the clap(?)

NOTE: **La chaude-lance**(!), **la chaude-pince**(!), **la chaude-pisse**(!) refer strictly to gonorrhea, while **la chtouille**(!) refers to both gonorrhea and syphilis. In standard French, **la maladie honteuse** refers to gonorrhea and syphilis.

ⓘ**«Ils ont chopé la chtouille**ⓘ **dans un claque**ⓘ **parisien et ont failli se faire casser la figure par le mac.»** ⓘ"They got a dose of the clap ⓘ in a Parisian whorehouse and almost had their faces smashed in by the pimp."

ⓘ**«Il a refusé de marchander avec une amazone dans une Mercédès mais il a baratiné une pute**ⓘ **qui faisait le trottoir près de son hôtel.»** ⓘ"He refused to bargain with a whore working from a Mercedes but sweet-talked a hooker/streetwalker working the street near his hotel."

TELEPHONE SEX

le sexe au téléphone telephone sex

les messageries roses (f) (*lit.*, pink parcel service), **le Minitel rose** sex chat lines (accessed on Minitel)

NOTE: **Le Minitel** is a public-access, information service which is peculiar to France. Users have a modem and a small screen with a keyboard; the system is used, for example, for a range of business, educational, and public services. Charges are put on the subscriber's telephone bill.

le téléphone rose (*lit.*, pink telephone) telephone sex lines, phone sex chat lines ■ **«Mon fiston est un passionné des messageries roses et ça me coûte les yeux de la tête.»** "My kid/son is obsessed with/[Br.] mad keen on sex chat lines, and it's costing me an absolute fortune."

See also "The Human Body," "Romance."

EXERCISES

C'est à vous maintenant!

A *Give an inoffensive French word for the following.*

1. homosexual ____________________
2. whorehouse/brothel ____________________
3. venereal disease (gonorrhea and syphilis) ____________________

B *Give a highly offensive French word for the following.*

1. sodomy/[Br.] buggery ____________________
2. a lesbian or nymphomaniac (one word for both) ____________________
3. sexual intercourse ____________________

C *Here is a list of English words for different types of fish and animals. Give the English translation(s) of the corresponding French word in its slang French meaning.*

EXAMPLE: mackerel—pimp (translation of *maquereau*)

1. whiting ______
2. cod ______
3. herring ______
4. pig (used adjectivally) ______
5. beaver ______
6. nanny goat and billy goat ______
7. (hot) rabbit ______

D *The following are literal translations of slang French expressions connected with sex or some form of sexual activity. Work out what the original French expression is and give the idiomatic English translation as your answer.*

1. To screw/[Br.] shag like a grocer

   ______

2. A hardworking flea

   ______

3. To nibble watercress

   ______

4. To pull out/to rip off someone's shavings

   ______

5. To be carried on the thing

   ______

6. To work on sails and steam

   ______

7. To lengthen one's macaroni

   ______

8. To play the mandolin

____

9. To do the pavement

____

10. The pink telephone

____

Sports

See also "Clothes" (Sportswear).

PRACTICING A SPORT

Athletes

affûter un athlète to bring an athlete to the top of his/her form

augmenter le rendement d'un athlète to improve an athlete's performance

contrôler un athlète (en vue d'un dépistage de stéroïdes) to test an athlete (for steroids)

le crack crack runner, top athlete

être en panne d'énergie to have run out of steam/energy

porter l'estocade (f) ([bullfighting] the death blow, the final thrust) to make the decisive move

avoir un bon finish to have a good finish

le coureur de fond/demi-fond long-/middle-distance runner

le leader race leader, front runner

le meneur de train pacesetter

décrocher un titre mondial to win a world title

le palmarès record (of achievement), list of medal winners

piquer un sprint/un cent mètres to sprint off, to go into top gear

être au top niveau to be at the top (of one's field)

des pointes (fpl) spikes

le quatre fois cent mètres four by one hundred meters relay

son record personnel his/her personal best, PB

le sprinter sprinter

le témoin (*lit.*, witness) baton

transmettre le témoin to pass the baton

«Le leader, qui est au top niveau depuis presque dix ans, a piqué un sprint qui lui a permis de décrocher encore un titre mondial. Il en a maintenant quatre à son palmarès.» "The race leader, who's been a top athlete for nearly ten years, went into top gear and this brought him the world title. He now has four (titles) under his belt."

«Dans le quatre fois cent mètres, le troisième sprinter n'a pas réussi à transmettre le témoin à son coéquipier, le véritable crack du groupe.» "In the four by one hundred meters relay, the third sprinter couldn't pass the baton to his teammate, the star of/top runner in the squad."

BASKETBALL

le basket basketball

NOTE: The standard French translation of "basketball" is **le basket-ball.**

les chaussures (fpl) **de basket** basketball shoes, [Br.] trainers

CYCLING

NOTE: Because cycling is such a popular sport in France—in terms of both watching and participating—it is the sport that has generated the most slang words and locutions.

faire l'accordéon (*lit.*, to do the accordion) (of main bunch of riders) to keep bunching and getting strung out alternately

l'autobus (m) (*lit.*, bus) trailing group (of riders)

becqueter de l'aile (*lit.*, to peck with one's wing) to lean on the fender/ [Br.] wing of a car

la bécane, le biclo, le biclou, le lové bike, bicycle

NOTE: **Lové** is another example of *verlan* and derives from **vélo.**

rouler la caisse (*lit.*, to roll/wheel along the crate/till/cash register) to lead the main group, to drag the main group along/behind

charger la mule (*lit.*, to load the mule) to take drugs

se coucher (*lit.*, to lie down, to go to bed) to retire (from a race)

crayonner (*lit.*, to scribble/jot down in pencil) to accelerate

le dégringoleur (*lit.*, faller, person who falls down) cyclist who is fast downhill/in descents

l'écureuil (m), **le pistard** track cyclist

la lanterne rouge (*lit.*, red lantern/light) back marker

les manivelles (f) (*lit.*, starting handles) legs

les manettes (f) (*lit.*, levers, taps) pedals

mordre le guidon (*lit.*, to bite the handlebars) to pedal in a forward position

pédaler en danseuse (*lit.*, to pedal like a dancer) to stand up on the pedals

pédaler en facteur (*lit.*, to pedal like a mailman/postman) to pedal in an upright position

le peloton (main) bunch/group of riders

la poussette (*lit.*, stroller/[Br.] pushchair) push

raccrocher (*lit.*, to hang back up; [Br.] to ring off) to give up competitive racing

faire rougir le treize (*lit.*, to make number thirteen blush) to pedal vigorously

le tintin (also, "no way!" in slang), **le tonton** (*lit.*, uncle) amphetamines

NOTE: **Tintin** is derived from **pervintin** and **tonton** is derived from **tonédron**.

la voiture-balai brush wagon (car following bike race)

«Il becquetait de l'aile car il était crevé et ne pouvait plus crayonner.» "He kept leaning on a car for a lift because he felt bushed/[Br.] knackered⑦ and couldn't accelerate any more."

«Ça faisait une demi-heure qu'on lui criait, ‹C'est toi la lanterne rouge!› Alors, quand il a vu la voiture-balai, il a décidé de se coucher.» "People had been shouting to him for half an hour that he was the back marker. So when he saw the brush wagon he decided to retire from the race."

«Il avait mal aux manivelles et il pédalait en facteur mais grâce à une poussette, il réussit à mordre le guidon.» "His legs were hurting him and he was in an upright position, but thanks to a push, he managed to start pedaling in a forward position."

SOCCER/FOOTBALL

jouer au foot to play soccer/football

faire un dernier essai/un dernier entraînement (*lit.*, to have a final try/ to do a final training session) to have a fitness test

être déclaré(e) bon pour le service to be declared/[Br.] passed fit

allumer le goal

l'occase (f) scoring chance

l'occase (f) **en or** golden opportunity, great scoring chance

la cage, les cages (*lit.*, cage[s]) goals

le portier (*lit.*, porter, commissionaire), **le goal** goalkeeper

la lucarne (*lit.*, skylight) top corner (of the net)

signer un but (*lit.*, to sign a goal) to score a goal

allumer le goal (*lit.*, to light [up] the goalkeeper) to shoot straight at the goalkeeper

NOTE: In slang French, the verb **allumer** has several other meanings: to arouse (sexually); **allumer les flics** (to watch out for the cops); **se faire allumer** (to get a bellyful of lead; to be told off).

le tir en boulet de canon cannonball (shot)

rater un but to miss a goal

prendre un carton rouge to be shown/given the red card

«On l'avait déclaré bon pour le service mais au bout de cinq minutes il a raté une occase en or.» "He had been declared fit (to play) but after five minutes he missed a golden opportunity."

«La première fois qu'il a shooté, il a allumé le goal; la deuxième fois, il a tiré dans les nuages mais la troisième fois il a signé un but sensass: il a envoyé le ballon en pleine lucarne.» "The first time he shot, it went straight at the goalie; the second time he shot miles over, but the third time he scored a magnificent goal; the ball went straight into the top corner of the net."

SWIMMING

le brasseur, la brasseuse breast-stroke swimmer

le crawler freestyle swimmer

le dos crawlé backstroke ▪ **«Ce crawler est minable comme brasseur mais quant au dos crawlé, il se défend pas mal.»** "This freestyle swimmer is a lousy breast-stroke swimmer but when he does the backstroke, he's not bad."

See also "Seaside and Mountains" (Swimming).

TABLE TENNIS

jouer au ping-pong to play table tennis, ping-pong

la raquette bat, paddle

la palette (surface of the) bat/paddle (used for hitting the ball)

donner de l'effet à sa balle to put spin on one's ball

le/la pongiste table tennis/ping-pong player ▪ **«Quand il joue au ping-pong, il donne de l'effet à sa balle avec la palette.»** "When he plays table tennis, he puts spin on the ball with his bat/paddle."

TENNIS

jouer sur terre to play on clay

gagner en deux/trois sets secs to win in two/three straight sets

le tennisman, des tennismen male tennis player(s)

la tenniswoman, des tenniswomen female tennis player(s)

balle (f) **de break/set/match** break/set/match point

le tennis tennis court

faire des/quelques balles to have a warm-up/[Br.] knock-up

«Quand elle joue sur terre, cette tenniswoman gagne presque toujours en trois sets secs mais aujourd'hui elle est incapable de gagner une balle de break. Elle aurait dû faire quelques balles avant la partie.» "When she plays on clay, this lady tennis player almost always wins in three straight sets, but today she just can't win a break point. She should have had a warm-up/[Br.] knock-up before the game."

RUGBY

(le quinze de) la Rose (*lit.*, [the fifteen of] the Rose) English rugby team

les Bleus (mpl) (*lit.*, the Blues, the men in blue) French rugby team

le Trèfle (*lit.*, clover) Irish rugby team

la (grosse) chandelle (*lit.*, [large] candle) a very high kick ahead/[Br.] up-and-under, [Br.] Gary Owen

NOTE: **Chandelle** is also used in soccer/[Br.] football and tennis, for example, meaning "a (high) lob."

caper un joueur to select a player for the national team, [Br.] to cap a player

«Les Bleus ont battu le Trèfle grâce à une grosse chandelle qui leur a permis de marquer un dernier essai cinq minutes avant la fin du match.» "France beat Ireland thanks to a high kick ahead/[Br.] an up-and-under/[Br.] Gary Owen which led to a final try five minutes from the end of the game."

SKIING

des lattes (f) (*lit.*, laths, boards, slats) skis

NOTE: **Lattes** in slang French also means "shoes" (flat-heeled) and "feet." The expression **filer un coup de lattes** means "to borrow."

SPORTS FANS

le club des supporte(u)rs fan/[Br.] supporters' club

supporter une équipe to support a team

NOTE: The standard verb phrase in French meaning "to support a team" is **être supporte(u)r d'une équipe.**

TRAINING

le kiné [kinésithérapeute] physical therapist, trainer, [Br.] physio(therapist)

faire la p.p.g. [préparation physique générale] to train, [Br.] to do circuit training

la gonflette bodybuilding

«Son kiné lui a dit de faire de la gonflette en plus de la p.p.g. qu'il fait tous les jours.» "His trainer/[Br.] physio has told him to do some bodybuilding in addition to the training/[Br.] circuit training he does every day."

See also "Clothes" (Sportswear).

EXERCISES

C'est à vous maintenant!

A *The following French and English phrases have become jumbled. Match the French expression on the left with the corresponding English expression on the right.*

____ 1. **becqueter de l'aile**
____ 2. **la lanterne rouge**
____ 3. **mordre le guidon**
____ 4. **un tir en boulet de canon**
____ 5. **gagner en deux sets secs**
____ 6. **une (grosse) chandelle**
____ 7. **faire la p.p.g.**
____ 8. **être en panne d'énergie**
____ 9. **faire l'accordéon**
____ 10. **transmettre le témoin**

a. a cannonball shot
b. to pedal in a forward position
c. to do circuit training, to train
d. a high kick ahead, [Br.] an up-and-under, [Br.] a Gary Owen
e. to pass the baton
f. to have run out of steam/energy
g. to lean on the fender/[Br.] wing of a car
h. to keep bunching and getting strung out alternately
i. the back marker
j. to win in two straight sets

B *Give the idiomatic French translation of the following English expressions.*

1. (cycling) to take drugs ____________
2. to shoot straight at the goalie/keeper ____________
3. to put spin on one's ball ____________
4. match point ____________
5. to play table tennis ____________
6. a middle-distance runner ____________
7. to give up competitive racing ____________
8. to be certified/[Br.] passed fit ____________
9. to play on clay ____________
10. to have a warm-up/[Br.] knock-up ____________

Travel and Transportation

See also "Cars," "Seaside and Mountains."

DESTINATIONS

Albion (la perfide)ⓘ (Perfidious) Albion (England) ■ **«Qu'est-ce que tu attends, c'est la perfide Albion qui s'y mêle de nouveau!»** "What do you expect? It's perfidious Albion getting involved again!"

NOTE: The term **Albion** is almost always used by French people as a sneering reference to treacherous England and particularly to the England of the era of colonial expansion. Whereas **Angleterre** still stands for Britain for most French people, **Albion** (from the Latin for the white cliffs of the Dover area) is exclusively Anglo-Saxon, and excludes the Celts of Ireland, Scotland, and Wales, whom the French often regard as kindred spirits.

le pays des Rosbifsⓘ (*lit.,* the land of the roast beefs) England

NOTE: Another picturesque term which can be either pleasantly humorous or mildly unpleasant, depending on the speaker's frame of mind. The expression has, however, taken on a somewhat ironic tinge since the advent of what is commonly known as mad cow disease.

le pays VFⓘ (*lit.,* the land of the mad cow [disease]) England

NOTE: **VF** stands for **vache folle** (mad cow). When news of this unfortunate disease first broke in the mid-1990s, French butchers panicked somewhat in the rush to assure their customers that their meat was French, and therefore safe, by advertising their beef as **VF**, which was intended to mean **viande française**. It did not take the French public very long to misinterpret their butchers' helpful notices as meaning the opposite of what was intended!

le pays des Amerloques Yankee-land ■ **«Le pays des Amerloques est terre neuve pour moi!»** "The land of the Yankees/[Br.] Yengis is virgin territory for me!"

NOTE: This term has an antique ring to it and is picturesque rather than pejorative, sounding as if it had been invented by the Iroquois, whose civilized social structures had such a strong influence on the drafting of the U.S. Constitution.

chez les Ricainsⓘ (*lit.,* at/to the Yank's place) in the States ■ **«Elle va faire un séjour chez les Ricains.»** "She's off on a trip to the States."

le ricain, une ricaine Yank(ee)

NOTE: The term is an abbreviation of **Américains** and is usually quite mild in its intent, though it can be somewhat pejorative when used by foreigners such as French-speaking Quebec people who live relatively close to the United States.

être du coin (*lit.*, to belong to the corner) to be local, to be from (a)round here

être de passage to be passing through ■ **«Je ne suis que de passage.»** "I'm only passing through."

pas la porte à côté not exactly next door ■ **«Bah oui, il y a une boîte de nuit. Mais, c'est pas la porte à côté!»** "Well, yes, there is a nightclub, but it's not exactly next door!"

NOTE: The expression omits the negative **ne**.

MEANS OF TRANSPORTATION

See also "Cars."

la bécane bike

le rafiot boat

le VTT mountain bike (see page 208)

aller à pince(s)⑦ (*lit.*, to go on one's paws/pincers) to go on foot, [Br.] to leg it, [Br.] to travel by Shanks's pony

prendre le train de onze heures to go on foot, [Br.] to leg it, [Br.] to travel by Shanks's pony ■ **«Dans un tel endroit, tu devras prendre le train de onze heures, si tu veux rentrer!»** "In a place like that, you're going to have to [Br.] leg it, if you want to get back!"

NOTE: The eleven o'clock nighttime train never comes. Hence, the need to walk.

TIMING YOUR TRAVEL

l'autoroute (f) **saturée** overcrowded freeway/expressway/[Br.] motorway, with traffic jams likely ■ **«Autoroute saturée—à cette époque de l'année, j'aurais dû savoir!»** "Traffic jams on the freeway/expressway/[Br.] motorway—at this time of the year, I should have known!"

le bison futé wily (wise) buffalo ■ **«Bison futé vous conseille l'itinéraire suivant... »** "The wily buffalo advises you to take the following route . . ."

NOTE: The Disney-like, friendly buffalo is a symbol thought up by the various French road safety agencies, to encourage Joe Public to think about alternative routes in the tourist season and at other peak travel times.

les flèches vertes (fpl) green arrows

NOTE: The **flèches vertes** are a system of green arrow signs that reroute motorists away from the main (crowded) thoroughfares.

«Moi, je suis flèche-vertiste, je prends toujours par les routes départementales.» "I'm a green arrow guy; I always take the B/country roads."

NOTE: This little piece of conversation is a good example of the **-iste** principle. It is theoretically possible to add **-iste** to almost any object, e.g., **fromagiste** (cheese lover) as a humorous way of stating that you are a fan or user. See also **peugeotiste**, page 36.

les journées rouges (fpl) red days (the days to avoid for travel, printed in red on official documentation) ▪ **«Vaut mieux éviter les journées rouges. Il y aura certainement des autoroutes saturées!»** "Best to avoid the red days. The freeways/expressways/[Br.] motorways will be jammed!"

le pont long weekend ▪ **«Tu vas faire le pont?»** "Are you going to make a long weekend of it?"

la rentrée return to work/school, usually after the long summer/holidays ▪ **«On ne va pas remonter pendant le dernier week-end d'août—C'est la rentrée!»** "We're not traveling back up during the last weekend in August—everyone will be going back!"

NOTE: Although most French people would not recognize it as such, **la rentrée** originates from Napoleon's sad retreat from Moscow. It still retains its negative charge, though this is nowadays nothing more sinister than resentment at the return to work or school, with the fall soon upon us.

DRIVING AND RIDING

See also "Cars."

passer un alcootest to take a breathalyzer test ▪ **«Tu ne vas jamais réussir à l'alcootest après tout ce que tu as picolé!»** "You'll never pass the breathalyzer after all you drank/[Br.] got down you!"

NOTE: Some humorous people use the term **l'alcootest** ironically to mean "the test to become an alcoholic," for example:

«Tu ne vas jamais passer l'alcootest, si tu ne bois (pas) plus que ça!» "You'll never get to be an alcoholic if you don't drink more than that!"

appuyer sur le champignon (*lit.*, to press on the mushroom), **écraser le champignon** (*lit.*, to crush/splatter the mushroom) to put your foot down on the accelerator ▪ **«Écrase le champignon, nous sommes déjà en retard!»** "Step on it/Put your foot down; we're already late!"

NOTE: This is a rural image for a not so rural activity.

le chauffard bad driver, road hog ■ **«Chauffeur? Chauffard? Tu n'as qu'à regarder son compteur quand tu es dans sa voiture. Un petit conseil: moi, je prendrais le siège d'arrière!»** "A good driver or a bad driver? You only have to look at his speedometer/[Br.] speedo when you're in his car. A little bit of advice: I'd sit in the back!"

NOTE: **-ard** is a pejorative suffix implying someone to look down on.

le conducteur, une conductrice du dimanche weekend/Sunday driver ■ **«C'est curieux, chéri—pour toi, les autres au volant, ce sont toujours les conducteurs du dimanche!»** "It's curious, isn't it, darling, for you anybody else at the wheel is always a weekend/Sunday driver!"

cracher **quelqu'un** (*lit.*, to spit someone out), **vomir** **quelqu'un** (*lit.*, to vomit/[Br.] sick someone up) to drop someone off ■ **«Où est-ce que je te crache?»** "Where shall I drop you off?"

faire un créneau to parallel park, to reverse into a parking spot ■ **«Mon mari n'a jamais compris comment faire un créneau—c'est moi qui dois toujours le faire pour lui!»** "My husband has never figured out/[Br.] sussed how to parallel park/reverse into a parking spot—I always have to do it for him!"

NOTE: **Les créneaux** are the crenellations in a castle wall. The idea of **un créneau** as a piece of parallel/reverse parking comes from the actual shape of the crenellation.

aller dans les décors (*lit.*, to go into the scenery) to drive off the road and hit something ■ **«Il y avait du verglas et pas pour la première fois il est allé dans les décors.»** "There was a patch of ice/black ice and, not for the first time, he drove off the road and hit/went into something."

faire demi-tour en trois temps (*lit.*, to do a half-turn in three movements) to do a U-turn/three-point turn ■ **«Je ne sais pas comment il a réussi au pratique. Il n'arrive jamais à faire demi-tour en trois temps!»** "I don't know how he got through his driving exam. He's never been able to do a U-turn!"

griller un feu rouge (*lit.*, to grill a red light) to go through a red light ■ **«N'oublie pas ta ceinture de sécurité—s'il voit un feu rouge, il le brûle!»** "Don't forget your seat belt—if he sees a red light, he goes through it!"

rouler à la papa/rouler pépère (*lit.*, to drive like grandpa) to amble, to meander gently along ■ **«Ça, c'est fin! Rouler pépère par une telle route, il y aura dix kilomètres de voitures derrière elle, avec nous les premiers!»** "That's the limit! Ambling along on a road like this, there'll be a ten kilometer backup/[Br.] tailback, with us at the front!"

s'arrêter pile to stop dead, to do an emergency stop ■ **«Heureusement que mes freins sont très forts! J'ai dû m'arrêter pile!»** "Thank goodness my brakes are very good! I had to stop dead!"

faire une queue de poisson à quelqu'un (*lit.*, to deal someone a fishtail) to cut someone off/[Br.] up, [Br.] to carve someone up ▪ **«C'est bien le gars dont je parlais—celui qui m'a fait une queue de poisson au rond-pont hier!»** "That's the guy I was talking about—the one who cut me off/[Br.] up/[Br.] carved me up at the traffic circle/roundabout yesterday!"

ACCIDENTS

bousiller sa voiture to crash/[Br.] pile up one's car ▪ **«Il ne trouvera plus d'assurance! C'est la troisième fois cette année qu'il a bousillé sa Mercédès!»** "He won't get insured again! It's the third time this year he's crashed/[Br.] piled up his Mercedes!"

le carambolage pile-up ▪ **«Il y a eu un carambolage énorme sur l'autoroute à cause du brouillard.»** "There's been an enormous pile-up on the freeway/expressway/[Br.] motorway because of the fog."

embrasser un platane to go smack into a tree ▪ **«Elle a embrassé un platane, pour avoir contourné trop vite!»** "She hit a tree, because she went (a)round the corner too quickly!"

NOTE: Literally "to embrace a plane tree," among the most common trees in France, planted on the roadsides to shelter traffic from the sun and less pleasant weather.

se mettre en portefeuille to jackknife [of an articulated vehicle] ▪ **«Le poids-lourd a pris le tournant trop vite et il s'est mis en portefeuille.»** "The heavy truck/[Br.] lorry took the corner too quickly and jackknifed."

NOTE: The term originates from the three-folded construction of traditional wallets.

se payer un trente tonnes (*lit.*, to buy oneself a thirty-tonner) to fight with/mix it (up) with/have it out with one of the heavyweights (truck, [Br.] lorry) ▪ **«Le jour même d'obtenir son permis, il a failli se payer un trente tonnes!»**. "The very day he got his license, he just missed fighting with/mixing it (up) with one of the heavyweights!"

NOTE: **Se payer** (to buy) stems from the classical idea of paying for your seat when the boatman (Death's henchman) ferries you across the River Styx to your final destination. Compare fighter pilots' wartime slang, "He bought it over Saigon!"

EXERCISES

C'est à vous maintenant!

A *In which countries would you be if you heard the following comments?*

«Il ne faut pas oublier qu'on est...

1. dans l'Hexagone!» ______________________
2. au pays des Rosbifs!» ______________________
3. au pays des Amerloques!» ______________________
4. chez les Ruskoffs!» ______________________
5. chez les Ricains!» ______________________
6. en Albion!» ______________________
7. chez les Chinetocs!» ______________________
8. chez les Espingouins!» ______________________

B *The following statements are taken from several traffic bulletins on the same French radio station just before and during a busy holiday weekend. Try to put them in the order in which they were spoken.*

1. Maintenant, comme prévu, autoroutes saturées, surtout l'A1 près de Montpellier.
2. Par suite des carambolages il y a enfin une série d'accidents. Sur l'autoroute près de Bordeaux, un poids lourd s'est mis en portefeuille.
3. N'oubliez pas, on est bientôt dans les journées rouges!
4. Quand vous serez en route, consultez le bison futé aux stations de service et aux aires de repos.
5. On est maintenant au début de la rentrée. Il y aura certainement des bouchons aujourd'hui.
6. Maintenant, il y a un autre carambolage sur l'A7 à l'entrée de Paris.
7. Alors, si vous rentrez demain de vos vacances, suivez de préférence les flèches vertes.

____, ____, ____, ____, ____, ____, ____

C *Put a ✓ by the driving habits that are acceptable and put an ✗ by those that are not.*

____ 1. griller un feu rouge

____ 2. rouler pépère sur l'autoroute

____ 3. faire un créneau

____ 4. faire une queue de poisson

____ 5. faire demi-tour

____ 6. vomir un passager

____ 7. appuyer sur le champignon en centre-ville

____ 8. aller dans les décors

Vacations

See also "Clothing," "Travel and Transportation."

DESTINATIONS

NOTE: The terms marked ⓞⓚ are standard French expressions.

le vieux coucou old plane/[Br.] kite

NOTE: **Coucou** (*lit.*, cuckoo) in slang French means "an old crate, a boneshaker" when applied to any vehicle.

le TOMⓞⓚ **[Territoire d'Outre-Mer]** (French) overseas territory

le DOMⓞⓚ **[Département d'Outre-Mer]** (French) overseas *département*

les vacs (fpl) **[vacances]** vacation, [Br.] hol(iday)s

le gîteⓞⓚ gîte, [Br.] self-catering cottage/apartment with kitchen

la guitoune tent

NOTE: **Gitoune** also means an "electric guitar" in slang French.

«J'ai toujours voulu passer mes vacs dans un TOM ou un DOM mais quand j'ai vu les vieux coucous dont ils se servent là-bas, j'ai décidé d'aller chez les espingouins.» "I've always wanted to spend my vacation/[Br.] hols in an overseas territory or *département,* but when I saw the old planes/[Br.] kites they use over there, I decided to go to Spain."

NOTE: **Espingouins** (Spaniards); see also "Foreigners."

«Notre vieille guitoune est foutue(!)**, alors cette année on va passer nos vacs dans un gîte.»** "Our old tent is finished/[Br.] knackered/buggered(?), so this year we're going to spend our vacation/[Br.] hols in a gîte."

VACATION ACTIVITIES

NOTE: The terms marked ⓞⓚ are standard French expressions.

le saut à l'élastiqueⓞⓚ bungee jumping

le VTTⓞⓚ **[vélo tout-terrain]** mountain bike

le mahomet sun

la planche

la planche surfboard

NOTE: The standard French expression for a surfboard is **une planche de surf**.

le parapente paragliding

faire du parapente to go paragliding

le parapente à ski paraskiing

l'ULM (m) **[Ultra-Léger Motorisé]** ultralight, [Br.] microlight (flying device)

le surfing, le surf surfing

faire du surf, surfer to surf, to go surfing

la planche à voile sailboard, (sport) windsurfing

NOTE: **Faire de la planche à voile** means "to windsurf"; "to go sailing" is **faire de la voile**.

se rôtir le cuir to sunbathe, to catch some rays

«Quand j'pars en vacs, je prends mon VTT et ma planche, mais quand le mahomet cogne, j'aime mieux me rôtir le cuir.» "When I go on vacation/[Br.] on my hols, I always take my mountain bike and my surfboard but when it's scorching (hot)/[Br.] it's a real swelterer, I prefer to catch some rays."

NOTE: An alternative slang expression for **le mahomet cogne** is simply **ça cogne**. In slang French, the verb **cogner (quelqu'un)** means "to beat (someone) up"; **se cogner** means "to fight," while **se cogner une corvée** means "to get stuck with a chore"; **s'en cogner** means "not to give a damn/shit (about something)."

See also "Clothing" (Vacation Clothes), *"Travel and Transportation."*

EXERCISE

C'est à vous maintenant!

Fill in the blanks in the following sentences, using an appropriate slang French term. There may be more than one suitable answer in some cases.

1. J'aimerais bien faire du camping mais notre ____________________ est déchirée et ne pourra plus servir. Alors, où est-ce qu'on va passer nos ____________________?
2. Si le ____________________ brille, je pourrai m'allonger sur la plage et me ____________________.
3. Qu'est-ce qu'il fait chaud! Ça ____________________! Mais ce soir, quand il fera moins chaud à marée haute, je ferai du ____________________ sur ma nouvelle ____________________.
4. Use standard French expressions to fill in the following blanks: Je veux bien faire de la ____________________ s'il n'y a pas trop de vent mais je n'oserais pas mettre un parachute pour faire du ____________________.

Verlan

NOTE: *Verlan* is a form of slang in which the syllables of the word are reversed and small changes in spelling may be made to aid pronunciation. It is far and away the most common form of slang among the young and some of it has passed quickly into general colloquial speech. Below is a list of the most common terms in *verlan*. By the time you read the list, more *verlan* will have entered into common French speech, since any word can be verlanized. Where examples of *verlan* appear elsewhere in our text, we have indicated this and given the original word, as we do here.

le/la babtou [*verlan*: **toubab**] Frenchman, -woman

la caillera [*verlan*: **rocaille**] scum

céfran (adj.) [*verlan*: **français**] French

chébran [*verlan*: **branché**] hip, trendy, "with it"

la chetron [*verlan*: **tranche**] chops, face, mug

à douf [*verlan*: **à fond**] very fast, [Br.] like the clappers

la drepou [*verlan*: **poudre**] charlie, coke, [Br.] scag, smack, snow

le féca [*verlan*: **café**] coffee

le/la feug [*verlan*: **juif**] Jewish

fonsdé [*verlan*: **défoncé**] stoned, out of one's mind/skin, wrecked

greum [*verlan*: **maigre**] thin

le keuf [*verlan*: **flic**] flatfoot, cop

le keum [*verlan*: **mec**] guy, [Br.] bloke

le keupon [*verlan*: **punk**] punk

le keusse [*verlan*: **sac**] 10 francs

faire lèche à quelqu'un⑦ [*verlan*: **chier**] to piss⑦ someone off

se faire lèche⑦ [*verlan*: **chier**] to be bored silly/shitless⑦

la meuf [*verlan*: **femme**] chick, [Br.] bird

le/la narzo [*verlan*: **zonard**] down-and-out

la negifran [*verlan*: **frangine**] sister, chick, [Br.] bird

pécho [*verlan*: **choper**] to catch, to grab, to nab

la québri [*verlan*: **brique**] 10,000 francs

le rasdep(?) [*verlan*: **pédéraste**] queer, fag(?), [Br.] poofter(?)

le rebeu [double *verlan*: **Arabe/beur**] second-generation French-born Arab

relou [*verlan*: **lourd**] unsubtle, in your face, [Br.] OTT

renoi (adj.) [*verlan*: **noir**] black

rench [*verlan*: **cher**] expensive, pricey

la reum [*verlan*: **mère**] old lady, an old dear

le reup [*verlan*: **père**] old man

la reuss [*verlan*: **sœur**] sister, girl

le ripou(x) [*verlan*: **pourri**] bad/corrupt cop, [Br.] bent cop

> NOTE: *Les Ripoux,* Claude Zizi's film of 1984, centers on the activities of a corrupt cop in Paris. The film was a notable success and drew the attention of the middle class and middle-aged to the way *verlan* was developing. Nowadays, people over forty are even known to use some *verlan* themselves, to add a humorous touch to their speech or to show that they, too, can be up to date!

le skeud [*verlan*: **disque**] record

la stonba [*verlan*: **baston**] slugfest, [Br.] punch-up

la tchon [*verlan*: **honte**] shame

tèj [*verlan*: **jeter**] to dump, to throw out, [Br.] to chuck out

la teuf [*verlan*: **fête**] party

la teup(!) [*verlan*: **pute**] tart(?), whore(?), pro(stitute), [Br.] slag(?), scrubber(?)

la touzepar [*verlan*: **partouze**] orgy

le trom, le tromé [*verlan*: **métro**] the subway, [Br.] tube, [Br.] underground

zarbi [*verlan*: **bizarre**] strange, odd, way-out, weird

la zicmu [*verlan*: **musique**] music, tunes, numbers

le zomblou [*verlan*: **blouson**] short jacket, [Br.] blouson

le zonga [*verlan*: **gazon**] grass, herb, weed (marijuana)

LE JAVANAIS

NOTE: An extensive section on *javanais* has not been included in the *Streetwise French Dictionary/Thesaurus* because it is not a real form of slang, but more a children's fun way of talking, rather like British "eg"-language, where the syllable "eg" is inserted before every vowel, for example "bregead" (bread), "fegootbegall" (football). *Javanais* is so called because it contains the syllable **"av,"** which along with **"va"** or **"ag"** can be inserted after a consonant or group of consonants, for example, **chavien** (for **chien**) and **Jagules** (for **Jules**).

Any French speaker could object to these two examples and say that he or she would insert other syllables where we introduced **av** and **ag.** That is exactly the point. *Javanais* can be what you want it to be, depending on your particular whim, and is not, therefore, genuine slang. However, if you are a young reader, one or two of your own inventions in the right company will impress!

EXERCISES

C'est à vous maintenant!

A *Turn the following* verlan *expressions back into the original French.*

1. céfran ________________
2. le féca ________________
3. tèj ________________
4. un keum ________________
5. zarbi ________________
6. un ripou ________________
7. un keusse ________________
8. le zonga ________________
9. un skeud ________________
10. greum ________________

B *Substitute a standard French equivalent from the column on the right for each expression in the column on the left.*

____	1. Elle n'est pas branchée, celle-là!	a. Arabe
____	2. D'accord, il est rasdep, et alors?	b. la police
____	3. Gare à la reum-là!	c. au courant
____	4. Appelle les veufs, il va y avoir une stouba!	d. honte
____	5. Il est aussi français que nous, même s'il est rebeu!	e. une bagarre
		f. homosexuel
____	6. Tu es trop jeune pour les touzepar!	g. m'ennuie
____	7. C'est mon frère, mais il me fait de la tchon!	h. vieille dame
____	8. Je me fais lèche ici!	i. orgies

C *Interpret the following* verlan *sentences into English for your friend who speaks no French, let alone* verlan*!*

1. T'as vu la reuss avec son reup?

   ____

2. Ce zoublon, il est rench!

   ____

3. Ils ont joué de la zicmu zarbi à la teuf.

   ____

4. Il a donné une québri aux pourris.

   ____

5. La negifran était fonsdé!

   ____

6. Le keuf a disparu dans le tromé.

   ____

7. La teup lui pécho son dernier keusse!

   ____

8. Il était babtou avec une chetron greum.

   ____

Weather

See also "Conversation and Invitations."

NOTE: The French are often said to be less obsessed with the weather and more with their health than the Americans and, particularly, the British. One reason put forward in support of this theory is that the French have such good food and drink to console them when the weather is bad! This is an attractive idea, but we are not sure it is much more than that, especially when you note how many more ways of talking about rainy weather there are than about the lovely, sunny weather, with which foreigners assume France to be perpetually blessed!

WEATHER GREETINGS

«Beau temps pour la saison!» (*lit.*, Fine weather for the season!) "Nice weather we're having!"

NOTE: This expression is also used when the speaker wishes to change the subject, avoiding embarrassment, gossip, etc.

Ça s'éclaircit! It's brightening up now!

Sacré temps! Nasty/[Br.] Flaming weather!

Quel temps de chien(s)! (*lit.*, What weather for dogs!) It's not fit for a dog (out there)!

RAINY WEATHER

NOTE: The French, like many Americans and most of the British, have to put up with a lot of rain. There are consequently many expressions in French that give a flavor of the people's relationship with what the clouds have to bring. It is interesting to note that, as with English, there are many more expressions relating to bad than to good weather!

Il pleut à verse! (*lit.*, It's raining torrents!) It's pouring!

Il pleut des hallebardes!

Il pleut des cordes! (*lit.*, It's raining ropes!), **Il pleut des hallebardes**(?)**!** (*lit.*, It's raining spears!), **Il tombe des cordes!** (*lit.*, There are ropes falling!), **Il pleut comme vache qui pisse!** (*lit.*, It's raining like a cow pissing!(?)) It's raining cats and dogs!

> NOTE: **Il tombe des cordes** will often cause a knowing smile, especially in areas with a ropemaking tradition. Compare **Faire des cordes (pour la marine)**(!) (to take a dump, to make turds(!)).

Il pleut à seaux. It's pouring/[Br.] bucketing down.

Ça dégringole. (*lit.*, It's tumbling down.) It's raining cats and dogs./[Br.] It's chucking it down.

la flotte water

prendre de la flotte (*lit.*, to take in water) to get soaked ■ **«Sans ton imperméable, tu vas prendre de la flotte!»** "Without your raincoat, you're going to get soaked!"

tomber de la flotte (*lit.*, there's water falling) to pour, to come down ■ **«Il tombe de la flotte aujourd'hui!»** "It's pouring (down) today!"

flotter to rain

péter to bang [of thunder]

> NOTE: **Péter** means "to fart, to explode." This use of **péter** harks back to the old belief that thunder was the gods farting.

Ça pète! Listen to that thunder!

> NOTE: This expression is also used humorously of a person plagued with gas.

pisser to piss with rain ▪ **«Voilà Dieu qui pisse!»** "There's the Good Lord relieving himself!"

NOTE: This use of **pisser** harks back in a similar way to **péter**, to the old belief that the rain was God relieving himself upon his creation and thereby providing the precious gift of water.

«Ça pisse dru!» "It's pouring down/[Br.] It's pissing it down/pissing thick and fast!"

la rincée, une saucée downpour

se faire rincer/saucer (*lit.*, to get rinsed/[Br.] sauced) to get drenched

HOT WEATHER

Il fait lourd. It's humid/[Br.] heavy/sticky.

Il fait de la chaleur! It's hot!

se chauffer au soleil to warm oneself in the sun

Il fait une chaleur terrible! It's terribly hot!

Quelle cuite! (*lit.*, What a cooking!) What a scorcher!

NOTE: Compare **un vin cuit** (page 75). The term **cuite** can also refer to a skinful of alcohol (see page 73).

C'est la canicule! It's a heat wave!

Quelle canicule! What a heat wave!

Quelle journée torride! (*lit.*, What a torrid day!) What a scorcher!

Il fait un soleil de plomb! (*lit.*, There's a lead sun!) The sun is scorching hot!

Ça dépasse l'échelle! It's going off the scale! (high temperatures)

FROM COOL TO COLD WEATHER

un peu de fraîcheur (*lit.*, a bit of coolness/freshness) cool spot ▪ **«Recherchons un peu de fraîcheur!»** "Let's find ourselves a cool spot!"

prendre le frais to take a breath of (fresh) air

à la fraîche (*lit.*, in the cool [period]) in the cool of the day

Il fait (un peu) frais! It's (a bit) cool/[Br.] fresh!

NOTE: Compare the expression **me voilà frais/fraîche!** (I'm in a fix!)

frileux, frileuse (adj.) sensitive to the cold, shivery ▪ **«Moi, je suis vraiment frileux!»** "I really feel the cold!"

Il fait frisquet. There's a chill/nip in the air. It's chilly/nippy.

Le fond de l'air est frais! (*lit.*, The air is cool right through!) It's nippy outside!

Ça caille! (*lit.*, That's coagulating!) It's freezing cold!

NOTE: **Cailler** means "to coagulate." It is cold enough to coagulate the blood!

Je me caille! (*lit.*, I'm coagulating!) I'm freezing!

Il fait un froid de canard/de loup. (*lit.*, It's cold enough for ducks/wolves!) It's bitterly cold/freezing.

Il fait froid/Il gèle à pierre fendre! (*lit.*, It's cold/freezing enough to split a stone!) It's freezing hard!

Il gèle à fond! (*lit.*, It's freezing through and through!) It's freezing cold!

se geler to freeze (of a person)

se les geler(!) (*lit.*, to freeze them) to be cold enough to freeze your balls off(!)

WINDY WEATHER

le Mistral powerful wind that blows down the Rhône valley, changing the weather rapidly ■ **«Le Mistral s'annonce!»** "There's a Mistral coming/[Br.] getting up!"

la Tramontane cold wind, blowing through the Languedoc and the Roussillon, named after the **tramontana**, the polestar, which was said to bring it on.

exposé(e) aux quatre vents open to the winds ■ **«Je ne voudrais pas habiter une maison exposée aux quatre vents comme ça!»** "I wouldn't like to live in a house open to the winds like that!"

le Bon Dieu lâche un vent! (*lit.*, the Good Lord is releasing a wind!) There's a wind coming/[Br.] getting up!

NOTE: Yet another reference to the toilet habits of the gods. Compare **entrer et sortir en coup de vent**, to dash in and out.

venter to be windy, to blow ■ **«Il vente fort à l'extérieur!»** "It's blowing hard outside!"

souffler en tempête (*lit.*, to blow a storm/tempest) to blow a gale ■ **«Après une telle chaleur, le vent souffle en tempête ici.»** "After such heat, there's a gale blowing/it blows a gale here!"

tempêter to rage, storm [of a person]

Il fait un vent à décorner les bœufs! (*lit.*, There's enough wind blowing to take the horns off the cattle!) It's blowing a gale/[Br.] great guns.

EXERCISES

C'est à vous maintenant!

A *Indicate which category each comment on the weather refers to.*

____	1. **Il tombe des cordes!**	a. Sun and/or heat
____	2. **Je me caille!**	b. Rain
____	3. **Ça s'éclaircit!**	c. Wind
____	4. **Quelle cuite!**	d. Cold
____	5. **Moi, je suis frileuse!**	
____	6. **Il vente fort!**	
____	7. **C'est la canicule aujourd'hui!**	
____	8. **Le Mistral s'annonce!**	

B **Off the scale!** *For each of the four types of weather below, arrange the expressions in order of rising intensity, e.g., from cool to freezing cold.*

1. a. **Je me suis trempée jusqu'aux os!** ____, ____, ____, ____
   b. **Il y a une averse!**
   c. **Il pleut à seaux!**
   d. **Il y a de la flotte!**
2. a. **Il fait de la chaleur!** ____, ____, ____, ____
   b. **C'est la canicule!**
   c. **Il commence à faire chaud!**
   d. **La terre se réchauffe!**
3. a. **Il fait plus froid!** ____, ____, ____, ____
   b. **Il y a un peu de fraîcheur!**
   c. **Il fait froid à pierre fendre!**
   d. **Il fait frisquet!**

4. a. Il souffle en tempête! ____, ____, ____, ____
   b. Il vente de plus en plus!
   c. Il fait un peu de vent!
   d. Le Bon Dieu lâche un vent!

C **God and his animals.** *The subject of God and God's creatures crops up frequently in expressions that deal with the weather. Translate the following expressions into English.*

1. Le Bon Dieu lâche un vent!

   ____

2. Il fait un froid de canard!

   ____

3. Il pleut comme vache qui pisse!

   ____

4. Quel temps de chiens!

   ____

5. Voilà Dieu qui pisse!

   ____

6. Il fait un vent à décorner les bœufs!

   ____

The World of Work

See also "Business," "Education."

WORK AND THE WORKPLACE

le bagne (*lit.*, penal colony) sweatshop, salt mine ■ **«Ça sent le bagne ici!»** "It's like a sweatshop here!"

> NOTE: **Un bagne** was originally a convict prison or prison ship, providing an unrelenting pattern of hard physical work and beatings.

la besogne ■ **«La compagnie, à la besogne!»** "Come on guys, let's get to work!/let's get down to it!"

> NOTE: If you come across the verb **besogner**, take care as it means to screw(!)/[Br.] shaft(!) and is likely to cause considerable offense in a work context.

la boîte workplace ■ **«Ta boîte, elle est bien nommée! C'est une vraie boîte à sardines!»** "The can/[Br.] tin is a good name for where you work! It's a real sardine can/[Br.] right sardine tin here!"

> NOTE: The term **boîte** originally developed as a name for the workplace, precisely because it implied a small, restricted place. It still has a negative ring to it.

le boulot job ■ **«Il en a marre de son boulot!»** "He's had enough of his job!"

le boulot peinard easy job, [Br.] cushy number, [Br.] easy billet ■ **«T'es bien tombé—c'est un véritable boulot peinard!»** "You landed well there—it's a real(ly) cushy job/[Br.] number!"

Métro, boulot, dodo! Subway, work, sleep!, [Br.] Tube, work, sleep!, the rat race ■ **«Ça ne m'a pas étonné que sa femme ait décampé! Pour lui, la vie n'est que métro, boulot, dodo!»** "I'm not surprised that his wife beat it! For him, life is just subway, work, sleep/the daily grind!"

> NOTE: This is the *cri de cœur* of the Parisians caught up in the daily triangle of commuting, work, sleep. Conversely, it has become a sneering judgment on Parisians by the rest of the French population, implying that their cousins in the metropolis need to get themselves a life.

WORK AND THE WORKERS

bosser, boulonner to work (hard) ■ **«Il ne bosse que pour impressionner sa nouvelle patronne!»** "He's only working hard to impress his new boss!"

bûcher to work hard, [Br.] to graft ■ **«Plus on bûche ici, moins on vous apprécie!»** "The harder you work here, the less they appreciate you!"

bûcheur hardworking, [Br.] grafting

le cadre, une femme cadre executive, manager ■ **«Un cadre bûcheur comme lui va se frayer un chemin rapide!»** "A hardworking executive like him is going to get up the ladder quickly!"

les cadres (m) management, the management team, the bosses ■ **«Dans cette usine, c'est les cadres contre les syndicats!»** "In this factory, it's the management against the unions!"

coincer la bulle(?) (*lit.*, to stick the bubble) to do nothing, [Br.] to do sweet Felicity Arkwright(?) (FA(?)) ■ **«Ici, ce sont les cadres qui coincent la bulle, pendant que les ouvriers boulonnent!»** "Here, it's the bosses who do nothing, while the workers do all the work!"

la cosse, la flemme laziness, idleness ■ **«J'ai la flemme d'y travailler!»** (*lit.*, I'm [too] idle to work at it!) "I can't be bothered to work at it."

se faire porter pâle (*lit.*, to pretend to be/act pale) to take a sick day/[Br.] sickie ■ **«Il a droit à une journée de mauvaise santé par mois. Tu vois, nous sommes le trente aujourd'hui. Demain, il va se faire porter pâle!»** "He's entitled to a sick day/[Br.] day's sickness a month. You see, today's the thirtieth. Tomorrow, he'll take a sick day/[Br.] sickie!"

tirer sa flemme (*lit.*, to go into lazy/lounging mode) to laze around ■ **«Ne tire pas ta flemme! Il y a toujours le classement à faire!»** "Don't laze around! There's always the filing to do!"

flemmard lazy, [Br.] skiving

glander(?)**, glandouiller**(?) to laze, to loaf around ■ **«Je voudrais lui passer un savon, parce qu'il glandouille tant!»** "I'd like to give him a real dressing-down; he loafs around so much!"

le gros bonnet, la grosse légume, l'huile (f) bigwig, one of the top people ■ **«Il ne va jamais être une grosse légume comme sa mère!»** "He'll never be one of the bigwigs like his mother!"

peigner la girafe(?) to fritter away your time, [Br.] not to do a right lot ■ **«Ceux qui peignent la girafe n'arrivent jamais au patronat.»** "Those who fritter their time away never get to be bosses."

Il a un poil dans la main, tout comme son père.

NOTE: Despite the apparently innocent, colorful image that this expression conjures up of someone combing the neck of a giraffe, it is best avoided in polite company, because of the barely disguised sexual connotation.

faire de la présence (*lit.*, to put in an appearance) to go through the motions, to just serve one's time ■ **«Il ne fait que de la présence dans son entreprise.»** "He's nothing but a timeserver with his firm."

avoir un poil dans la main (*lit.*, to have a hair in one's hand) to be on the lazy side, [Br.] to be bone idle ■ **«Il a un poil dans la main, tout comme son père!»** "He's a lazy bum/[Br.] bone idle, just like his father!"

le rond de cuir paper pusher, pen pusher ■ **«C'est un rond de cuir, qui va rester rond de cuir toute sa vie!»** "He's a paper pusher, who'll be a paper pusher all his life!"

faire suer le bournos⑦ to exploit

NOTE: This expression can easily offend sensibilities, since it means to make you sweat through your robe and harks back to the hard labor inflicted on Arabs by their colonial masters.

tirer au flanc (*lit.*, to shoot for the side) to sit around, [Br.] to skive ■ **«Elle est flemmarde de nature et cherche toujours un prétexte pour tirer au flanc!»** "She's a lazy devil and is always looking for an excuse to sit around/[Br.] skive!"

se tourner les pouces to twiddle one's thumbs ■ **«Ne reste pas là en te tournant les pouces! Il y a du boulot à faire!»** "Don't sit there twiddling your thumbs! There's work to be done!"

HIRING/GETTING AHEAD

faire du lèche-cul① to go in for ass② ([Br.] arse②)-licking① ▪ **«S'il fait du lèche-cul avec la patronne, il va avoir une rude déception!»** "If he tries any ass② ([Br.] arse②)-licking with the boss, he's in for a big shock!"

NOTE: This unpleasant expression, which can cause great offense, is found in all the major world languages and in many others besides, stemming as it does from an ancient method of humiliation used by tribal leaders.

graisser la patte à quelqu'un (*lit.*, to grease someone's paw) to grease someone's palm

avoir du piston/se faire pistonner (*lit.*, to have some piston [power]) to pull strings ▪ **«Il graisse toujours la patte à quelqu'un pour se faire pistonner!»** "He's forever greasing someone's palm to pull a few strings!"

NOTE: The expressions with **piston** stem from the idea of adding "piston power" to your engine.

le piston string pulling, pulling strings

pistonner quelqu'un to pull strings for someone

retrousser ses manches to roll up one's sleeves ▪ **«Si tu veux réussir dans la vie, tu dois retrousser tes manches!»** "If you want to succeed in life, you've got to roll up your sleeves!"

NOTE: This expression is used figuratively, as in English, to indicate that you are prepared to get down to the hard work/nitty-gritty (**les aspects pratiques**).

ne rien faire de ses dix doigts (*lit.*, to do nothing with one's ten fingers) not to do a damned/darned/[Br.] blind thing ▪ **«Il n'a rien fait de ses dix doigts depuis son arrivée!»** "He's not done a darned thing since he came!"

NOTE: Because of the current fashion for jokes relating to masturbation, you may wish to avoid this expression to save you from knowing smiles in polite company.

tirer le bon numéro (*lit.*, to draw the right number) to strike it lucky ▪ **«T'as tiré le bon numéro avec ton boulot!»** "You got/struck it lucky with your job!"

NOTE: This expression is used generally to indicate a piece of good luck, but is often used to suggest that someone has found an easy, comfortable job. Compare with the English "he's on an easy job/[Br.] a good number."

faire du zèle (*lit.*, to put on the zeal) to be overenthusiastic, [Br.] to be super keen ▪ **«Je ne peux pas supporter les jeunes cadres qui font du zèle comme ça!»** "I can't bear overenthusiastic/[Br.] super keen young executives like that!"

EXERCISES

C'est à vous maintenant!

A *For each colloquial or slang expression in italics, choose the standard French version from the list on the right.*

____ 1. Mon *boulot* me fait du stress.

____ 2. Moi, je cherche *un boulot peinard.*

____ 3. Cherchez-le dans *sa boîte.*

____ 4. Son idée de travailler, c'est de *se tourner les pouces.*

____ 5. Avec son travail, il *a tiré le bon numéro*!

____ 6. Il ne faut pas *peigner la girafe*!

____ 7. *À la besogne* et faites vite!

____ 8. Lui, aussi, *il faisait du zèle* quand il était jeune!

a. ne rien faire

b. travailler avec tant d'énergie

c. au travail

d. gaspiller ton temps

e. lieu de travail

f. métier

g. est tombé bien

h. travail facile

B *Find the pairs or small groups of expressions that have a connection.*

1. le bagne
2. boulonner
3. le boulot
4. glander
5. une huile
6. tirer au flanc
7. une grosse légume
8. se faire porter pâle
9. tirer sa flemme
10. un gros bonnet
11. bosser
12. faire suer le bournos
13. glandouiller
14. la besogne

____—____

____—____—____

____—____

____—____—____

____—____

____—____

C *Find the pairs of opposites, using one expression from each column.*

____ 1. retrousser ses manches		a. boulot peinard
____ 2. se tourner les pouces		b. avoir un poil dans la main
____ 3. le bagne		c. un gros bonnet
____ 4. bûcher		d. faire du zèle
____ 5. bûcheur		e. faire de la présence
____ 6. un rond de cuir		f. flemmard

Answer Key

Acronyms and Initials

A. 1. HP 2. RU 3. SF 4. JT 5. WW 6. PDG 7. CRS 8. BD

B. 1. hangovers 2. a broken-down car 3. toilet paper 4. the term "fag/queer" 5. a very short female 6. drugs

Animals

A. 1. de chat *or* d'âne 2. mouche 3. chevaux 4. grenouille 5. cerf

B. 1. chat (I've got a frog in my throat.) 2. chien (et) chat (My mother and I go at it like cat and dog.) 3. chien (She leads a dog's life.) 4. mouton (The [arm]chair he's bought is really unusual/is a genuine rarity.) 5. chien (de sa) chienne (Since she left him, he's been wanting to get even with her/he's really had it in for her.) 6. lapin (Her jewels are totally worthless/[Br.] aren't worth a monkey's fart.) 7. vache (I can't stand this woman; she's a real bitch.) 8. vache (The whole family speaks pidgin/lousy English.) 9. chameau (This woman is unbearable. She's a nasty piece of work.)

Art

A. 1. f 2. a 3. e 4. h 5. d 6. g 7. c 8. b

B. 1. décor 2. Marie-Chantal 3. planches 4. locomotive 5. branchée 6. artistique

C. 1. (Pour moi) c'est un roman de gare! 2. Non, Billy s'est ramassé/planté (avec son film). 3. C'est une grosse légume. 4. Il oublie son texte. 5. C'est le grand manitou/le ponte au studio. 6. Elle tâte de la sculpture.

Beauty

A. 1. Elle va **se faire refaire les seins**. 2. Sa fille **s'est fait faire un lifting**. 3. Elle est allée **chez le coiffeur**. 4. Sa fille **s'est maquillée**.

B. 1. fesse (His/her little sister has drooping buttocks.) 2. gaufre (She's going to do her face before she goes out.) 3. poches/valises (His/her father has bags under his eyes.) 4. clou (He's as thin as a rake.) 5. armoire (His/her son is a real hulk.)

Business

A. 1. Président-Directeur Général (Chairman and Managing Director) 2. Salaire Minimum Interprofessionnel de Croissance (the [official] minimum wage) 3. Agence Nationale pour l'Emploi (Employment Office/Job Center) 4. La Banque de France (the Bank of France)

B. 1. menuise (m) 2. électro (m) 3. plombard (m) 4. barbouilleur (m)

C. 1. (a) has made loads of dough/lots of money (b) is filthy rich 2. (a) the top brass/the men in (gray) suits/the suits (b) white-collar workers 3. (a) wheeler-dealers (b) to swindle 4. (a) is out of work/[Br.] on the dole (b) was fired/[Br.] sacked 5. (a) worker (b) is paid in cash/under the table

Cars

A. 1. amocher, bousiller 2. prendre le volant, se mettre au volant 3. chandelles (meaning "candles")

B. 1. le rodéo 2. le propergol 3. le chauffard 4. faire du stop 5. amazone 6. faire du lèche-cul 7. esquinter

C. 1. déglinguée 2. pas 3. diable 4. pédibus 5. pratique 6. pétrolette

D. 1. b, c, a 2. b, d, a, c 3. c, d, a, b 4. d, b, a, e, c

City

A. 1. gueuleton (m) 2. frichti (m) 3. beuverie (f) 4. casse-croûte (m) 5. tortore (f)

B. 1. store/shop 2. discount/special price 3. clothes/[Br.] gear 4. secondhand trade 5. secondhand dealer

C. 1. un maraudeur 2. le bahut/sapin/tacot 3. un copeau 4. une bouche de métral/de métro 5. un carnet

D. 1. faire un footing 2. se payer un piéton 3. brûler un feu rouge 4. faire le bitume/le macadam

E. 1. la Santaga 2. le Latin 3. Paname 4. la Raffinerie/l'Usine à gaz 5. le Poireau

Clothing

A. 1. être mal fagotée 2. avoir un look d'enfer 3. s'habiller en pingouin 4. être ficelée 5. être tirée à quatre épingles

B. 1. Mom/[Br.] Mummy is wearing a cheap dress. 2. He's a victim of fashion/ a slave to fashion. 3. She went to the Paris fashion shows. 4. Topless bathing is forbidden here. 5. I put on my sweat suit/tracksuit to go for my daily jog/run.

C. 1. une minouse 2. des écrase-merde 3. un zomblou 4. une serpillière 5. un string/un cache-frifri

D. 1. shoes 2. basketball shoes/[Br.] trainers 3. briefs/underpants 4. a shirt 5. stockings/nylons

Conversations and Invitations

A. 1. aller au chagrin, porter le pet 2. passer l'arme à gauche, avaler son bulletin de naissance 3. lever le coude 4. faire de la musique, renauder 5. il fait un temps de chien 6. un pébroque, un pépin 7. vos gueules! 8. gambiller, guincher 9. aller au cinoche 10. rencarder quelqu'un

B. au revoir—ciao; bonjour—salutas; bonjour, mes amis—salut, les gars; ça va—ça boume; je vous présente mes parents—voici mes vieux; manger—becter; le rhume/la grippe—la crève; le vent—le zef

Disputes

A. 1. d 2. g 3. a 4. f 5. b 6. c 7. e

B. 1—8—11; 2—9—16; 3—6—14; 5—7—10—15; 4—12—13

C. 1. He was putting his two cents in/[Br.] sticking his oar in (interfering). 2. He was pushing it! 3. He was getting me hopping mad! 4. He was looking for a fight! 5. I told him to mind his own business! 6. Then things started heating up . . . 7. and I gave him a slap. That's all!

Drinks

A. The captain found a drop of red for his number two. There was also some white rotgut/[Br.] gut-rot. It was too terrible! The captain had a glass of red as well. Afterwards, the servants cleared away the glasses.

B. 1. pot 2. baptise 3. arrosons 4. verre 5. cuve 6. aile 7. carburant 8. cinquante-et-un

C. 1. Would you like a pastis with grenadine? 2. After a beer with grenadine, I always get indigestion. 3. I had a light beer. 4. Look at that comedian with his liter of beer! 5. I'm a doctor, but I'm offering you some pastis. (*The pun on official poison is lost in the translation.*) 6. We'll both have a beer with mint syrup. 7. There's a fly in the champagne!

Education

1. h 2. k 3. b 4. a 5. e 6. j 7. g 8. i 9. n 10. d 11. o 12. c 13. l 14. f 15. m

Emotions

A. 1. con (j) 2. trouillomètre (h) 3. nickelés (i) 4. poing, gueule (a) 5. peau (c) 6. cinéma (d) 7. mousser (f) 8. cloque (e) 9. pisser (g) 10. fard, soleil (b)

B. 1. to be afraid, to shit(!) a brick, to be shit-scared(!) (scared shitless(!)) 2. to be afraid, to wet oneself (with fear) 3. to have one's head in the clouds 4. to look for a fight 5. in seventh heaven (to be over the moon)

Entertainment

A. 1. a wild party 2. a nightclub 3. a party/bash 4. a (young people's) party 5. an orgy 6. a local dance 7. a children's vacation camp 8. a lousy film

B. 1. ✗ 2. ✓ 3. ✗ 4. ✓ 5. ✗ 6. — 7. ✓ 8. ✓ 9. — 10. ✗

C. 1. We lived it up! 2. It brought the house down! 3. It wasn't (up to) much. 4. It was a (great) barrel of laughs! 5. As usual, coarse/gross and ridiculous! 6. It was a drag.

D. 1. jouer devant les banquettes 2. un frimant 3. les vieux routiers de la variété française 4. une bistouille 5. un bordel, un claque, un baisodrome 6. un saxo 7. sortir en boîte 8. courir les théâtres 9. jouer à guichets fermés 10. s'en jeter un derrière la cravate

E. 1. In this bar, they're all alkies/lushes/[Br.] dipsos. I don't really want to have (fancy having) my aperitif here. 2. In the nightclub/jazz club where we went, we wanted to dance to rap music but a jazzman and the bouncer/doorman told us to go somewhere else. 3. I wanted to do the rounds of the Paris theaters and see the big stars but my kid brother said that he preferred to go nightclubbing.

Food and Eating

A. 1. ✗ 2. — 3. ✗ 4. ✓ 5. ✓ 6. — 7. ✗ 8. ✗ 9. — 10. ✓ 11. ✗ 12. —

B. (*Below is a reasonable model for your side of the conversation. What you wrote may vary considerably and still be perfectly acceptable.*) 1. Je me gave de bricheton. 2. J'aime (bien) la soupe à l'oignon, mais je n'aime pas la lavasse! 3. Je voudrais manger du calendos. 4. J'aime bien les patates et les fayots.

C. (*Again, the material below is a reasonable model. What you have to say may vary in small ways and still be acceptable.*) 1. Are you hungry, Alex? 2. Great, let's chow down/[Br.] get stuck in, then! 3. What time do you eat at home, normally? 4. Don't pay any attention to our daughter. She eats like a horse! 5. And, as a contrast, our son just picks at his food! He's in love! 6. Well, Alex, we feed our faces here, don't we?

Foreigners

A. 1. d 2. h 3. f 4. b 5. g 6. e 7. c 8. a

B. 1. l'anglaise 2. maghrébin (marocain) 3. kiwi (néo-zélandais) 4. rosbifs/biftecks 5. porto, espagnole 6. nègre

Health

A. 6, 3, 8, 2, 7, 5, 1, 4

B. 1. e 2. f 3. b 4. g 5. c 6. a 7. d

C. 1. I went to see the quack. 2. Then I went to the hospital. 3. I thought I was dying! 4. The surgeon had me on the operating table. 5. And I didn't seem to have long to go! 6. But, now there's no stopping me!

Hobbies and Pastimes

A. 1. un(e) mordu(e) d'informatique 2. un(e) cinéphile 3. un bricoleur/une bricoleuse 4. un(e) accro du rap 5. un(e) fana de football 6. un(e) mordu(e) de lecture 7. un amateur de jazz 8. un(e) mélomane

B. 4, 6, 2, 1, 3, 5

C. 1. e 2. d 3. a 4. b 5. c

Human Body

A. 1. la moustache 2. la bite 3. la chatte

B. 1. cafetière 2. coffre 3. aile 4. éponge 5. citron 6. théière 7. plumes 8. piège 9. soufflet 10. prunes 11. radis 12. œufs sur le plat 13. as de trèfle

C. 1. She's got really big/great tits.(?) 2. I'm fed up to the back teeth (to here). 3. They've got no nuts(?)/balls(?). 4. He's always worn bell-bottoms/[Br.] flares/ flared trousers. 5. She's hooked a real sucker/mug. 6. He's racking his brains. 7. He's a good talker/He's got the gift of (the) gab.

Immigrants and Immigration

1. Ce clandestin est en situation irrégulière. 2. «Touche pas à mon pote» ont crié les beurs. 3. Le mullah/mollah est sorti de son HLM pour aller à la mosquée. 4. Les intégristes ont toujours un tapis de prière. 5. Le cloporte/concepige/ pipelet/la pipelette/le (la) concierge dit que beaucoup de locataires travaillent au noir mais qu'ils paient toujours leur loyer.

Information Technology

1. piratage 2. logiciel, logithèque 3. internaute, surfer 4. modem, e-mail 5. disque, fichier, disquette

Land and Countryside

A. 1. Colin Maillard 2. Frou-Frou Beljambe 3. Boris 4. Colette 5. Thierry Tomalin, Benjamin Lecadet

B. 1. Il faut revenir à terre. 2. Moi, je suis très terre à terre. 3. Elle ne touche pas terre! 4. Je resterai/vais rester sur terre ferme! 5. Ça va tout foutre par terre! 6. C'est un paradis sur terre!

The Movies

A. 1. c 2. d 3. f 4. a 5. b 6. e

B. 1—6; 3—10; 4—9; 2—7—11; 5—8

C. 4, 6, 2, 7, 5, 3, 1

Music

A. 1—12; 2—7; 3—10; 5—11; 8—9

B. 1. That singer deserves an (old) vinyl record, not a gold record! 2. For that kind of blaring music, you don't need a ghetto-blaster! 3. With that weird music, he ought to be playing at La Villette! 4. In their damn restaurant they make you listen to their bad musician/[Br.] muso! 5. That's not the Bastille Opera!

If you ask me, it's a rockers' (rock 'n' roll) gig! 6. He plays too slow on that squeeze-box of his! 7. You call them star quality? Not at all, they're nothing but rabble-rousers!

C. 1. feeling 2. amphi 3. accro 4. bémol 5. palmarès 6. chanson 7. explosé

D. 1. un slow 2. le swing 3. le tango 4. la tarentelle

E. en tête d'affiche; tube; chanter en play-back

F. 1. un Walkman 2. un skeud/squeud 3. aller faire dodo 4. sa boîte 5. un bobo

Names

A. 1. Alphonse, Étienne 2. Arthur, la Camarde, Ducon 3. Bastoche, Lutèce 4. Blanche-Neige 5. Tintin

B. 1. d 2. f 3. h 4. g 5. c 6. b 7. e 8. a

Press, Magazines, Books

A. 1. Apostrophes 2. Galligrasseuil 3. la PAO 4. CAO 5. la TAO 6. le BVP 7. IPSOS, l'IFOP

B. (*Possible answer*) Guy was wandering along the bookstalls on the Left Bank and found a book that was a pocket edition of a famous whodunnit. He spotted a publicity editorial in it, inviting the reader to the *L'Humanité* book festival, an invitation that he took up.

Regions and Francophone Countries

A. 1. Monsieur Bons Offices 2. Marianne 3. l'Arlésienne 4. les Belges 5. les Canaques 6. l'Élysée 7. France

B. 1. f 2. h 3. a 4. b 5. d 6. g 7. c 8. e

C. 1. du Maghreb 2. la Métropole 3. le noctambus 4. à Paname/en Lutèce 5. maquisarde 6. les TER 7. de souche

Romance

A. The suspect, one Jean Dax, has arrived at the Café Huron, looking for some chicks/[Br.] a bit of skirt. He's coming on to/[Br.] chatting up one of the hostesses. He's giving her the eye. She's making sheep's eyes at him. Ah, there's a problem now . . . The owner of the café is not happy. Dax is playing footsie with the girl. The owner is shouting "Stop staring at her!/[Br.] Wash your eyes out!" at Dax. He's not happy about the girl catching Dax's fancy/Dax coming on to the girl. Now there's a fight.

B. 1. d 2. c 3. h 4. a 5. f 6. g 7. b 8. e

C. 1. — 2. ✓ 3. ✗ 4. ✗ 5. — 6. ✗ 7. ✓ 8. ✓ 9. ✓ 10. —

Seaside and Mountains

A. foutre à poil; rôtir le cuir; maître nageur; topless; frimeur

B. 1. des lunettes de ski 2. des chaussures de ski 3. une combinaison de ski

C. 1. sailor, marine 2. the drink, the Naval College 3. tub, bucket (boat), broken-down machine (*in standard French*: clog; hoof [of cow, etc.]; wheel clamp)

D. 1. un(e) skieur(-euse) 2. un crawler 3. un(e) volleyeur(-euse)

Sex

A. 1. un gay 2. un lupanar, une maison close 3. une maladie honteuse

B. 1. l'enculage (m) 2. une gousse 3. la baise

C. 1. pimp (*merlan*) 2. whore, hooker (*morue*) 3. pimp or policeman (*hareng*) 4. dirty-minded, horny/[Br.] randy (*cochon/cochonne*) 5. male prostitute (*castor*) 6. passive and active homosexual (*bique et bouc*) 7. sex maniac (*chaud-lapin*)

D. 1. baiser(!) en épicier (not to enjoy screwing/a screw) 2. une puce travailleuse (a lesbian) 3. brouter le cresson (to perform cunnilingus) 4. arracher le copeau à quelqu'un (to get someone off, [Br.] to ring someone's bell) 5. être porté(e) sur la chose (to be obsessed with sex, to have a one-track mind) 6. marcher à la voile et à la vapeur (to be bisexual, to be AC/DC) 7. s'allonger le macaroni (to masturbate) 8. jouer de la mandoline (to jerk/[Br.] finger oneself [off]) 9. faire le trottoir (to be a hooker/streetwalker; [Br.] to be on the game) 10. le téléphone rose (telephone sex lines; phone sex chat lines)

Sports

A. 1. g 2. i 3. b 4. a 5. j 6. d 7. c 8. f 9. h 10. e

B. 1. charger la mule 2. allumer le goal 3. donner de l'effet à sa balle 4. balle de match 5. jouer au ping-pong 6. un coureur de demi-fond 7. raccrocher 8. être déclaré bon pour le service 9. jouer sur terre 10. faire des/quelques balles

Travel and Transportation

A. 1. France 2. England 3. the USA 4. Russia 5. America 6. England 7. China 8. Dagoland (*Please remember that most of these expressions can be offensive and even racist.*)

B. 3, 7, 5, 4, 1, 6, 2

C. 1. ✗ 2. ✗ 3. ✓ 4. ✗ 5. ✓ 6. ✓ 7. ✗ 8. ✗

Vacations

1. guitoune, vacs 2. mahomet, rôtir le cuir 3. cogne, surf, planche 4. voile *or* planche à voile, parapente

Verlan

A. 1. français 2. café 3. jeter 4. un mec 5. bizarre 6. un pourri 7. un sac (= 10 fr) 8. le gazon (= herb, grass, weed) 9. un disque 10. maigre

B. 1. c 2. f 3. h 4. b, e 5. a 6. i 7. d 8. g

C. 1. Did you see the girl with her old man? 2. That blouson is expensive! 3. They played some way-out music at the party! 4. He gave the corrupt/[Br.] bent cop 10,000 francs. 5. The chick was stoned out of her skin! 6. The cop disappeared into the subway. 7. The hooker/[Br.] slag nicked his last 10 francs from him. 8. He was French with (a) thin mug/chops.

Weather

A. 1. b 2. d 3. a 4. a 5. d 6. c 7. a 8. c

B. 1. b, d, c, a 2. d, c, a, b 3. b, d, a, c 4. c, d, b, a

C. 1. There's a wind coming/[Br.] getting up! 2. It's bitterly cold/freezing! 3. It's raining cats and dogs! 4. It's not fit for a dog! 5. That's God relieving himself! 6. It's blowing a gale!

The World of Work

A. 1. f 2. h 3. e 4. a 5. g 6. d 7. c 8. b

B. 1—12; 2—11; 3—14; 4—9—13; 5—7—10; 6—8

C. 1. e 2. d 3. a 4. b 5. f 6. c

Bibliography

Blum, Geneviève. *The Idiomatics*. Paris: Éditions du Seuil, 1989.

Brunet, François and McCavana, Declan. *Dictionnaire bilingue de l'argot d'aujourd'hui. Bilingual Dictionary of Today's Slang. Français-anglais, anglais-français*. Paris: Pocket (Langues pour tous), 2nd edition, 1996.

Caradec, François. *Dictionnaire du français argotique et populaire*. Paris: Larousse, 1998.

Chiflet, Jean-Loup. *Sky my husband! Ciel mon mari!* Paris: Éditions Hermé, 1985.

Chiflet, Jean-Loup. *Sky my wife! Ciel ma femme!* Paris: Carrère, 1989.

Colin, Jean-Paul, Mével, Jean-Pierre, Leclère, Christian. *Dictionnaire de l'argot*. Paris: Larousse, 1994; new edition Larousse-Bordas, 1997.

Geneviève. *The Complete Merde! The REAL French You Were Never Taught at School*. London: HarperCollins Publishers (paperback edition), 1996.

Levieux, Michel and Eleanor. *Beyond the Dictionary in French. A Handbook of Colloquial Usage*. London: Cassell and Company, 1967; fifth impression (with revisions), 1974.

Levieux, Michel and Eleanor. *Insiders' French. Beyond the Dictionary*. Chicago and London: The University of Chicago Press, 1999.

Pierron, Agnès. *Dictionnaire des expressions populaires*. Paris: Éditions Marabout, 1999.

Pilard, Georges and Stevenson, Anna (eds). *Harrap's Slang. Anglais-français/français-anglais*. Edinburgh: Chambers Harrap, 1998.

French-English Dictionary/Index

French-English Dictionary/Index

Numbers cross-refer to entries in the main thesaurus, where further details on literal translations, register, and usage, example sentences, and related terms may be found.

Note: The following words are not alphabetized within an entry:

definite and indefinite articles: **la, le, l', les, un, une, des;**
the prepositions **à, au, aux, en;**
the possessive adjectives **mon, ma, mes, son, sa, ses;**
avoir, être, and their conjugated forms;
quelqu'un.

A

les abattis (mpl) limbs 125; arms 126
abîmer le portrait de/à quelqu'un to bash someone's face in 67, 90
accaparer la vedette to hog the limelight 149
l'accro (f/m) nut, fanatic 120; **l'accro** (f/m) **du rap** raphead 120; **un/une accro du jazz** jazz freak 151
être accro à to be hooked on, to be a fan of 120
l'adaptation (f) **à l'écran** screen adaptation 147
l'adresse (f) address 140
être adroit(e) de ses mains to be good with one's hands 121
l'affairisme (m) wheeling and dealing 30
un affairiste wheeler-dealer 30
être à l'affiche to be on the bill 155
affûter la forme to get into top shape 22
affûter un athlète to bring an athlete to the top of his/her form 194
l'afro afro 130
agacer le sous-préfet to masturbate 189
les agates (fpl) eyes 130
l'agent (m) agent 155
les agobilles (fpl) testicles 128
l'aile (f) arm 125
l'aileron (m) arms 126
aimer son pinard to like one's wine 70
avoir l'air con to look (bloody) stupid 88
avoir l'air tout chose to look really peculiar 114
les airbags (mpl) breasts 131
Albion (la perfide) (Perfidious) Albion (England) 201
l'alcool blanc (m) colorless spirit(s) 93
l'alcoolo (m) alkie, lush, [Br.] dipso, souse 93
l'alfa (m) hair 126
aller au chagrin to lodge/register/put in a complaint 55
aller dans les décors to go crashing off the road 17, 204
aller faire dodo to go beddy-bye, [Br.] to go to beddy-byes 154
aller faire un malheur to be about to blow it, to do something nasty 64
aller à pince(s) to go on foot, [Br.] to leg it, [Br.] to travel by Shanks's pony 202
aller au ski to go skiing 181
aller tout doux to be fair/middling 114
allonger une baffe/gifle à quelqu'un to give someone a slap 65
les allonges (fpl) arms 126
allumer to arouse (sexually) 197
allumer le goal to shoot straight at the goalkeeper 197
allumer les flics to watch out for the cops 197
l'allumeuse (f) cock-teaser, prick-teaser 188
Alphonse: téléphoner à Alphonse to go to the john 159
l'amateur (m) filmgoer, cinema goer 147
l'amateur (m) **de** fan of, into 120; **être grand amateur de** to be into . . . in a big way 120
l'amateur de jazz jazz fan 120
l'amazone (f) prostitute who works from a car 35, 190

un amerloque, un amerluche Yank 111
amocher quelqu'un to bash/smash someone's face in 66
amocher la bagnole, amocher la tire to smash up one's car 35
amocher un phare to smash a headlight/ [Br.] headlamp 34
les amortisseurs (mpl) breasts 131
l'amphi (m) lecture hall 85; music hall, stadium 151
amuser Charlot to masturbate 189
l'andouille (f) dork, jerk 88
l'âne: Il est monté comme un âne. He's got a really big prick/dick. 12
être aux anges to be in seventh heaven, [Br.] to be over the moon 89
l'anorexie (f) **mentale** anorexia 22
l'apéro (m) aperitif 93
Apostrophes literary talk show on French TV 164
l'appart (m) apartment, [Br.] flat 97
avoir un appétit d'oiseau to eat like a bird 106
appuyer sur le champignon to put your foot down on the accelerator 203
l'araignée: Elle a une araignée au plafond. She has bats in the belfry. 13
l'arbalète (f) penis 127
l'arche (f) bottom, ass 132
l'ardillon (m) penis 127
l'ardoise (f) credit (in a bar), [Br.] slate 93
l'Arlésienne the invisible man or woman, character 167
une armoire à glace, une armoire normande well-built man, hunk 22
l'Armor coastal Brittany 167
l'arnaque (f) scam, racket, caper 30
arnaquer to scam, to rip off 30
l'arpète (m), **l'arpette** (m) bricklayer's apprentice/laborer 27
l'arpion (m) foot 128
arracher le copeau (à quelqu'un) to get someone off 186
arracher son copeau to come, to get it off 186
arranger le portrait de/à quelqu'un to rearrange someone's face 67, 90
l'arrière-train (m) bottom, ass 132
arroser to water, to wash down 72
arroser un événement to celebrate an event 72
Arte culture vulture 16
Arthur: se faire appeler Arthur to get bawled out, to get your head bitten off 159
l'artiche (m) bottom, ass 132
l'as (m) **de trèfle** anus 132
les aspects (mpl) **pratiques** hard work, nitty-gritty 224
l'asperge (f) penis 127
des asperges (f) shoes, high heels; also, penis, "beanpole" 51
l'assiette (f)**: ne pas être dans son assiette** to be under the weather 56, 114
astap hysterical, sidesplitting 98
astiquer quelqu'un to bring someone off, to play with someone 189
les Athéniens: C'est là que les Athéniens s'atteignirent. That's when things started to go downhill. 159
avoir les atomes crochus to hit it off 174
attaquer to start 107
attendre jusqu'à la Saint-Glinglin to wait till Doomsday 162
attraper to tell someone off 64
attraper la crève to catch a stinking/nasty cold 56
l'aubergine (f) red nose; female traffic warden, meter maid 131
une augmentation mammaire breast enlargement 21
augmenter le rendement d'un athlète to improve an athlete's performance 192
aujourd'hui c'est la canicule it's a real scorcher today 57
l'autobus (m) trailing group (of riders) 195
l'autoroute (f) **saturée** overcrowded freeway/[Br.] motorway 202
avaler le pépin to get pregnant 57
avaler son bulletin de naissance to kick the bucket 56
les avantages (mpl) breasts 131
l'avant-scène (f) bust 131
avoir quelqu'un to take someone for a ride 176

B

le baba bottom, ass 132
le babin mouth 131
les babines (fpl) lips 131
les babouines (fpl) lips 131
le/la babtou Frenchman, -woman 211
le bac, le bachot the baccalaureate 78
les bacantes/bacchantes (fpl) moustache 125

le bachelier, la bachelière student who has passed the bac 78
le bachotage cramming 78
bachoter to cram for an exam 78
le bachoteur, la bachoteuse student cramming for an exam 78
les badigoinces (fpl) lips 130
la badine legs 133
la baffe slap (on/in the face) 65
la baffi moustache 126
bâfrer to feed one's face, to pig out, [Br.] to pig oneself 107
le bâfreur, une bâfreuse hog, glutton, [Br.] greedy guts 107
le bagad Breton (pipe) band 156
la bagarre brawl, scrap 66, 82; **c'est la bagarre** to have it in for 66
le bagne sweatshop, salt mine 221
bagot(t)er to walk, to go on foot 44
les bagougnasses (fpl) lips 131
la bagouse, la bague anus 132
les baguettes (fpl) hair 126, legs 133
le bahut senior high school 78, 79; taxi 42
le baigneur bottom, ass 132
la baille drink 180; **tous à la baille!** everyone into the water/[Br.] the drink! 180
la baise fucking, screwing 186
baiser quelqu'un to bang 186
baiser en canard to fuck doggie fashion 186
baiser en cygne to fuck with the woman's legs on the man's shoulders 186
baiser en épicier not to enjoy screwing 186
baiser en hussard/à la hussarde to have a quick screw 186
baiser en levrette to fuck doggie fashion 186
baiser à la papa to have a slow screw, to have the hots for someone 186
baiser à la riche to have anal sex 186
le baiseur, la baiseuse horndog, [Br.] randy/horny bugger 186
le baisodrome brothel, whorehouse 94, 188, 190
un baladeur a Walkman 151
le balai à chiottes moustache 126
être balaise/balèze/balèse en informatique to be a computer whiz kid/whiz 139
la balayette penis 127
la balayeuse long hair 130
le balcon bust 130, 131; **y a du monde au balcon** she's got great tits 134
une balle money 26
balle (f) **de break/set/match** break/set/match point 198
les ballochards (mpl) breasts 131
les balloches (fpl) testicles 128
avoir le ballon to be pregnant 87, 177
le baloche local dance 97
la bamboula wild party 97
un bamboula wog 112
la banane French plait; [of man] teddy-boy haircut 130
Bande (f) **d'enculés!** What a load of fucking dickheads! 184
bander to have an erection 13, 186
bander: ne bander que d'une to be afraid 89
bander mou to be afraid 89
la banlieue suburbs 167
baptiser son vin to dilute one's wine 72
baquer to go for a dip 98
le baquet stomach 127
la baraque cowboy firm, crap company; pad 28
baratiner quelqu'un to come on to someone 173
la barbaque tough meat 105
la barbe drag 99; **Quelle barbe!** What a drag!/[Br.] What a bloody bore! 3
le barbeau pimp 190
le barbillon small-time/young pimp 190
barboter le copain/la copine à quelqu'un to steal someone's boyfriend/girlfriend 177
le barbouilleur painter 27
la barbouse/barbouze beard 125
le barbouze plainclothes cop 67
le barbu pubic hair 132
barder: Ça barde. Things are heating up. 63; **Ça va barder.** There's going to be trouble. 64
le barsli briefs, underpants 52
le basket basketball 195
des basks (fpl) basketball shoes, [Br.] trainers 51
la Bastaga/la Bastoche Bastille area of Paris 45, 159
la baston free-for-all, [Br.] punch-up 82
le bavard bottom, ass 132
la bavarde tongue 131
le Baz Grand lycée Louis-le-Grand 45
BCBG preppy, [Br.] Sloane(-ranger) 8

BD cartoon, comic strip 8
le/du beau linge beautiful people, celebs, top people 15, 48
Beau temps pour la saison. Nice weather we're having. 215
beauf redneck, square; brother-in-law 17, 139
le beaujolpif Beaujolais 74
la bébine weak, poor quality wine 70
la bécane computer 159; bike, bicycle 195, 202
un bécot a kiss 177
becqueter to grab a bite (to eat) 40, 59, 107
becqueter de l'aile to lean on the fender/[Br.] wing of a car 195
la bectance meal, food 41
becter to grab a bite (to eat) 40, 59, 107
la bédé (strip-)cartoon 147
avoir le béguin pour quelqu'un to have a crush on someone 175
les Belges Belgians 167
ma belle my beautiful 177
un bémol flat [mus.], damper, downer, [Br.] dampener 152
le bénard pants, trousers 49
le bénouze briefs, underpants 52
la Bérézina disaster 99, 159
avoir la berlue to be seeing things 91
des bernicles (fpl), **des besicles** (fpl) glasses, [Br.] specs 52
berzingue: à tout berzingue at top speed, like sixty, [Br.] like the clappers 36
à la besogne let's get to work 221
besogner to screw/[Br.] shaft 221
le beur, la beurette second-generation Arab 111, 136, 167
le beurre money 26
être beurré(e) to be drunk/plastered 72
la beuverie binge, [Br.] piss-up 40
la BGV fast food 40
un bic Arab 111
ma biche my darling 177
le biclo, le biclou bike, bicycle 195
la bicoque jerry-built house 28
un bicot Arab 111
la bide stomach, belly 125
le bide failure, flop 17, 147
le bidochard pimp 190
la bidoche meat 105
le bidon stomach 127
bidonnant(e) hysterical(ly funny), sidesplitting 99
être bien en point to be fit, healthy 115
bien tassé a good measure 75
le biffeton, le bifton ticket, banknote, doctor's prescription 44
un bifteck Brit, Englishman 111
les bijoux (mpl) **de famille** sex(ual) organs 128
le bikini bikini 52
le billard operating table 117
la bille head 126
la binette head 126
le biniou Breton bagpipe 156
mon biquet, ma biquette my love 14
la biroute penis 127
une bise a kiss 177
le bison futé wily (wise) buffalo 202
un bisou a kiss 177
la bistouille mixture of coffee and alcohol 93
la bistouquette penis 127
le bistro(t), le bistroquet watering hole, bar, pub 93
le bistrot bar owner; bar 28
le bistrot du coin local (watering hole) 93
la bite penis 127
le bitos hat, [Br.] tifter 49
le bizut, le bizuth freshman, first-year student, [Br.] fresher 80
le bizutage hazing, [Br.] ragging 80
bizuter to haze/[Br.] rag a freshman 80
black, blanc, beur racist tricolor 167
les blagues (fpl) **à tabac** drooping breasts 131
le blair nose 130
le/la Blanche-Neige coon, wog 159
le blase/blaze nose 131
le blé money 26
le bled village, small town, dump 142
les Bleus (mpl) French rugby team 198
blindé(e) drunk, plastered 73
blinder to bomb/[Br.] belt along 36
la bloblote fear 88
avoir la bloblote to be afraid 89
la blonde light beer 74
le blot discount, special price 41
la B.N. French National Library 85
Bobino concert hall in Paris 153
le bobo [to/from small children] hurt, sore 116; sore, cut 154
un boche Kraut 111
un bœuf: souffler comme un bœuf to fight for one's breath 12

À boire! Give me a drink! 4
boire un coup to have a drink 59, 71
boire la goutte (to have) a drop of brandy 74
la boîte workplace, firm, business, school 30, 32, 79, 221; the can 147
la boîte à bachot cram(ming) school 78
la boîte aux lettres vagina 132
la boîte à mensonges mouth 131
la boîte de nuit nightclub 30, 95, 97
la boîte à ragoût stomach 127
les boîtes (fpl) **à lait** breasts 131
le/la boit-sans-soif drunkard 72
le bol bottom, ass 132
avoir du bol to be in luck 90
le bolide rocket, fast car 35
la bombarde type of Breton oboe 156
bomber to bomb/[Br.] belt along 36
Le Bon Dieu lâche un vent! There's a wind coming/getting up! 218
le bonbon clitoris 133
les bonbons (mpl) testicles 128
le bonhomme penis 127
le bordel brothel, whorehouse 94, 97, 190
la borne kilometer 35
le boss boss, director 28
bosser to work (hard), [Br.] to slog 85, 222
botter les fesses à quelqu'un to kick someone up the ass 66
la bouche de métral/métro subway/underground entrance 44
la bouffe chow, food, grub 40, 104
bouffer to grab a bite (to eat) 40, 107
bouffer comme un chancre to eat like a horse 107
bouffer à la pelle to shovel it down 108
bouffer du pédé to gay-bash, to go queer-bashing 185
le bouffeur pig, [Br.] guzzler 107
un bougnoule Arab, wog 111, 112
le boui-boui brothel; cheap café 94
le Boul' Mich Boulevard St-Michel, Latin Quarter 45, 160
la Boulange aux faffes La Banque de France, the Bank of France 26
Les boules! Scary!/It scared me to death! 5
avoir les boules to shit a brick 89
les boules (fpl) **de loto** eyes 130
boulonner to work (hard) 32, 222
le boulot work, job 32, 221
le boulot peinard easy job, [Br.] cushy number 221
le boulot précaire casual/occasional job with no security 31
la boum (young people's) party, dance 81, 97
le bouquin book 85, 164
bouquiner to read; to frequent the bouquiniste stalls 164
le/la bouquiniste bookstall holder 164
bourge classy/[Br.] Sloane-rangerish 8
être à la bourre to be short of time 60
bourré(e) drunk/plastered 4, 73
être bourré(e) de fric to be filthy rich 27
bousiller sa bagnole to wreck one's car 34
bousiller sa voiture to pile up/crash one's car 205
la boustif poor/nasty grub 104
la boustiffe, la boustifaille chow, food, grub 40, 104
le bout penis 127
au bout du monde out in the boonies, [Br.] at the back of beyond 142
la boutanche bottle 74
la boutique sex(ual) organs 125; vagina 132
le bouton clitoris 133
les brancards (mpl) legs 133
branché(e) with it, trendy, [Br.] switched on 16
brancher to interest, to turn on 16
le brandillon arms 126
le brandon penis 127
branler quelqu'un to play with someone, [Br.] to bring someone off 189
le braquemart penis 127
le brasseur, la brasseuse breast-stroke swimmer 198
la brêle scooter, moped; fathead, jerk, [Br.] tosspot 35
la Brésilienne transvestite or transsexual Brazilian prostitute 160
le bricheton bread 105
le bricolage home improvement, do-it-yourself/[Br.] DIY 121
bricoler to go in for home improvement/do-it-yourself 120; to masturbate 120
être bricoleur(-euse) to be good with your hands 120
le bricoleur, la bricoleuse home-improvement/[Br.] DIY enthusiast 120
un bridé Chinaman 111
la briffe food, meal 41

brimer quelqu'un to haze/bully someone 80
la brioche stomach 127
une brique 10,000 francs 26
le broc, le broco secondhand goods dealer 42
la brocante secondhand trade 42
la brocasse secondhand goods 42
le Bronx: mettre le Bronx là-dedans to make a (right) mess of it 160
la brousse sticks, boonies, [Br.] the back of beyond 142
brouter le cresson/la motte to perform cunnilingus 185
brouter la tige to perform fellatio 185
la brouteuse lesbian 185
brûler le dur to travel on the subway/tube/train without a ticket 44
brûler un feu rouge to go through a red light 36, 44
brutaliser quelqu'un to bully someone 80
bûcher to work hard, [Br.] to graft, to cram 85, 222
bûcheur hardworking, [Br.] grafting 222
le buffet stomach 127; **n'avoir rien dans le buffet** to have no guts 129
le burelain office worker 30
les burettes (fpl) testicles 128
le burlain, le burlin office worker 30
les burnes (fpl) testicles 128
buter quelqu'un to bump somebody off 91
le buveur, la buveuse drinker 72
le BVP French advertising standards commission 164
Byzance: C'est Byzance. It's the last word in luxury. 160

C

câblé(e) with it, trendy, [Br.] switched on 16
la caboche head 126
le cabot mutt, pooch, doggy; boss, [Br.] gaffer 13
le cabotin, une cabotine ham actor 147
le cache-frifri G-string, skimpy panties 52
un cache-sexe G-string 52
le cachet the takings 96
le cachetonneur, la cachetonneuse pick-up/[Br.] jobbing actor/actress 96
les cadavres (mpl) empties 71
le cador mutt, pooch, doggy; boss, [Br.] gaffer 13, 28
le cadre executive, manager 222
les cadres (m) management, the management team, the bosses 222
avoir le cafard to feel blue, to have the blues 56, 176
le café-calva coffee with calvados 93
la cafetière head 125
la cage, les cages goals 197
la cage à lapins [apartments, etc.] rabbit hutch 85
la cage à poules jungle gym, [Br.] climbing frame 82
le cahier d'appel attendance register/sheet 80
le cahier de cours exercise book, workbook 80
le cahier de devoirs notebook, homework book 82
le cahier de textes homework notebook/diary, journal 82
cailler: Je me caille! I'm freezing! 218; **Ça caille!** It's freezing cold! 218
la caillera scum 211
le caillou head 126
la caisse old car 35; head 126
le caisson head 126; **se faire sauter le caisson** to blow one's brains out 128
le calbar boxer shorts 52
calcer quelqu'un to bang 186
le calcif briefs, underpants 52
les Caldoches white New Caledonians 167
le calebar boxer shorts 52
le calendos Camembert 105
caler to be full 108
le calfouette boxer shorts 52
le calot eyes 130
la calouse legs 133
la calpette tongue 131
le calva calvados (apple brandy) 74
la Camarde: La Camarde l'attend. Death is waiting for him. 160
la cambrousse countryside 142
la camelote worthless goods, junk, [Br.] trash gear 30
les Canaques indigenous, Melanesian population of Nouvelle Calédonie 167
mon canard duck 14
le caneçon boxer shorts 52
caner to be afraid; to die, to give up 89
la canicule: C'est la canicule! It's a heat wave! 217; **Quelle canicule!** What a heat wave! 217
la canne legs 133
canon stunning, a stunning chick 22

la CAO CAD (computer-aided design) 164
caper un joueur to select a player for the national team, [Br.] to cap a player 199
le capésien, la capésienne holder of the CAPES 79
la capote anglaise rubber, condom, [Br.] French letter 188
le carafon head 126
le carambolage pile-up 205
le carburant drink that keeps you going 74
la carne (tough) meat 105
le carnet (de tickets) book of ten tickets 44
le caroline bottom man, butt boy, transvestite 184
la Caroline du Nord/du Sud homosexual 184
la carotte (soprano) saxophone 94
carotter to swindle, to con 30
des carreaux (mpl) glasses, [Br.] specs 52; eyes 130
la carte orange long-term ticket for public transportation in the Paris region 44
la casbah place, pad 97
casquer to cough up, to fork out 98
la casse (bodily) violence, broken bones 64
casse-couilles annoying, pain-in-the-neck 62
le casse-croûte snack, sandwich 40, 104
le casse-dalle sandwich, [Br.] butty, [Br.] sarny 105
le casse-graine snack 104
casse-pieds annoying, pain-in-the-neck 62
casser la baraque to bring the house down 99
casser les couilles à quelqu'un to get on someone's nerves 62
casser la croûte to have a bite to eat, to snack 104
casser la figure à quelqu'un to bash/ smash someone's face in 66
casser la graine to have a bite to eat 108
casser la gueule à quelqu'un to beat somebody up, to smash somebody's face in 66, 90
casser: ne pas casser des briques not to be up to much 99
casser du pédé to gay-bash, to go queer-bashing 185
casser les pieds à quelqu'un to get on someone's nerves 62
casser sa pipe to die, to kick the bucket 117
casser le portrait à quelqu'un to bash/smash someone's face in 66
casser la tronche à quelqu'un to bash/smash someone's face in 66
le cassis head 126
la castagne fighting, [Br.] punch-up 90
Castle-Pump water 160
le castor male prostitute, homosexual 184
céfran (adj.) French 211
le centre vagina 132
le cerf: bander comme un cerf to get a real hard-on 13
la chaille tooth 131
le chameau: être un vrai chameau to be a nasty piece of work 13
le champ champagne, bubbly 74
les Champs (m) the Champs-Élysées 45, 160
la chandelle very high kick ahead, [Br.] up-and-under, [Br.] Gary Owen 199
changer de boîte to change labels/record companies 155
changer de disque to change the record 153
chanter en play-back to lip-sync, to mime 155
le chantier building site 28
le chapeau de soleil sun hat 52
le char old car 35
charger la mule to take drugs 195
les charmeuses (fpl) moustache 126
charrier un prof to hassle a teacher 81
le châsse eyes 130
le châssis (woman's) body 130
le chat: appeler un chat un chat to call a spade a spade 12
le chat: avoir d'autres chats à fouetter to have other fish to fry/better things to do 12
le chat: C'est du pipi de chat. It's undrinkable. 12
le chat: avoir un chat dans la gorge to have a frog in one's throat 12
le chat: Il n'y a pas un chat. There's not a soul about. 12
le chat: Il n'y a pas de quoi fouetter un chat. It's not worth making a fuss about it. 12
le chat: vivre comme chien et chat to go at it like cat and dog 12
le Château-la-Pompe (tap) water 160
la chatte vagina 132

la chaude-lance, la chtouille VD, the clap, the pox 190
le chaud-lapin sex maniac 187
la chaude-pince, la chaude-pisse VD, the clap, the pox 190
le chauffard road hog, dangerous driver 36, 44, 204
chauffer: Ça va chauffer. There's going to be trouble. 64
les chaussures (fpl) **de basket** basketball shoes, [Br.] trainers 195
des chaussures (fpl) **de jogging** running shoes, [Br.] trainers 51
le chauve à col roulé penis 127
chébran with it, trendy, [Br.] switched on 16, 99, 211
le chèque en bois bad check/cheque, a check/cheque that bounces 26
un chèque sans provision bad check/cheque 26
le chèqueton check/cheque 26
chercher la bagarre to look for a fight 66
chercher des crosses to look for trouble 90
chercher de la fesse to go looking for a bit of skirt/the other/[Br.] crumpet 173
chercher un peu de fesse to look/go looking for a bit of skirt/[Br.] some crumpet 189
chercher le rif/rififi to look for a fight 90
mon chéri, ma chérie my darling, love, sweetie-pie 14, 177
la chetron chops, face, mug 211
le cheval: Il est monté comme un cheval. He's hung like a horse. 12
les chevaux: monter sur ses grands chevaux to get on one's high horse 13
chez les Ricains in the States 201
chialer to cry, to blubber 88
le/la chialeur(-euse) whiner, crybaby 88
chiant(e) dead (utterly) boring 99
la chiasse fear 88
avoir la chiasse to be scared shitless 89
le chien: être chien avec quelqu'un to be nasty to someone 13
le chien: Elle a du chien. She's a real good looker. 13
le chien: Je lui garde un chien de ma chienne. I've been wanting to get even with him. 13
le chien: Je me suis donné un mal de chien pour te rembourser. I've done everything. 13
le chien: Quel métier de chien! What a crummy job! 13
le chien: Quelle chienne de vie! Life's a bitch! 13
la chienlit utter shambles 99
chier dans son froc/sa culotte to shit a brick 89
la chignole old car 35
la chine secondhand trade 42
chiner to hunt around for antiques/secondhand goods 42
un chinetoque Chinaman 111
chinois: c'est plutôt chinois it's pretty difficult 112
le chinois penis 127
la chiotte shithouse; old car; motor scooter 35
la chipolata penis 127
un chleuh Kraut 111
chocotter to tremble with fear 89
avoir les chocottes to be afraid 89
être au chômage/au chômedu, être chômedu to be unemployed/[Br.] on the dole/out of work 31
choper la chtouille to get a dose of the clap 190
choper la crève to catch a stinking/nasty cold 56
mon chou my darling, love, sweetie-pie 177
la choucroute curly hairdo, beehive 130
la chouette anus 132
la chouille party, bash 97
chouiller to party 98
la choune vagina 132
la choupette tuft 130
la chtouille VD, the clap 191
Chut! Quiet! 7
Ciao! Ta-ta!, Bye(-bye)! 60
le ciel: être au septième ciel to be on cloud nine 89
le cigare à moustaches penis 127
la Cigogne law courts, the police headquarters 44
le ciné, le cinoche flicks, movies 59, 147
le/la cinéphile film buff 120, 147
le cinoche movies 97
le cinq-à-sept quick screw during the day 186
le cinquante-et-un pastis 74

le cirque: Quel cirque pour sortir du supermarché. What a hassle/drag getting out of the supermarket. 94
le cirque d'hiver winter circus 94
la cité phocéenne Marseille 170
le citron head 126; **se creuser le citron** to rack one's brains 128
la citrouille head 126
clamecer to die, to kick the bucket 117
le clandestin illegal worker/immigrant 136
le clapet mouth 130; **ferme ton clapet** shut your face 133
le claque brothel, whorehouse 94, 190
claquer to die, to kick the bucket 117
la clarinette penis 127
le clébard, le clebs mutt, pooch, doggy 13
avoir la cliche to be scared shitless 89
la cliche fear 88
le clicli clitoris 133
le clip clip, videoclip 147
la cliquette clitoris 133
le clito clitoris 133
le cloporte janitor/concierge/caretaker 137
être en cloque to be pregnant 87
cloquer le nase/le naze to get/to pass on a dose of the clap 56
le clou old car 35
le club de remise en forme spa, health club/[Br.] farm 24
le club des supporte(u)rs fan/ [Br.] supporters' club 199
le c.m. lecture 84
avoir le cocard to have a black eye 116
le cochon piggy 11; **Ce qu'il a fait, c'est un travail de cochon.** He's made a mess of it. [Br.] He's made a pig's ear of it. 11
cochon/cochonne (adj.) dirty-minded, horny/[Br.] randy 187
mon coco, ma cocotte my darling, love, sweetie-pie 177
la cocotte hen 11
ma cocotte chicken, honey 14
le cocu cuckold 187
cocufier to cheat on one's male partner 176
le coffre chest 125
cogner: ça cogne it's scorching hot 209; **cogner (quelqu'un)** to beat (someone) up 209
le coiffe-tifs hairdresser 23
être du coin to be local, from (a)round here 143, 202
coincer la bulle to do nothing, [Br.] to do sweet Felicity Arkwright (FA) 222
le colas neck 131
le colbac neck 130
collant(e) skintight, tight fitting, clinging 48
coller un PV à quelqu'un to book someone 84
la colo children's summer camp 97
avoir les colombins to be afraid 89
la coloquinte head 126
le combinard wheeler-dealer 30
la combine scam, racket, caper 30
la comédie musicale musical 147
comme ci comme ça so-so, fair to middling 114
comme un combat de nègres dans un tunnel as clear as mud 112
comment va la santé? how are you? [Br.] how are you keeping? 55
le commerçant (market) trader, shopkeeper 42
le compas legs 133
Complètement dingue! Absolute nutcase! [Br.] Barking mad! 6
la comptine nursery rhyme 154
le con vagina 132
le concepige janitor/concierge/caretaker 137
le conducteur/la conductrice du dimanche weekend/Sunday driver 204
le conseil de classe staff meeting 80
la conso drink (in a bar, café, or club) 74
le contrecoup foreman 27
des contrées lointaines (fpl) distant parts 143
contrefiche (f) foreman 27
contrôler un athlète to test an athlete 192
convoler to get hitched, to tie/[Br.] splice the knot 175
le copeau short journey, trip 42
avoir les copeaux to be afraid 89
le coq: sauter du coq à l'âne to jump from one subject to another 11
la coquette penis 127
la corde à sauter skipping rope, jump rope 82
le cornet stomach 127
la cosse laziness, idleness 222
le costard suit 51
couci-couça so-so, fair to middling 55

D

le dada horsey, [Br.] gee-gee 11
la dalle mouth 131; **avoir la dalle** to be hungry 106
avoir quelqu'un dans la peau to be smitten by someone 174
dans une merde noire up shit creek 142
dans les parages in the vicinity 142
dans le secteur in the area; [Br.] roundabouts 142
être dans les vapes to be out for the count (with drink, drugs, etc.), out cold 116
danser le swing to jive, to swing dance 154
danser un slow to do a slow dance 154
le dard penis 127
le dargeot bottom, ass 132
le dargif bottom, ass 132
le darrac penis 127
la DATAR Metropolitan France government agency for regional development 168
la daube pits, end 147
le dé à coudre anus 132
être déclaré(e) bon pour le service to be declared/passed fit 196
déconner to cause trouble, to act up, [Br.] to play up 116
en décor naturel on location 17
décrocher un titre mondial to win a world title 192
le défilé de mannequins fashion parade 50
défoncer to work hard 43
défoncer la plaque to work beyond permitted hours 43
défoncer le portrait à quelqu'un to bash somebody's face in, to rearrange someone's features 90
la défonceuse penis 127
déglingué(e) bust, busted, falling apart, [Br.] knackered 35
dégobiller to vomit, to puke 117
dégringole: Ça dégringole. It's raining cats and dogs. [Br.] It's chucking it down. 216
le dégringoleur cyclist who is fast downhill/in descents 195
dégueuler to vomit, to puke 117
le dégueuloir mouth 131
le déj breakfast 104
le délire great success 147
avoir le démon de midi to be suffering from the male menopause, midlife crisis 187
avoir les dents du fond qui baignent to have pigged out, to be full to bursting 108
dépasser: Ça dépasse l'échelle! It's going off the scale! [high temperatures] 217
dépoter to go like a bomb/the wind 36
le dernier cri latest fashion 48
descendre quelqu'un to do in, to kill, to bump off, to knock off someone 67
la descente: avoir une sacrée descente to be able to put it away/knock it back 72
destroy blaring, loud, violent [music] 151
la deuche Citroën 2CV (2 horsepower) 35
le DEUG university diploma 83
être à deux doigts de la mort to be at death's door 56
le devoir homework exercise, paper 82
le devoir sur table class or written test 80
les devoirs (mpl) homework 82
le diable au volant devil at the wheel 36
au diable vauvert stuck out in the sticks, miles from anywhere 142
le diaphragme diaphragm, [Br.] Dutch cap 188
le/la difficile picky/[Br.] faddy eater 107
être dingue de quelqu'un to be mad about someone 174
dire des personnalités to talk about someone, to bad-mouth 63
le directeur, la directrice headmaster, headmistress, principal 81, director, supervisor (of hall, etc.) 85
le dirlo director 16
le disco disco music 95
la discothèque discotheque 95
un disque noir/vinyle long-playing record 151
un disque d'or gold record, [Br.] golden disc 153
le dix anus 132
le doctorat doctorate 84
le DOM (French) overseas *département* 168, 206
les DOM-TOM (m) the *départements d'outre-mer* and the *territoires d'outre-mer* (see page 170) 168
les dominos teeth 131
avoir un don naturel pour to have a gift for, to be cut out for 121

l'esclave (m/f) **de la mode** fashion victim, slave to fashion 48
l'esgourde (f) ear 125
esgourder to hear/listen 151
des espadoches (fpl), **des espagas** (fpl) espadrilles, fabric sandals 52
un espingouin Hispanic 111
esquinter to bust (up), to wreck, [Br.] to knacker 36
l'estom' (m) stomach 127
l'ETA Basque separatist movement 168
l'établissement pour cures d'amaigrissement et de rajeunissement spa, health club 24
l'établissement (m) **de remise en forme** spa, health club 24
l'étagère (f) **à mégots** ears 126
Étienne: À la tienne, Étienne! Cheers! 160
les étiquettes (fpl) ears 126
étrangler le borgne/Popaul to masturbate 189
l'Europe passoire Europe open house 168
Euzkadi Basque 168
l'exhib (m) flasher 187
exploser to explode 151
exposé(e) aux quatre vents open to the winds 218
l'extase (f) climax 187

F

la fac university 83
le faffe greenback, banknote 27
les faffes (mpl) identity papers 27
avoir un faible pour quelqu'un to have a soft spot for someone 174
avoir une faim de loup to be as hungry as a bear 106
faire l'accordéon [of main bunch of riders] to keep bunching and getting strung out alternately 195
faire de l'après-ski to play the nineteenth hole 123
faire du bachotage to cram/[Br.] swot for an exam 78
faire des/quelques balles to have a warm-up/[Br.] knock-up 198
faire la bamboula to live it up, [Br.] to go on the razzle 98, 112
faire du baratin à quelqu'un to come on to someone, [Br.] to chat someone up 173
faire du barouf to cause a commotion 65
faire son beurre to make lots of dough 26
faire la bise à quelqu'un to kiss someone (on both cheeks) 58
faire le bitume to walk the streets, to be a hooker, [Br.] to be on the game 44
faire un bœuf to have a jam session 98
faire la bombe to party 98
faire bondir quelqu'un to make someone hopping mad 64
faire la bringue to party, to go on the town/[Br.] razzle 98, 112, 122
faire chier quelqu'un to make someone sick 63
faire chômedu to be unemployed/[Br.] on the dole/out of work 31
faire de la chine to hunt around for antiques/secondhand goods 42
faire du cinéma to put on an act, a performance 17; to make a song and dance 148; to cause a scene 176
faire du cinoche to cause a scene 176
faire les collections parisiennes/londoniennes to go to the Paris/London fashion shows 50
faire des cordes (pour la marine) to take a dump, to make turds 216
faire le coup du lapin à quelqu'un to give somebody a rabbit punch 35
faire un créneau to parallel park, to reverse into a parking spot 204
faire une croix dessus to settle, close (it), [Br.] to draw a line under 65
faire demi-tour en trois temps to do a U-turn/three-point turn 204
faire un dernier essai/un dernier entraînement to do a final training session 196
faire dodo to go to sleep, to be asleep 154
faire une fiesta (à tout casser) to have a (hell of a) party 98
faire un foin terrible to kick up/make one hell of a fuss 63
faire un footing to go for a jog 44
faire un fromage to kick up/make a fuss 63
faire du genou à quelqu'un to play footsie with someone 174
faire du gringue à to come on to someone, [Br.] to chat someone up 173
faire une grosse tête à quelqu'un to bash someone's face/head in 66
faire: Il fait de la chaleur! It's hot! 217

faire suer le bournos to exploit 223
faire suer quelqu'un to be a pain to someone 62
faire du surf to surf, to go surfing 209
faire un tabac to kick up/make a fuss 63
faire du tam-tam to make a big song and dance (about something) 63
faire la tambouille to do the cooking 105
faire une tartine to kick up/make a fuss 63
faire du topless to go topless 180
faire une touche to score (a hit), to make it 174
faire un tour to go for a spin 37
faire la tournée des grands ducs to have a night out, to paint the town red, to hit the high spots 122
faire tourner quelqu'un en bourrique to push someone over the edge, [Br.] to drive someone round the bend 62
faire du tout-debout not to switch on the meter 43
faire un travail posté to work (on) shifts 32
faire le trottoir to be a streetwalker, [Br.] to be on the game 190
faire vieux (vieille) to look old 116
faire de la voile to go sailing 209
faire les yeux doux à quelqu'un to make sheep's eyes at someone 173
faire du zèle to be over enthusiastic, [Br.] to be super keen 224
faire zizi-panpan to get it on 129
le falzar pants, trousers 49
le fana de football soccer/[Br.] football fan 120
le/la fana de jazz jazz freak 120
le/la fana de théâtre theater buff 16
le fast-food fast food, fast-food restaurant 40
le faubourg bottom, ass 132
faucher le copain/la copine à quelqu'un to steal someone's boyfriend/girlfriend 177
la Faucheuse Grim Reaper (Death) 160
les fayots (mpl) beans 105
le féca coffee 211
au feeling by intuition 153
une femme cadre executive, manager 222
le fendant pants, trousers 49
le fendard pants, trousers 49
le fendu men's pants/trousers 49
la fente vagina 132
le fer à souder big nose 131
La ferme! Shut your mouth/face! 7
Ferme ta gueule! Shut your face/trap! 58
avoir la fesse triste/tombante to have drooping buttocks 21
la fête bamboula wild party 97
la fête de l'Huma *Huma(nité)* festival 164
le feu gun 67
avoir le feu au cul to feel horny 133
le/la feug Jewish 211
la feuille: être dur de la feuille to be hard of hearing 128
les feuilles (fpl) ears 126
un feuj Jew 112
être ficelé(e) to be dolled/[Br.] tarted up, to be very chic 49
ficher une baffe/gifle à quelqu'un to give someone a slap 65
ficher une balle dans la peau to shoot 67
ficher les jetons à quelqu'un to scare someone 90
ficher une raclée/trempe à quelqu'un to beat someone up 66
le fignard, le fignolet anus 132
la figue vagina 132
les figues (fpl) testicles 128
filer à l'anglaise to take unauthorized time off/[Br.] to take French leave 81, 112
filer un coup de lattes to borrow 199
filer les flubes to be afraid 89
filer de la jaquette (flottante) to be gay 184
filer un mauvais coton to be (in) a sorry state 115
filer un rencard to make/set up a date 174
le film de cul/de fesse(s) porn movie, skin flick 148
la fine-gueule gourmet 107
le finish: avoir un bon finish to have a good finish 192
le fion anus 132
le flageolet penis 127
le flanc: être sur le flanc to be laid up 116
flanquer une baffe/gifle à quelqu'un to give someone a slap 65
flanquer une beigne/une châtaigne/ un gnon/un marron/une pêche/une taloche à quelqu'un to slug someone 66
flanquer une trempe/raclée à quelqu'un to beat someone up 66
flasher sur quelqu'un to fall head over heels for someone 175

F.L.E. French as a foreign language 84
les flèches vertes (fpl) green arrows 203
flemmard lazy, [Br.] skiving 222
la flemme laziness, idleness 222
le flic cop, policeman 67
la flicaille the cops, the fuzz 67
le flingue, le flingo gun, rifle 67, 91
flinguer quelqu'un to shoot/gun down someone 67, 91
le flingueur, la flingueuse contract killer 91
flirter to flirt 174
la flotte water 216
flotter to rain 216
avoir les flubes to be afraid 89
la flûte legs 133
un flyer a rave [evening] 151
avoir les foies (blancs) to be afraid 89
le foiron bottom, ass 132
folklo weird (and wonderful) 99, 151
la folle fairy, queen 184
Le fond de l'air est frais! It's nippy outside! 218
fonsdé stoned, out of one's mind/skin, wrecked 211
forcer la dose to push it (too far) 63
la forme: être en pleine forme to be on (in) (top) form 115; **avoir la forme** to be in great shape 115
la formule à 120 francs menu at 120 francs 40
fouetter to be afraid 89
la foufoune vagina 132
le four failure, flop 17
la fourchette du père Adam fingers 126
le fourgat, le fourguem receiver (of stolen goods), fence 30
fourguer to palm off, to unload, [Br.] to flog 30
le fourreau pants, trousers 49
fourrer quelqu'un to bang 186
foutre quelqu'un à la baille to chuck/throw someone into the water 180
foutre une baffe à quelqu'un to give someone a slap 65
foutre le camp to clear out 133
foutre une balle dans la peau to shoot 67
foutre les flubes to be afraid 89
foutre une gifle à quelqu'un to give someone a slap 65
foutre les jetons à quelqu'un to scare someone 90
foutre par terre to mess up, to screw up 145
foutre le poing sur la gueule de quelqu'un to punch somebody's face in 90
foutre une raclée/trempe à quelqu'un to beat someone up 66
à la fraîche in the cool of the day 217
la fraîcheur: un peu de fraîcheur cool spot 217
frais/fraîche: me voilà frais/fraîche! I'm in a fix! 217
la framboise clitoris 133
la France profonde the real heart of France; backward-looking France 168
les francforts (mpl) fingers 126
Francilien(-ienne) belonging to or an inhabitant of the Île de France 168
la Francilienne expressway/[Br.] motorway that encircles the Paris region 168
freiner à mort to slam on the brakes 37
le fric money 26; **être plein(e) de fric** to be filthy rich 27
le frichti (cooked) meal 41, 104
le fricot chow, food, grub, [Br.] tucker 104
le Fridolin/fridolin Kraut 111, 160
le frifri vagina 132
frileux, frileuse (adj.) sensitive to the cold, shivery 217
le frimant walk-on, bit-part player 96
le frimeur poser, show-off 180
la frimousse face 23
avoir la fringale to be hungry, to have the munchies 106
les fringues (fpl) clothes, [Br.] gear 41, 48; **des fringues** (fpl) **de coulisse** underwear, lingerie 52
le Frisé/frisé Kraut 111, 160
un fritz Kraut 111
le froc pants, trousers 49
le fromage foot 128
le frome/le frometon cheese 105
être en fumasse to be sore/steamed up 87
les fumerons (mpl) feet 128; **avoir les fumerons** to be afraid 89
le fumiste cowboy, [Br.] skiver 28
le funk funk 96
être furax/furibard(e)/furibond(e) to be livid 65
les fusains (mpl) thighs 133
le fusil stomach 127
fusiller to overcharge, to rip off; to wreck, to smash up, [Br.] to knacker 30

le futal pants, trousers 49
le fute pants, trousers 49

G

la gâche: c'est une bonne gâche it's a piece of cake 32
le gadin head 126
le gagne-pain bottom, ass 132
gagner en deux/trois sets secs to win in two/three straight sets 198
la gagneuse whore earning good money 190
le galérien driver of a taxi that has a roof rack 42
Galligrasseuil fictitious publisher 164
le galure, le galurin hat 49
gambergeailler to daydream 91
la gambette leg 130
la gambille dancing, [Br.] bopping 59
gambiller to dance, to boogie 59
garder la ligne to keep trim 115
gargariser de mots to be taken in by one's own words 164
la gargue mouth 131
du gâteau piece of cake 104
la gaufre waffle 40
avoir la gaule to have an erection, to have/get a hard-on 186
gauler (une femme) to have sex/get it on/ [Br.] have it off (with a woman) 186
la gavousse lesbian 185
le gay homosexual 184
le gazon hair 126; pubic hair 132
GDB hangover 8
gégène great, terrific 99
geler: Il gèle à fond! It's freezing cold! 218
geler: Il gèle à pierre fendre! It's freezing hard! 218
le genre artiste artsy-fartsy, [Br.] arty-farty 16
le gésier stomach 127
un ghetto-blaster a ghetto-blaster 151
le gicleur mouth 131
la gifle slap (on/in the face) 65
un gig a gig, concert 151
le gigolo des bars bar lizard, lounge lizard 16
le gigot thigh 133
le gîte gîte, [Br.] self-catering cottage/ apartment with kitchen 208
le giton young, passive homosexual 184
le gland penis 127
glander, glandouiller to laze, to loaf around 222
le glouton, la gloutonne hog, glutton 107
gnangnan (adj. inv.) corny, [Br.] twee 148
le goal goalkeeper 197
des godasses (f) shoes 51
le gode, le godemiché dildo 188
le goinfre hog, glutton 107
la gonflette bodybuilding 199
la gonzesse chick, babe; wife, old lady 133
le gorgeon drink 74
le gorille bodyguard, bouncer 67
la goudou lesbian 185
la gougnot(t)e lesbian 185
la gouine lesbian 185
la goule mouth 131
le gourdin penis 127
le gourmand glutton, [Br.] greedy guts 107
le gourmet gourmet, discerning eater 107
la gousse lesbian, nymphomaniac 185
le grabuge trouble 64
la graille food, meal, grub 41, 104
grailler to grab a bite (to eat) 40, 108
le graillon burned fat 104
le grain de café clitoris 133
grainer to grab a bite (to eat) 40
graisser la patte à quelqu'un to bribe/ grease someone's palm 129, 224
le grand amateur de cinéma filmgoer, cinema goer 147
le grand écran the big screen 147
un grand format 500 franc note 26
le grand magasin department store 41
le grand manitou the big boss, big shot, big white chief 17, 161
la Grande Bibliothèque National Library 85
la grande bleue Mediterranean Sea 168
la Grande Boulange the Bank of France 26, 44
la grande surface supermarket 41
les grands couturiers great fashion designers 48
le grappin hand 126
le gras-double stomach 127
une gratte a guitar 151
gratter les cordes to play the guitar 151
les Grecs: Va te faire enculer/faire chez les Grecs! Eat it! 160
le greffier puss, pussy, pussycat 12

la greffière vagina 132
les grelots (mpl) testicles 128; **avoir les grelots** to be afraid 89
grelotter to be afraid 89
une grenouille de bénitier a narrow-minded old bigot 13
greum thin 211
la grille d'égout set of teeth 131
griller un feu rouge to go through a red light 204
le grimpant pants, trousers 49
grimper au cocotier to fly off the handle 87
la grinque food 41
la grip(p)ette vagina 132
le grisbi money 26
des grolles (f) shoes 51
gros(se) fat, cuddly 70
le gros bonnet big noise, star performer, leading light, VIP, top brass 18, 29, 222
les supérieurs, les gros bonnets top brass 29
le gros lard fatty, fatso, big fat slob 22
mon gros loup (my) pet 14
un gros-plein-de-soupe fatty, fatso, big fat slob 22
le gros rouge ordinary red wine 70
une grosse egghead 66
la grosse chandelle very high kick ahead, [Br.] up-and-under, [Br.] Gary Owen 199
la grosse dondon fatty, fatso, fat cow 22
la grosse légume bigwig, one of the top people 18, 222
les grosses légumes top brass, men in (gray) suits 28
la gueule mouth 131; **Ta gueule!** Shut your face!/trap! 58; **Vos gueules!** Shut up, the lot of you! 58
avoir la gueule de bois to have a hangover 74
le gueuleton blowout, feast 40, 105
la guibolle thigh 133
la guimbarde old car 35
le guinche hop, dance 81
guincher to dance, to boogie 59, 98, 122
en guincher une to dance, to shake a leg, [Br.] to have a spin 122
guindé(e) uptight, stiff, starchy, anal retentive 17
le guise, le guizot penis 127
la guitoune tent; electric guitar 206
la gumbarde heap, rust bucket, [Br.] banger 35

H

H hash, [Br.] blow 8
être habile de ses mains to be good with one's hands 121
être hanté(e) par to be obsessed by 122
un hardeur, une hardeuse a rocker, rock chick 152
le hareng pimp; gendarme 190
Heureux(-euse) de vous revoir. Nice to see you again. 58
l'Hexagone (m) metropolitan France 168
le/la HLM public housing, low rent, subsidized apartment, (low rent) apartment building 137
l'homo (m) homosexual 184
l'hosto (m) hospital 117
le hot hot jazz 95
HP psychiatric hospital 8
HS bust, kaput, out of order, [Br.] knackered 8
l'huile (f) important person, VIP, big cheese, big wig 29, 222
les huiles top guys, big guns 29
hyper, hypra mega 99
l'hypokhâgne first-/second-year preparatory course for the **Grandes Écoles** 78
l'hypotaupe first-/second-year preparatory course for the **Grandes Écoles** 78

I

l'IFOP a polling institute 165
l'image (f) **à l'écran** screen image 147
l'immigré (m) **de la deuxième génération** second-generation immigrant 136
l'immigré (m) **(qui est) en situation irrégulière** immigrant whose papers are not in order 136
impec perfect!, [Br.] great (stuff)! 100
l'imper (m) raincoat 49
l'industrie (f) **du bâtiment** the building industry/trades 28
info ou intox information or intoxication 165
l'instit (m/f) primary-school teacher 81
l'intégrisme (m) fundamentalism 169
intello intellectual, egghead 17
l'internaute (m/f) Web surfer 161
les Invalos, les Invaloches Invalides 45
IPSOS a French polling institute 165
l'iroquoise (f) Mohican haircut 130
être ivre to be drunk 72

J

le Jacquot (taxi) meter 42
le jacquot penis 127
la jaffe food or meal 41
le jambon thigh 130
le jambonneau thigh, guitar, mandolin, banjo 133
un jap Jap 111
la jaquette (male) homosexuality 184; **être de la jaquette (flottante)** to be gay 184
le jaune pastis 74
la java popular waltz 154
le jazz jazz 95
le jazzman jazzman 95
le jazz-rock jazz-rock 95
être jazz-tango to be bisexual, to be AC/DC 188
le jean nu-tête penis 127
avoir les jetons to be afraid 89
le job work, job 32
le jogging sweat suit, tracksuit 51
jouer au basket to play basketball 82
jouer au foot to play soccer/[Br.] football 82, 196
jouer dans la cour des grands to play with the big boys/older children; to play in the major league 80
jouer devant les banquettes to play to an almost empty house 96
jouer à guichets fermés to play to a full house 96
jouer de la mandoline to finger oneself (off) 189
jouer à la marelle to play hopscotch 82
jouer au ping-pong to play table tennis, ping-pong 198
jouer sur terre to play on clay 198
le joufflu bottom, ass 132
jouir to come, to get it off 186
jouissif barrel of laughs 100
les journées rouges (fpl) red days (the days to avoid for travel) 203
les joyeuses (fpl) testicles 128
JT television news 8
le Jules man, boyfriend, [Br.] squeeze 161
la Julie girlfriend, [Br.] squeeze, bird 161
les jumelles (fpl) bottom, ass 132
Juste un chouïa. Just a drop. 4
le jute sperm, spunk, cum 186
juter to come, [Br.] to cream, to pop one's cork 187

K

la K7 a cassette [audio or video] 152, 155
les Kanaks indigenous Melanesian population of Nouvelle Calédonie 167
un kangourou Aussie, Australian 111
un kebla/keubla nigger 112
le keuf flatfoot, cop 211
le keum guy, [Br.] bloke 211
le keupon punk 211
un keuss/un keusse 10 francs 26
le keusse 10 francs 211
la khâgne first-/second-year preparatory course for the **Grandes Écoles** 78
Khâgneux (m)/**khâgneuse** (f) student 79
le kiki neck 131
un kilo 1000 francs 26
un kiwi New Zealander 111
la kro Kronenbourg beer 74

L

le lac vagina 132
lâcher to ditch someone 176
lâcher son fou to have a great time 99
laisser choir to ditch someone 176
laisser tomber to ditch someone 176
la laitue vagina, pubic hair 132
la lampe stomach 127
la lampe à souder big nose 131
le lampion stomach 127; neck 131
le lance-fusées rocket launcher 35
la langouse tongue 131
la languetouse tongue 131
la languette tongue 131
la lanterne rouge back marker 196
le lapin: Ça (ne) vaut pas un pet de lapin. It's totally worthless./[Br.] It's not worth a monkey's fart. 12
le lapin: Elle lui a posé un lapin. She's stood him up. 12
le larfou scarf 49
le Latin Latin Quarter, Boulevard St-Michel 45
la latte foot 128
des lattes (f) feet, skis, shoes 51, 199
la lavasse dishwater, [Br.] watery, piddly soup 105
laver to launder (money), to sell off (stolen goods), to fence 30
le laziloffe venereal disease, the clap 56
le leader race leader, front runner 192
le lèche-vitrines window-shopping 121
lever le coude to be a heavy drinker 56

lever le pouce to hitchhike, to thumb a lift 37
la licence degree (university) 83
licencier to fire, to dismiss, [Br.] to sack 31
la limace, la limouse shirt 49
les limaces (fpl) lips 131
limer to have a slow screw, to have the hots for someone 186
un linvé 20 francs 26
la liquette shirt 49
des lisses (fpl) stockings, nylons 49
le litron bottle of red wine 74
la loche cabbie, cabdriver 42
les loches (fpl) ears 126
la locomotive trendsetter, leader 17
les lolos (mpl) breasts; milk 131
le long métrage feature film 148
avoir un look d'enfer to look great/cool/ [Br.] wicked 50
la lopaille homosexual 184
la lope, la lopette homosexual 184
la louche hand 126
lourder to fire, to dismiss, [Br.] to sack 31
le lové bike, bicycle 195
LSD shorty, squirt, [Br.] titch 8
le Lucal, le Luco the Luxembourg Gardens 45
la lucarne top corner (of the net) 197
la lucarne enchantée anus 132
la lune bottom, ass 132
des lunettes noires/de soleil shades, sunglasses 52
Lutèce Paris 161, 169
le lycéen, la lycéenne high-school student, [Br.] sixth-former 78

M

le mac pimp 190
le macab corpse, stiff 117
un macaroni Italian 111, 112
le macaroni penis 127
le macchabée corpse, stiff 117, 161
le macdo hamburger, burger 40
le maçon bricklayer, [Br.] brickie 27
être madame je-sais-tout to be a bit of a know-it-all/[Br.] know-all 121
le magaze shop 41
le magazine de fesses porn magazine 148
le Maghreb, un Maghrébin, une Maghrébine Arab 111, 169
magouiller to do some wheeling and dealing 30
le magouilleur wheeler-dealer 30
le mahomet sun 206
le mahomet cogne it's scorching hot 209
être maigre comme un clou to be as thin as a rake 22
le maillot de bain swimsuit, [Br.] swimming costume 52
avoir la main baladeuse to be a groper, to have roving hands 187
avoir la main verte to have a green thumb/[Br.] green fingers 121
la maison royco police station, [Br.] the cop shop 67
le maître nageur lifeguard 180
être mal en point to be in a poor/bad way 115
être mal fagoté(e) to be badly dressed, [Br.] to be dressed like a dog's dinner 49
la maladie honteuse gonorrhea and syphilis 190
le manche (à balai/à couilles) penis 127
les mandarines (fpl) small breasts 131
les manettes (fpl) ears 126; pedals 196
la mangeaille chow, food, grub 40
manger de l'ail to be/to appear to be a lesbian 185
manger les pissenlits par la racine to be pushing up (the) daisies 56
manger trois fois rien to eat next to nothing 106
manger quelqu'un des yeux to devour someone with one's eyes 173
manger de la vache enragée to go through hard times 12
le mangeur, la mangeuse (good) eater 107
la mangeuse d'hommes man-eater 187
la manif demonstration 136
les manivelles (fpl) arms 126, thighs 133; legs 196
le mannequin fashion model 50
le manœuvre laborer, unskilled worker 27
manquer (à l'appel) to be absent (at registration/attendance/roll call) 81
la mansarde head 126
le maquereau pimp 190
le maquereautin small-time pimp 190
la maquerelle madam(e) 190
le maquis Resistance (World War II) 169
le maquisard, une maquisarde member of the French Resistance 169
la maraude soliciting fares away from taxi stands 42

marauder to solicit/[Br.] tout for hire, to solicit/[Br.] tout for customers on the streets 42
le maraudeur taxi driver soliciting fares from taxi stands 42
le marcel vest 161
le marchand de soupe owner of a cheap restaurant 41
le marché aux puces flea market 41
marcher à la voile et à la vapeur to be bisexual, to be AC/DC 188
la margoulette mouth 131
les marguerites (fpl) white hairs 126
Marianne symbol of France; compare Uncle Sam, Britannia, John Bull 169
la Marie-Chantal highbrow snob 17; preppy, [Br.] Sloane-ranger 161
la Marie-couche-toi-là slut, [Br.] slag, pro(stitute) 161
la marie-jeanne grass, weed, Mary Jane 82
le marlou pimp 190
marquer midi to have an erection, to have/get a hard-on 186
marquer son territoire to mark out one's territory 145
marrant(e) funny 100
le marsouin sailor 180
le mastodonte large/heavy truck; [Br.] juggernaut 35
la masure (f) dump, hovel 28
mater quelqu'un to give someone the eye 173
la matraque penis 127
les mécaniques (fpl) shoulders 125
Me-Lèche-les-Prunes Sticksville 144, 161
mélo over-the-top, [Br.] OTT 100
le/la mélomane music lover 120, 152
le melon head 126
la même chanson the same old song/tune/story 153
mener quelqu'un en bateau to lead someone up the garden path, to string someone along 176
mener le petit/prosper au cirque to make love 94
le meneur de train pacesetter 192
Ménilmuche Ménilmontant 46
la menteuse tongue 130
la menuise carpenter, [Br.] chippie 27
le merlan pimp 190
les messageries (f) **roses** sex chat lines (accessed on Minitel) 191
le métallo steelworker 32
un métèque wop 112
le/la métèque foreigner, usually of mixed French and foreign blood 169
le métral subway, [Br.] metro, tube, underground 43
Métro, boulot, dodo! Subway, work, sleep!, the rat race 221
la métropole continental France, including Corsica 169
mettre du beurre dans les épinards to improve one's living standards, to grease the wheels 26
mettre quelqu'un en boîte to annoy someone, [Br.] to wind someone up 62
mettre quelqu'un en boule to raise someone's hackles, to infuriate someone 63
mettre en cloque to put someone in the family way 177
mettre le grappin to hook 129
mettre sur les endosses de quelqu'un to make someone take the rap 129
mettre le turbo to get a move on 37
mettre en vedette to give someone star billing, to highlight 149
mettre: y mettre son grain de sable to put one's two cents in, to interfere, [Br.] to stick one's oar in 63
la meuf chick, [Br.] bird 211
les meules (fpl) teeth 130; bottom, ass 132
la meu-meu moo-cow 11
les miches (fpl) breasts 131
les miches (mpl) bottom, ass 132
avoir les miches à zéro to be afraid 89
avoir les miches qui font bravo to be afraid 89
le micky nobody, nonentity 161
le micro mouth 131
le mille-feuille vagina 132
mimi cute 17
mimile square (old-fashioned) 17
minable pathetic, useless, wretched 148
le minet puss, pussy, pussycat 12; vagina 132
la minette puss, pussy, pussycat 12, 130
le Minitel rose sex chat lines (accessed on Minitel) 191
le minou puss, pussy, pussycat 12
la minouse panties, [Br.] knickers, pants 52
la mirette eye 130
la mirette: s'en mettre plein les mirettes to blow one away 133

N

le nœud penis 127; **c'est une tête de nœud** he's a dickhead 133
un noiche Chinaman 111
le noirot late-night taxi 42
les noisettes (fpl) testicles 128
la noix bottom, ass 132
avoir la nostalgie du pays/de la terre natale to be homesick 144
le nougat foot 128
le nuitard late-night taxi 42

O

être obsédé(e) par to be obsessed by 122
l'occase (f) scoring chance 197
l'occase (f) **en or** golden opportunity, great scoring chance 197
Mon œil! My eye! My foot! 4
avoir l'œil au beurre noir/avoir l'œil poché to have a black eye 116
l'œil de bronze anus 132
l'œillet (m) anus 132
les œufs sur le plat breasts 131
les oignes (mpl) feet 128
les oignons (mpl) feet 128
les olives (fpl) testicles 128
Olympia major concert hall in Paris 153
l'Opéra Bastille modern Paris opera house 153
une opération de chirurgie esthétique cosmetic surgery 21
les oranges (fpl) small breasts 131
les orphelines (fpl) testicles 128
l'Orsec national system of disaster relief 170
l'os à moelle penis 127
l'oseille (f) money 26
oublier son texte to forget one's lines 17
l'outil (m) penis 127
outre Quiévrain Belgium 170
l'ouvrier (m) **du bâtiment** construction worker 27
l'ouvrier (m) **(qui est) en situation irrégulière** worker whose papers are not in order 136

P

pacser to cohabit 175
paf drunk, plastered 73
le paf penis 127
le Palais Garnier the old Paris opera house 153
la palette (surface of the) bat/paddle (used for hitting the ball) 198
le palmarès the winners, honors list, prizewinners, record (of achievement) 153, 192
le palpitant heart 127
la paluche hand 125
Paname Paris 44, 161, 170
le panard foot 128
le panier bottom, ass 132
le panier à salade police van 67
être en panne d'énergie to have run out of steam/energy 192
le pantouflard stay-at-home 187
Pantruche Paris 44
la PAO desktop publishing 165
le papillon du Sénégal penis 127
papouiller à quelqu'un to grope someone 188
la pâquerette vagina 133
le paradis paradise 144
le parapente paragliding 209
le parapente à ski paraskiing 209
le pare-brise glasses, [Br.] specs, goggles 52
les pare-chocs (mpl) breasts 131
le parigot, Parigot Parisian 44, 170
la parigote, une Parigote Parisian 44, 170
le Paris-Dakar car race from France to Senegal 170
parler français comme une vache espagnole to speak pidgin French 112
la partie carrée foursome 97
le/la partousard(e), le/la partouzard(e) person taking part in an orgy 97
la partouse orgy 97
partouser to take part in an orgy 98
pas net(te) shady, [Br.] dodgy 100
pas la porte à côté not exactly next door 202
Pas de vagues! Don't make trouble! 62
le pascal 500 franc bill 162
être de passage to be passing through 202
passer l'arme à gauche to kick the bucket 56
passer un alcootest to take a breathalyzer test 203
passer bien to be/look good on film/camera 149
passer devant monsieur le maire to get married 175
passer à l'écran to screen, to show 148
passer l'éponge là-dessus to forget/wipe the slate clean of something 65

picorer to pick at one's food 108
le picrate wine, vino 74
la pièce de dix ronds anus 132
le pied: avoir bon pied bon œil to be hale and hearty 55
avoir les pieds nickelés to have the luck of the devil, [Br.] to be jammy, to be lucky 89
le piège beard 127
le piège à macaronis/à poux beard 127
pieuter to crash, [Br.] to kip 59
le pif nose 131
la pignole masturbation 189
pignoler quelqu'un to play with someone, [Br.] to bring/toss/wank someone off 189
le pilon foot 128
le/la pilote driver 36
piloter to drive (race cars) 37
la pin up pinup 180
le pinard wine, vino 74
le pinardier wine merchant, [Br.] plonk seller 42
la pince hand 125
le pinceau foot 125
pincer le copain/la copine à quelqu'un to steal someone's boyfriend/girlfriend 177
en pincer pour quelqu'un to be smitten by someone 174
la pine penis 127
le pinglot foot 128
le pingouin foot 128
un pion older student 80
le pion, la pionne supervisor, monitor 80
le pipelet, la pipelette janitor/concierge/caretaker 137
piquer le copain/la copine à quelqu'un to steal someone's boyfriend/girlfriend 177
piquer quelqu'un to stab 67
piquer un fard/un soleil to go as red as a beet(root) 88
piquer un sprint/un cent mètres to sprint off, to go into top gear 194
piquer une crise to throw a fit, to fly off the handle 87
la piquette cheap wine, [Br.] plonk 70
pisser to piss with rain 217; **Ça pisse dru!** It's pouring down! 217
pisser de l'œil to cry, to burst into tears 88
le pistard track cyclist 195
le piston string pulling, pulling strings 224; **avoir du piston** to pull strings 224
pistonner quelqu'un to pull strings for someone 224
le plafond head 126
planant(e) mellow [music] 100
la planche (de surf) surfboard 209
la planche à voile sailboard, windsurfing 209
le plancher des vaches dry land, terra firma 144
planer to be high (as a kite), [Br.] to be over the moon; to be stoned (on drugs); to be cut off from reality 90
le/la planqué(e) person with an easy job/[Br.] cushy number 32
la planque, la planquouse easy job, [Br.] cushy number 32
planter là to ditch someone 176
planter quelqu'un to stab 67
la plaque license/registration plate 43
plaquer to ditch someone 176
pleuvoir: Il pleut à seaux. It's pouring/[Br.] bucketing down. 216
pleuvoir: Il pleut à verse! It's pouring! 215
pleuvoir: Il pleut comme vache qui pisse! It's raining cats and dogs! 216
pleuvoir: Il pleut des cordes! It's pouring! 57, 216
pleuvoir: Il pleut des hallebardes! It's raining cats and dogs!/It's pouring! 57, 216
pleuvoir: Il tombe des cordes! It's pouring! 216
le plombard plumber 27
les plumes (fpl) hair 126
le pneu love handle 125
le poche paperback, pocket edition 165
avoir des poches sous les yeux to have bags under the eyes 21
le podium catwalk 50
la pogne hand 125; masturbation 189
le pognon money 26
le pogo dance 97
pogoter to dance 98
poignarder quelqu'un to stab 67
la poignée d'amour love handle 125
le poil: être de mauvais poil to be in a bad mood 87; **être de bon poil** to be in a good mood 87; **avoir un poil dans la main** to be on the lazy side, [Br.] to be bone idle 223
le point noir anus 132
pointer (sa fiche horaire) to clock in/on, to clock out 31

le principal headmaster, principal 81
un problème de maths vachement balaise really hard math(s) problem 81
à la prochaine! be seeing you! 60
un produit amincissant reducing/slimming aid 22
le prof teacher, teach 80
le prof d'histoire-géo history and geography teacher 83
le prof de gym gym teacher 83
le prof de maths math(s) teacher 83
le prof de sciences-nat' natural science teacher 83
le prof de sciences-po political science teacher 83
le programme à deux longs métrages double-feature program 148
projeter to screen, to show 148
le propergol rocket fuel 36
le prose/proze, le prosinard bottom, ass 132
le proviseur headmaster, principal 81
le proxo pimp 190
les prunes (fpl) testicles 128
la puce travailleuse lesbian 185
le puceau virgin 187
le pue-la-sueur workman 32
la pute whore, hooker 94, 190
le PV, le p.-v. student transcript/profile 84; police fine/ticket 84

Q

le quai de Javel location of the famous Citroën car factory 170
le quart de brie big nose 131
le quatre fois cent mètres four by one hundred meters relay 194
la québri 10,000 francs 212
la journée: Quelle journée torride! What a scorcher! 217
le métier: Quel métier de chien! What a crummy job! 13
le temps: Quel temps de chien(s)! What lousy weather!/It's not fit for a dog (out there)! 13, 215
la vie: Quelle vie de chien! What a rotten life! 13
les quenottes (fpl) baby teeth 131
la quéquette, la queue penis 127
la queue de canard DA, duck's ass/ [Br.] arse 130
la queue de cheval ponytail 130
la quille thigh 133
les quilles: ne tenir plus sur ses quilles to be unable to stand up 134
la Quincampe la rue Quincampoix 45
le quinquet eyes 130
le quinze de la Rose English rugby team 198
le quiqui neck 131

R

raccrocher to give up competitive racing 196
raconter: Tu me racontes des histoires! You're telling fibs!/You're lying! 4
le radis toe 125, 128
la Raffinerie the Pompidou Center 45
le rafiau tub, bucket (boat) 180
le rafiot tub, bucket (boat) 180, 202
le ragga ragga(muffin) 96
la ragougnasse swill, pig swill 105
le raï rai 96
raide plastered; drugged 56
le Rambo (Paris Railways) security officer 162
la ramener to kick up/make a fuss 63
ramener sa fraise to butt in, [Br.] to get stroppy 63
la rampe footlights 149
le rancard appointment, meet(ing), date 59
rancarder quelqu'un to arrange to meet someone, to make a date with someone 60
le rap rap 95, 152
rapper to rap, to play rap, to dance to rap music 96
le rappeur, la rappeuse rapper 96
rapports sexuels (mpl) sexual intercourse 186
la raquette foot 128; bat, paddle 198
ras le bol: J'en ai ras le bol! I've had it up to here!/I'm totally pissed off! 3
rasant(e) deathly (deadly) dull, a real drag 100
Ras l'Front! Down with the National Front! 170
le rasdep homosexual, queer 184, 212
la rasta rasta 152
le rata food, meal; bean and potato stew 41, 105
rater l'écrit to fail the written test 37
rater le pratique to fail the practical/ the road test 37
rater un but to miss a goal 197

la ratiche tooth 131
un raton Arab 111
la RATP the Paris transport authority 44
ravaler sa façade to put on one's war paint/makeup 23
ravaler sa frimousse to put on one's makeup 23
le raymond square (person) 162
le rebeu second-generation French-born Arab 212
son record personnel his/her personal best, PB 194
la récré recess, break, [Br.] break time, time-out 79
refiler de la jaquette (flottante) to be gay 184
le reggae reggae 96
relou unsubtle, in your face, [Br.] OTT 212
reluquer to ogle (someone)/[Br.] to eye (someone) up 23
le rembour, le rencard appointment, meet(ing), date 59
remuer le potage to stir things up 62
renauder to complain, to bitch 55
le rencard date, rendezvous 59, 174, 177
rench expensive, pricey 212
renoi (adj.) black 212
la rentrée return to work/school, usually after the long summer/holidays 203
renvoyer un élève to expel a student/pupil 81
le RER rapid-transit train service in the Paris region 44
le restau, le resto, le restif restaurant 40
le restau(-)U, le resto(-)U student restaurant/canteen 40
rester en strasse [of taxi] to be/to wait at a taxi stand 42
retomber sur ses pattes to land on one's feet 129
retrousser ses manches to roll up one's sleeves 224
retrouver la forme to get fit/in shape 115
la reum old lady, an old dear 212
le reup old man 212
la reuss sister, girl 212
revenir sur terre to come back down to earth 143
des ribouis (m) shoes 51
le ricain, un ricain, une ricaine Yank(ee) 111, 202
le/la richard swell, [Br.] off, [Br.] nob 162
la rincée downpour 217
Rince-toi l'œil! Wash your eye out! 174
ringard(e) square (old-fashioned) 17
ringard(e), ringardos tacky, [Br.] naff 100
la ringardise tackiness 100
les ripatons feet 128
le ripou(x) bad/corrupt cop, [Br.] bent cop 212
un rital Italian, wop 111, 112
la robe de quatre sous cheap dress 48
la robe très mode really trendy dress 49
les roberts (mpl) breasts, tits 131, 162
le robinet d'amour penis 127
le rock rock ('n' roll) 95
le rocke(u)r, le rockie, le rocky, la rockeuse rocker, rock musician, rock fan, headbanger 95
le rodéo joyride (in a stolen vehicle) 37
le rofou pants, trousers 49
les rogatons (mpl) leftovers 105
la rogne bad temper 87
les rognons (mpl) testicles 128
le roi tycoon 29
le roi du béton concrete tycoon 29
le roi des cons a prize idiot, a real dickhead, a complete prick 29
le roi de l'édition publishing tycoon 29
le roi de l'épicerie supermarket tycoon 29
le roi de l'immobilier property tycoon 29
le roi du pétrole oil tycoon 29
le roman de gare pulp/trashy novel, potboiler 17, 165
romano (adj.) gypsy, [Br.] gippo 162
le rond de cuir paper pusher, pen pusher 223
rond(e) (comme une bille) drunk, plastered 73
les rondins (mpl) breasts 131
les roploplots (mpl) breasts 132
un rosbif Brit, Englishman 111
les roseaux (mpl) hair 126
les rotoplots (mpl) breasts 132
les roubignolles (fpl) testicles 128
les rouleaux (mpl) testicles 128
rouler la caisse to lead the main group, to drag the main group along/behind 195
rouler à la papa/rouler pépère to amble/meander gently along 204
rouler au pas to crawl along 37
la roulure slut, [Br.] scrubber 187
la roupane dress 48
les roupettes (fpl) testicles 128

le rouquin red wine with a bit more body 70
rouspéter to moan, to grouse 55
le rouspéteur, la rouspéteuse moaner, complainer 55
le roussi a rise in temperature, things heating up 64
les roustons (mpl) testicles 125, 128
le RU university cafeteria, canteen 9
la RU, la r.u. residence hall 85
la ruche nose 131
un ruski, un ruskof Russian 111, 162
rustaud(e) hillbilly 143

S

s'accrocher à to keep at, to stick at (to, with) 121
s'allonger to masturbate 189
s'allonger le macaroni to masturbate 129
s'amuser comme Charlot to masturbate 189
s'arrêter pile to stop dead, to do an emergency stop 204
s'arroser: Ça s'arrose! This calls for a celebration! 72
s'astiquer (la colonne) to masturbate 189
s'en branler not to give a damn 189
s'en cogner not to give a damn/shit (about something) 209
s'en coller plein la lampe to pig out 129
s'éclaircir: Ça s'éclaircit! It's brightening up now! 215
s'éclater to freak out 122; to hit it off 174
s'emballer to get carried away, to get overexcited 89
s'empiffrer to stuff oneself, to feed one's face 108
s'en foutu plein la lampe to pig out 129
s'en jeter un dernier to have one for the road 71; **s'en jeter un derrière la cravate** to have a drink, to knock one back 93
s'enamouracher de quelqu'un to fall head over heels for/[Br.] to be besotted by someone 175
s'enivrer to get oneself drunk 72
s'envoyer quelqu'un to get/have it off with someone 188
s'exhiber to flash 187
s'habiller en pingouin to wear a dinner/dress suit; to wear tails 51
s'habiller mode to wear the latest fashion 48
s'en mettre plein la lampe to feed one's face, to pig out 108, 129
s'occuper: T'occupe! Mind your own (darned) business! 64
s'en payer une tranche to have a great time 122
s'en avoir plein le cul to be pissed off 133
s'en avoir ras le cul to be pissed off 133
le sabot tub, bucket (boat) 180
le sabre penis 127
le sable: y mettre son grain de sable to put one's two cents in, to interfere, [Br.] to stick one's oar in 63
Sacré temps! Nasty/[Br.] Flaming weather! 215
Saint Ger Saint-Germain-des-Prés 45
Sainte-Ginette Sainte-Geneviève library 45
sainte-nitouche Goody Two-shoes 162
Saint-Glinglin Doomsday 162
le saladier mouth 131
la salle à manger mouth 131
les salsifis (mpl) fingers 126
Salut! Ta-ta!, Bye(-bye)! 60
Salut, les gars! Hi, you guys! Hello, guys! 57
Salutas! Howdy! 57
avoir le sang chaud to be a sex maniac 187
la Santaga/la Santoche Santé prison 46
la santé: être en pleine santé to be hale and hearty 55
être saoul(e) to be drunk 72
le sapin taxi, cab 42
le satyre flasher 187
une saucée downpour 217
le sauciflard salami 106
le sauret pimp 190
le saut à l'élastique bungee jumping 206
sauter to skip class, to play hooky, [Br.] to bunk off (a class) 81
sauter à la corde to skip, jump rope 82
sauter du coq à l'âne to jump from one subject to another 11
sauter une femme to bang/[Br.] have it off with a woman 188
savoir: ne savoir rien de rien to be clueless 122
le saxo sax(ophone), sax player 95
schlass drunk, plastered 73
la Scolarité Registrar, Academic Office 84
se bagarrer to brawl, to fight 66, 82
se bagot(t)er to walk, to go on foot 44

se baguenauder to wander/saunter around 44
se baquer to go for a dip 98
se barrer: Barrons-nous!/Je me barre! Let's get out of here!/I'm off! 6
se bastonner to scrap, to fight, to brawl 82
se bécoter to neck 177
se berlurer to delude oneself 91
se bouffer: Ça me bouffe! It really gets me! 107
se bouffer le nez to be at each other's throats 65
se branler to masturbate 189
se branler les couilles to masturbate/[Br.] to do sweet FA 189
se bricoler to masturbate 120
se castagner to scrap, to fight, to brawl 82, 90
se chamailler to squabble 65
se chauffer au soleil to warm oneself in the sun 217
se cogner to fight 209
se cogner une corvée to get stuck with a chore 209
se coller un rassis to masturbate 189
se coucher to retire (from a race) 195
se crasher to crash 36
se crever to ruin one's health, to wreck oneself 116
se cuiter to get drunk 73
se débrouiller (tout seul[e]) to get by, to manage (on one's own) 122
se dormir: ne pas se dormir sur le rata not to fall asleep on the job 105
se faire allumer to get a bellyful of lead; to be told off 197
se faire avoir to be had 177
se faire une bouffe to eat together, to have a meal together 107
se faire boum to masturbate 189
se faire choper to catch a dose of, to get laid down (low) by 115
se faire du cinéma to imagine things 91
se faire faire un lifting to have a face-lift 21
se faire faire un ravalement to have a face job/a face-lift 21
se faire lèche to be bored silly/shitless 211
se faire les ongles to manicure one's nails 23
se faire licencier avec prime à la clé to get the golden handshake 31
se faire lourder avec prime à la clé to get the golden handshake 31
se faire un macdo to go for a burger 40
se faire péter l'anneau/la rondelle to get buttfucked/[Br.] buggered 185
se faire pistonner to pull strings 224
se faire porter pâle to take a sick day/[Br.] sickie 222
se faire une pogne to masturbate 189
se faire ravaler la façade to have a face job/face-lift 21
se faire refaire le nez to have a nose job 21
se faire refaire les nichons to have a boob job 21
se faire refaire les seins to have a breast implant 21
se faire rincer/saucer to get drenched 217
se faire soigner les pieds to have a pedicure 23
se faire tailler les crayons to have a haircut 128
se faire taper dans la lune to get buttfucked/[Br.] buggered 134
se faire tartir to be bored to death/shitless/[Br.] witless 100
se faire une touche to masturbate 189
se faire virer avec prime à la clé to get the golden handshake 31
se farcir to stuff oneself 108
se farcir quelqu'un to get/have it off with someone 188
se finir (à la manivelle) to masturbate 189
se flanquer la trouille to scare stiff 129
se flinguer to blow one's brains out 91
se foutre (à poil) to strip (off), to peel (off) 180, 188
se foutre en rogne/boule to get cross/annoyed 65
se foutre en pétard to go ballistic 87
se foutre en rogne to blow one's top, to get one's dander up 87
se fréquenter to masturbate 189
se fringuer (chic) to get dolled up/[Br.] tarted up 48
se gargariser de mots to be taken in by one's own words 164
se geler to freeze (of a person) 218
se les geler to be cold enough to freeze your balls off 218
se gondoler to crack up, to fall over/[Br.] fall about laughing 99
se griffer to masturbate 189

se griffer la devanture to put on makeup 23
se griffer la tronche to put on makeup 23
se laisser prendre to allow oneself to be taken in 174
se lever du pied gauche to get up on the wrong side of the bed/[Br.] to get out of bed on the wrong side 56
se maquiller to put on makeup 23
se mettre à cinq contre un to masturbate 189
se mettre pétard to go ballistic 87
se mettre à poil to strip (off), to peel (off) 180
se mettre en portefeuille to jackknife [of an articulated vehicle] 205
se mettre en renaud to blow a gasket/fuse, to lose one's temper 87
se mettre au volant to get behind the wheel of a car 34
se monter la tête to blow one's top 63, 87
se monter le bourrichon to get worked up, [Br.] to get het up 87
se nipper to get dolled up, to get dressed up 23, 49
se palucher to masturbate 189
se payer to be full (up)/full to bursting/[Br.] full as an egg 108
se payer quelque chose to treat oneself to something 41
se payer un piéton to hit a pedestrian 44
se payer un trente tonnes to mix it (up) with/have it out with one of the heavyweights (truck, [Br.] lorry) 205
se payer une bonne cuite to get drunk 73
se planter to fail, flop 17
se pogner to masturbate 189
se pointer to turn up, [Br.] to roll up, to put in an appearance 32
se polir le chinois to masturbate 129
se polir la colonne to masturbate 129
se porter comme un charme to be as fit as a fiddle/[Br.] flea 115
se pourlécher les babines to lick one's lips 133
se ramasser to fail/flop 17
se reloquer to get dressed 23
se rencarder to get information in advance 82
se retrouver comme un con to be left feeling like a complete asshole 88
se rôtir le cuir to catch some rays, to sunbathe 180
se rôtir le cuir to sunbathe, to catch some rays 209
se saouler to get oneself drunk 72
se saper to get dolled up 23
se sentir ___ ans de moins to feel ___ years younger 115
se sentir patraque to be under the weather/[Br.] off color 114
se sentir tout con to feel like a (right) prick 88
se sentir un peu chose to feel funny/peculiar 114
se sentir: ne pas se sentir d'attaque to be under the weather, [Br.] to not be up to the mark 114
se sentir: ne pas se sentir très vaillant to be a bit under the weather/[Br.] off form/off it/off 114
se shooter to inject (drug), to shoot, to mainline 82
se soûler to get oneself drunk 72
se sucrer la gaufre to do one's face 23
se tabasser to fight 66
se taper dessus to fight 66
se taper la cloche to feed one's face, [Br.] to have a slap-up/first-rate meal 108
se taper la colonne to masturbate 189
se taper une pignole to masturbate 189
se taper une pogne to masturbate 189
se taper un rassis to masturbate 189
se téléphoner: On s'téléphone. I'll give you a call/ring/[Br.] bell. 7
se terrer to hide, [Br.] to go to earth/ground 145
se tirer: Je me tire! to sit around/[Br.] skive 223
se tordre (de rire) to be doubled up with laughter 100
se toucher to masturbate 189
se tourner les pouces to twiddle one's thumbs 223
se tripoter to masturbate 189
se tuyauter to get information in advance 82
se vouloir artistique to think oneself artsy-fartsy/[Br.] arty-farty 17
le Sébasto le boulevard Sébastopol 45
secouer le petit homme to masturbate 189
secouer les puces à to tell someone off 64
semer la merde to stir up, [Br.] to wind up 62
sent-bon (m) perfume 48

sentir: ça sent le sapin (s)he doesn't have long/[Br.] (s)he's not long to go now 117
sentir l'ail to be/to appear to be a lesbian 185
la série noire famous whodunnit series 165
le sérieux liter of beer 75
séropo HIV-positive (person) 117
être séropositif(-ive) to be HIV positive 187
la serpillière dress, rag 48
serrer la cuiller to shake hands 129
serrer la louche to shake hands 129
serrer les fesses to be afraid 89
le service trois-pièces sex(ual) organs 128
le sexe au téléphone telephone sex 191
la SF science fiction 9
le shit hashish, shit, dope 82
le short shorts 52
le Sida AIDS 187
le siège à morts death seat (front passenger's seat) 36
signer un but to score a goal 197
le singe boss man, [Br.] guv'nor 28
le singe: On n'apprend pas à un singe comment faire la grimace. You can't teach an old dog new tricks. 13
le sinoquet head 126
le skeud platter, disc, record 155, 212
le slibar briefs 52
le slip de bain swim(ming) trunks 52
le slow slow dance, fox-trot 154
SMIC minimum gross hourly wage 31
Snif! Boo-hoo! 88
sniffer to cry; to sniff (drugs), to huff (solvents), to snort (cocaine) 88
la sœur effeminate young man 184
le soft soft porn 97
le software software 140
le/la soiffard(e) drunkard 72
une soirée rave a rave [evening] 152
les 75 Parisians 170
sonner les cloches to tell someone off 64
la sono sound system 152
la sorbonne head 126
des sorlots (m) shoes 51
sortir du placard to come out (of the closet) 185
sortir en boîte to go nightclubbing 95
SOS Racisme anti-racist organization 136, 170
le sostène, le soutif bra, boulder-holder 52
de souche native-born (often with certain racist connotations) 170
souffler en tempête to blow a gale 218
souffler le copain/la copine à quelqu'un to steal someone's boyfriend/girlfriend 177
le soufflet lung 127
être soûl(e) to be drunk 72
le/la soûlard(e) drunkard 72
le/la soûlot(te) drunkard 72
la soupape lung 127
le sous-entrepreneur/sous-traitant subcontractor, [Br.] subbie 28
le sous-fifre humble employee, underling, junior 30
le sous-verge humble employee, underling, junior 30
le souteneur pimp 190
le sprinter sprinter 194
le staff personnel 28
la star star 96, 149
le step nose 131
la stonba slugfest, [Br.] punch-up 212
être en strasse (of taxi) to be/to wait at a taxi stand 42
le string G-string, thong 52
le studio apartment, flat 85
subir le coup de foudre to fall in love at first sight 174
avoir un succès fou to be a smash hit 148
être en suif to be sore/steamed up 87
le SUIO Student Information Service 84
super super, great 100
super marrant(e) mega (funny) 100
superchiant(e) deadly/[Br.] bloody boring 141
les supérieurs top brass 29
supernana great chick 141
être supporte(u)r d'une équipele kiné physical therapist, trainer 199
supporter une équipe to support a team 199
surfer to surf, to go surfing 209
le surfing, le surf surfing 209
le surgé chief, head, supervisor, dean of students 80
le survêt' sweat suit, tracksuit 51
le swing (dance) jive, (music) swing 154
sympa nice, friendly, pleasant 100

T

les tabourets (mpl) teeth 131
le taco(t) taxi, cab 42

le tacot old car 35
le taf fear 88
le tafanard bottom, ass 132
taffer to be afraid 89
tailler une branlette à quelqu'un to get/[Br.] bring someone off 186
tailler une pipe/une plume/un pompier to give a blow-job 133
avoir du talent pour to have a talent for 121
la tambouille chow, food, grub, [Br.] tucker 105
le tango beer with grenadine syrup 75
la tante homosexual 184
la tantouse, la tantouze homosexual 184
la TAO computer-assisted translation 165
le tape-cul old car 35
taper dans l'œil de quelqu'un to catch someone's fancy 174
taper l'ail to be/to appear to be a lesbian 185
la tapette tongue 131; homosexual 184
le tarbouif nose 131
la tarentelle tarantella 154
les targettes (fpl) clodhoppers; feet 51, 128
le tarin nose 131
tarte thick, ridiculous, [Br.] dim, [Br.] naff 100
Tartempion thingy, what's her/his name 162
tartignole ridiculous, [Br.] naff 100
des tartines (f) shoes 51
le tasseau nose 131
des tatanes (f) shoes 51
tâter de to try (to), to take up, [Br.] to have a go at 18
la taule prison 67
le taulier owner, boss (of pub, bar, restaurant, lodging house) 28
la taulière madam(e) 190
la taupe first-/second-year preparatory course for the **Grandes Écoles** 78
taupin (m) student 79
la tchon shame 212
les t.d. (mpl) seminar(s) 84
le tébi penis 127
la techno techno 96, 152
tèj to dump, to throw out, to chuck out 212
la téloche TV, tube, [Br.] telly 97
le témoin baton 192
tempêter to rage, storm [of a person] 218
le temps est au beau fixe the weather's fine/it's going to be beautiful 57
tenir la forme to keep in shape/trim/one's figure 115
tenir: ne tenir pas sur les guibolles to be shaky on the old pins 134
le tennis tennis court 198
le tennisman, des tennismen male tennis player(s) 198
la tenniswoman, des tenniswomen female tennis player(s) 198
le ténor big noise, star performer, [Br.] leading light, VIP 18
le TER local/regional/cross-country train 170
terre à terre down-to-earth, matter-of-fact 143
terre ferme dry land, terra firma 144
la Terre sainte area between the **esplanade des Invalides** and the Champs-Élysées 45
être terré(e) dans to be holed up in, [Br.] to go to earth (ground) in 145
la terrine head 126
les tétasses (fpl) withered breasts 132
la tête: Ça va pas la tête? Are you crazy?/Are you off your rocker?/[Br.] your trolly? 6
être en tête d'affiche to be top of the bill 155
la tête de nœud dickhead 88
le teube penis 127
la teuche vagina 133
la teuf party 212
la teup tart, whore, pro(stitute), [Br.] slag 212
teushou (m) a fix 82
le théâtre de boulevard light comedies (performed in the theaters of the Paris boulevards) 96
la théière head 126
une thune 5 francs 26
avoir le/un ticket avec quelqu'un to hit it off with someone 174
le ticson ticket (for transportation, theater) 44
les tifs (mpl) hair 125
la tige penis 127; foot 128
des tiges (f) shoes; feet; penis 51
la tignasse hair 126
Tintin! No way, José!/[Br.] Not on your nelly! 162

le vin cuit vermouth 75
virer to fire, to dismiss, [Br.] to sack 31
virer homo to become/turn gay 184
le virus bug, passion 18
vivre comme chien et chat to go at it like cat and dog 12
Voici mon frangin. This is my brother. Meet my brother. 58
Voici mes meilleurs amis. These are my best friends. 58
Voici mes parents. These are my parents./Meet my parents. 58
me voilà frais/fraîche! I'm in a fix! 217
voir trente-six chandelles to see stars 34
la voiture-balai brush wagon (car following bike race) 196
le volley volleyball 182
vomir quelqu'un to drop someone off 204
le vrai Beaubourg! real bit of contemporary design 16
avoir le vresson clairsemé to be going thin on top 128
la vrille lesbian 185
le VTT mountain bike 36, 202, 208; 4×4, off-roader 36
vulgos vulgar, coarse, gross 100

W

le walkman Walkman 155
un whisky bien tassé a good measure of whisky 75
WW marking on temporary license plates 9

X

la X [ecstasy] X 9

Y

un yankee Yank 111
un youpin, un youtre Jew 112

Z

zarbi strange, odd, way-out, weird 212
le zeb, le zébi penis 127
le zef the wind 57
les avoir à zéro to be afraid 89
le zib, le zibar penis 127
la zicmu music, tunes, numbers 94, 212
le zigouigoui penis 127
zigouiller to do in, to kill, to bump, to knock off 67
le zinzin (annoying) hum/buzz; violin; thingamajig; bonkers, loopy 94
le zizi penis 127
la zizique music, tunes, elevator music 94, 152
le zob/zobi penis 125
le zomblou bomber jacket , short jacket 49, 212
le zonga grass, herb, weed (marijuana) 212
les zozores (fpl) ears 126